An imaginative blend of memoir and history, *Of Woman Born* is a view of women's role as mother throughout history. Drawing on anthropology, medicine, psychology, literature, history and her own experiences, Adrienne Rich triumphantly explores the pleasures and pains of motherhood. The result, a bestseller in America, is a study of universal importance for all mothers, daughters, fathers and sons.

Adrienne Rich was born in Baltimore in 1929. She graduated from Radcliffe College in 1951, the year her first volume of poems *A Change of World* was published. Since then she has published seven more collections, and is regarded as one of the most distinguished modern American poets. *Diving into the Wreck* was co-winner of the National Book Award. She has taught at Swarthmore College, Columbia University, the City University of New York, Brandeis University and now teaches at Douglass College. Adrienne Rich has three sons and lives in New York. *Of Woman Born* is her first work of prose.

VIRAGO
is a feminist publishing company:

'It is only when women start to organize
in large numbers that we become a
political force, and begin to move towards
the possibility of a truly democratic society
in which every human being can be brave,
responsible, thinking and diligent in the struggle
to live at once freely and unselfishly'

SHEILA ROWBOTHAM
Women, Resistance and Revolution

VIRAGO
Advisory Group

OF WOMAN BORN

By Adrienne Rich

ADRIENNE RICH

OF WOMAN BORN

MOTHERHOOD AS EXPERIENCE AND INSTITUTION

Virago
London

First published in Great Britain by VIRAGO Limited 1977
3 Cheyne Place, Royal Hospital Road, London SW3 4HH.

First published in the U.S.A. 1976
Copyright ©W. W. Norton & Company, Inc. All rights reserved.

ISBN 0 86068 030 4   Casebound Edition
ISBN 0 86068 031 2   Paperback Edition

Printed in Great Britain at the Anchor Press Ltd.
and bound by Wm Brendon & Son Ltd.
both of Tiptree, Essex.

Grateful acknowledgment is made for permission to quote from the following: "To a Boy-Child," by Sue Silvermarie, copyright © Winter 1974 by *Women: A Journal of Liberation*, 3028 Greenmount Avenue, Baltimore, Maryland 21218, pp. 26–27, reprinted by permission of the author and the publisher; "The Child," Part IV of "The Network of the Imaginary Mother," copyright © 1976 by Robin Morgan, reprinted from *Lady of the Beasts*, by Robin Morgan, by permission of Random House, Inc. and Georges Borchardt, Inc.; "Mother and Child" in *Like the Iris of an Eye* by Susan Griffin, copyright © by Susan Griffin, reprinted by permission of Harper & Row, Publishers, Inc., and the author; Lines from an Egyptian hymn from *Birth*, by David Meltzer, translated by John A. Wilson, Ballantine Books, 1973, reprinted by permission of Ballantine Books; a poem by Alta, *Momma: A Start on All the Untold Stories*, pp. 72–73, copyright © 1974 by Times Change Press, reprinted by permission of the publisher and the author; the "Third Elegy" of the *Duino Elegies*, by Rainer Maria Rilke, translated by Lilly Engler, reprinted by permission of the translator; "The Hanging of Sam Archer," a folk poem reported, with music, in *Hoosier Folklore*, 5 (1946): 30, reprinted by permission of *Hoosier Folklore*.

To my grandmothers

Mary Gravely   Hattie Rice

whose lives I begin to imagine

CONTENTS

. . . ma per trattar del ben ch'i vi trovai,
    diro dell' altre cose, ch'io v'ho scorte.

(. . . but to treat of the good that I found there,
    I will tell of other things I there discerned.)

—Dante, *Inferno,* 1:3

FOREWORD

All human life on the planet is born of woman. The one unifying, incontrovertible experience shared by all women and men is that months-long period we spent unfolding inside a woman's body. Because young humans remain dependent upon nurture for a much longer period than other mammals, and because of the division of labor long established in human groups, where women not only bear and suckle but are assigned almost total responsibility for children, most of us first know both love and disappointment, power and tenderness, in the person of a woman.

We carry the imprint of this experience for life, even into our dying. Yet there has been a strange lack of material to help us understand and use it. We know more about the air we breathe, the seas we travel, than about the nature and meaning of motherhood. In the division of labor according to gender, the makers and sayers of culture, the namers, have been the sons of the mothers. There is much to suggest that the male mind has always been haunted by the force of the idea of *dependence on a woman for life itself*, the son's constant effort to assimilate, compensate for, or deny the fact that he is "of woman born."

Women are also born of women. But we know little about the effect on culture of that fact, because women have not been makers and sayers of patriarchal culture. Woman's status as childbearer has been made into a major fact of her life. Terms like "barren" or "childless" have been used to negate any further identity. The term "nonfather" does not exist in any realm of social categories.

Because the fact of physical motherhood is so visible and dramatic, men recognized only after some time that they, too, had a part in generation. The meaning of "fatherhood" remains tangential, elusive. To "father" a child suggests above all to beget, to provide the sperm which fertilizes the ovum. To "mother" a child implies a continuing presence, lasting at least nine months, more often for years. Motherhood is earned, first through an intense physical and psychic rite of passage— pregnancy and childbirth—then through learning to nurture, which does not come by instinct.

A man may beget a child in passion or by rape, and then disappear; he need never see or consider child or mother again. Under such circumstances, the mother faces a range of painful, socially weighted choices: abortion, suicide, abandonment of the child, infanticide, the rearing of a child branded "illegitimate," usually in poverty, always outside the law. In some cultures she faces murder by her kinsmen. Whatever her choice, her body has undergone irreversible changes, her mind will never be the same, her future as a woman has been shaped by the event.

Most of us were raised by our mothers, or by women who for love, necessity, or money took the place of our biological mothers. Throughout history women have helped birth and nurture each others' children. Most women have been mothers in the sense of tenders and carers for the young, whether as sisters, aunts, nurses, teachers, foster-mothers, stepmothers. Tribal life, the village, the extended family, the female networks of some cultures, have included the very young, very old, unmarried, and infertile women in the process of "mothering." Even those of us whose fathers played an important part in our early childhood rarely remember them for their patient attendance when we were ill, their doing the humble tasks of feeding and cleaning us; we remember scenes, expeditions, punishments, special occasions. For most of us a woman provided the continuity and stability—but also the rejections and refusals— of our early lives, and it is with a woman's hands, eyes, body, voice, that we associate our primal sensations, our earliest social experience.

2

Throughout this book I try to distinguish between two meanings of motherhood, one superimposed on the other: the *potential relationship* of any woman to her powers of reproduction and to children; and the *institution*, which aims at ensuring that that potential—and all women—shall remain under male control. This institution has been a keystone of the most diverse social and political systems. It has withheld over one-half the human species from the decisions affecting their lives; it exonerates men from fatherhood in any authentic sense; it creates the dangerous schism between "private" and "public" life; it calcifies human choices and potentialities. In the most fundamental and bewildering of contradictions, it has alienated women from our bodies by incarcerating us in them. At certain points in history, and in certain cultures, the idea of woman-as-mother has worked to endow all women with respect, even with awe, and to give women some say in the life of a people or a clan. But for most of what we know as the "mainstream" of recorded history, motherhood as institution has ghettoized and degraded female potentialities.

The power of the mother has two aspects: the biological potential or capacity to bear and nourish human life, and the magical power invested in women by men, whether in the form of Goddess-worship or the fear of being controlled and overwhelmed by women. We do not actually know much about what power may have meant in the hands of strong, prepatriarchal women. We do have guesses, longings, myths, fantasies, analogues. We know far more about how, under patriarchy, female possibility has been -literally massacred on the site of motherhood. Most women in history have become mothers without choice, and an even greater number have lost their lives bringing life into the world.

Women are controlled by lashing us to our bodies. In an early and classic essay, Susan Griffin pointed out that "rape is a form of mass terrorism, for the victims of rape are chosen indiscriminately, but the propagandists for male supremacy broad-

cast that it is women who cause rape by being unchaste or in
the wrong place at the wrong time—in essence, by behaving
as though they were free. . . . The fear of rape keeps women
off the streets at night. Keeps women at home. Keeps women
passive and modest for fear that they be thought provocative."*
In a later development of Griffin's analysis, Susan Brownmiller
suggests that enforced, indentured motherhood may originally
have been the price paid by women to the men who became
their "protectors" (and owners) against the casual violence of
other men.† If rape has been terrorism, motherhood has been
penal servitude. *It need not be.*

This book is not an attack on the family or on mothering,
except as defined and restricted under patriarchy. Nor is it a
call for a mass system of state-controlled child-care. Mass child-
care in patriarchy has had but two purposes: to introduce large
numbers of women into the labor force, in a developing economy or during a war, and to indoctrinate future citizens.†† It
has never been conceived as a means of releasing the energies of
women into the mainstream of culture, or of changing the
stereotypic gender-images of both women and men.

* "Rape: The All-American Crime," in Jo Freeman, ed., *Women: A Feminist Perspective* (Stanford, Calif.: Mayfield Publishing, 1975).
† *Against Our Will: Men, Women and Rape* (New York: Simon and
Schuster, 1975). Reviewing Brownmiller's book, a feminist newsletter commented: "It would be extreme and contentious . . . to call mothers rape
victims in general; probably only a small percentage are. But rape is the
crime that can be committed because women are vulnerable in a special
way; the opposite of 'vulnerable' is 'impregnable.' Pregnability, to coin a
word, has been the basis of female identity, the limit of freedom, the futility of education, the denial of growth." ("Rape Has Many Forms," review in *The Spokeswoman*, Vol. 6, No. 5 [November 15, 1975].)
†† To these American capitalism is adding a third: the profit motive. Fran-
chised, commercially operated child-care centers have become "big business." Many such centers are purely custodial; overcrowding limits physical
and educational flexibility and freedom; the centers are staffed almost
entirely by women, working for a minimum salary. Operated under giant
corporations such as Singer, Time Inc., and General Electric, these profit-
making preschools can be compared to commercial nursing homes in their
exploitation of human needs and of the most vulnerable persons in the society. See Georgia Sassen, Cookie Arvin, and the Corporations and Child
Care Research Project, "Corporate Child Care," *The Second Wave: A
Magazine of the New Feminism*, Vol. 3, No. 3, pp. 21–23, 38–43.

3

I told myself that I wanted to write a book on motherhood because it was a crucial, still relatively unexplored, area for feminist theory. But I did not choose this subject; it had long ago chosen me.

This book is rooted in my own past, tangled with parts of my life which stayed buried even while I dug away at the strata of early childhood, adolescence, separation from parents, my vocation as a poet; the geographies of marriage, spiritual divorce, and death, through which I entered the open ground of middle age. Every journey into the past is complicated by delusions, false memories, false naming of real events. But for a long time, I avoided this journey back into the years of pregnancy, child-bearing, and the dependent lives of my children, because it meant going back into pain and anger that I would have preferred to think of as long since resolved and put away. I could not begin to think of writing a book on motherhood until I began to feel strong enough, and unambivalent enough in my love for my children, so that I could dare to return to a ground which seemed to me the most painful, incomprehensible, and ambiguous I had ever traveled, a ground hedged by taboos, mined with false-namings.

I did not understand this when I started to write the book. I only knew that I had lived through something which was considered central to the lives of women, fulfilling even in its sorrows, a key to the meaning of life; and that I could remember little except anxiety, physical weariness, anger, self-blame, boredom, and division within myself: a division made more acute by the moments of passionate love, delight in my children's spirited bodies and minds, amazement at how they went on loving me in spite of my failures to love them wholly and selflessly.

It seemed to me impossible from the first to write a book of this kind without being often autobiographical, without often saying "I." Yet for many months I buried my head in historical research and analysis in order to delay or prepare the way for the plunge into areas of my own life which were painful and problematical, yet from the heart of which this book has come. I believe increasingly that only the willingness to share private and sometimes painful experience can enable women to create a collective description of the world which will be truly ours. On the other hand, I am keenly aware that any writer has a certain false and arbitrary power. It is *her* version, after all, that the reader is reading at this moment, while the accounts of others—including the dead—may go untold.

This is in some ways a vulnerable book. I have invaded various professional domains, broken various taboos. I have used the scholarship available to me where I found it suggestive, without pretending to make myself into a specialist. In so doing, the question, *But what was it like for women?* was always in my mind, and I soon began to sense a fundamental perceptual difficulty among male scholars (and some female ones) for which "sexism" is too facile a term. It is really an intellectual defect, which might be named "patrivincialism" or "patriochialism": the assumption that women are a subgroup, that "man's world" is the "real" world, that patriarchy is equivalent to culture and culture to patriarchy, that the "great" or "liberalizing" periods of history have been the same for women as for men, that generalizations about "man," "humankind," "children," "blacks," "parents," "the working class" hold true for women, mothers, daughters, sisters, wet-nurses, infant girls, and can include them with no more than a glancing reference here and there, usually to some specialized function like breast-feeding. The new historians of "family and childhood," like the majority of theorists on child-rearing, pediatricians, psychiatrists, are male. In their work, the question of motherhood as an institution or as an idea in the heads of grown-up male children is raised only where "styles" of mothering are discussed and criticized. Female sources are rarely cited (yet these sources exist, as the feminist historians are showing); there are virtually no primary sources from women-as-mothers; and all this is presented as objective scholarship.

It is only recently that feminist scholars such as Gerda Lerner, Joan Kelly-Gadol, and Carroll Smith-Rosenberg have begun to suggest that, in Lerner's words: "the key to understanding

women's history is in accepting—painful though it may be—
that it is the history of the *majority* of mankind. . . . History,
as written and perceived up to now, is the history of a minority,
who may well turn out to be the 'subgroup.' "*

I write with a painful consciousness of my own Western
cultural perspective and that of most of the sources available
to me: painful because it says so much about how female culture is fragmented by the male cultures, boundaries, groupings
in which women live. However, at this point any broad study of
female culture can be at best partial, and what any writer hopes
—and knows—is that others like her, with different training,
background, and tools, are putting together other parts of this
immense half-buried mosaic in the shape of a woman's face.

ACKNOWLEDGMENTS

There are people I need to thank. Without my three sons, this
book might not have existed; but in particular their love, intelligence, and integrity have been resources for me since we
first began to talk to each other. There are so many women
with whom I have talked, as mothers and as daughters, that it
is impossible to acknowledge all my debts. Phoebe DesMarais
and Helen Smelser have generously shared their experiences and
their wisdom with me since our undergraduate days, regardless
of time zones, distances, children, husbands, lovers, and life-
styles. Barbara Charlesworth Gelpi and Albert Gelpi, both in
argument and in support, have each freely contributed their
perceptions of the visions we share. Jane Cooper's imagination
and insight have been activating and healing forces in my work
and my life. With Robin Morgan I had vital conversations during the book's gestation; her mind and her affection have been
important to me throughout. Jane Alpert, under the most
difficult personal conditions, has generously encouraged and
criticized. Mary Daly has given emotional and intellectual com-
radeship; I cannot separate one from the other. Susan Griffin
has criticized at the deepest, most loving level. Tillie Olsen

* "Placing Women in History: Definitions and Challenges," in *Feminist
Studies*, Vol. 3, No. 1–2 (Fall 1975), pp. 8, 13.

sternly and tenderly demands, through her work and her example, that we all search more relentlessly into our hidden life as women, and the language in which we name it. Kirsten Grimstad and Susan Rennie provided insights, crucial resources, and the spur of emulation, through their friendship and their work. Janice Raymond began as a vital critic and has become a friend as well. Kenneth Pitchford gave me the benefit of a sensitive critique of Chapter VIII. Richard Howard gracefully recreated in English the words of a seventeenth-century French midwife for Chapter VI. John Benedict, my editor, contributed a close, honestly responsive reading, and many suggestions which helped me to clarify the structure of the book; he more than once said the right words at the right time, and more than once have we argued the themes pursued here. Michelle Cliff was a superb and stimulating copy editor. I have all along been fortunate in the support of W. W. Norton, my publishers.

Lilly Engler read, reread, and commented on the manuscript; she translated afresh for me the lines quoted from Rilke's "Third Duino Elegy" in Chapter VIII; and she has been with this book, in the deepest possible sense, from the first.

Throughout the writing of the book I also received help, in the form of references, unpublished papers, reprints, letters, encouragement, and counsel, from women, many of whom I had not met or barely knew, who are working along some of the same lines, both within and outside the academic world. Books were lent, work-in-progress shared, with a generosity that made me realize concretely how much I was part of a working community of women. I want to thank in particular Alta, Kathleen Barry, Emily Culpeper, Nancy Fuller, Liselotte Erlanger Glozer, Mary Howell, Brigitte Jordan, Jane Lazarre, Jane Lilienfeld, Helen McKenna, Marian Oliner, Grace Paley, Alice Rossi, Florence Rush, Myra Schotz, Elizabeth Shanklin, Patricia Traxler; and Karyn London and Fabi Romero-Oak of Womanbooks, West Ninety-second Street, New York, for bibliographical resources, correspondence, and conversation. Rhoda Fairman and Lisa George not only typed the manuscript at various stages; they made me feel it was worth reading. Finally, Simone de Beauvoir and Shulamith Firestone created pioneering feminist insights to which I shall always stand in debt.

Needless to say, I owe much to many people unnamed here. No one whom I thank necessarily shares all my opinions and conclusions; the final responsibility throughout is my own.

Of course I am indebted to libraries: to the Schlesinger Women's Archives at Radcliffe College, the New York Public Library, the Library of the New York Academy of Medicine, the A. A. Brill Collection of the New York Psychoanalytic Institute, the New York Society Library, the Widener and Countway Libraries of Harvard University, the Douglass College Library at Rutgers University; to Joseph Hickerson of the Music Division of the Library of Congress; and to the libraries of my friends. The Ingram Merrill Foundation kindly provided a grant to cover research expenses, typing, and other practical costs; I am grateful to them for understanding that this book was as important for me to write as the poetry they would have preferred to encourage.

Finally, I cannot imagine having written this book without the presence in my life of my mother, who offers a continuing example of transformation and rebirth; and of my sister, with and from whom I go on learning about sisterhood, daughterhood, motherhood, and the struggle of women toward a shared, irreversible, liberation.

New York City
February 1976

I ANGER AND TENDERNESS

═══════════════════════════════

... to understand is always an ascending movement; that is why comprehension ought always to be concrete. (one is never got out of the cave, one comes out of it.)
—Simone Weil, *First and Last Notebooks*

Entry from my journal, November 1960

My children cause me the most exquisite suffering of which I have any experience. It is the suffering of ambivalence: the murderous alternation between bitter resentment and raw-edged nerves, and blissful gratification and tenderness. Sometimes I seem to myself, in my feelings toward these tiny guiltless beings, a monster of selfishness and intolerance. Their voices wear away at my nerves, their constant needs, above all their need for simplicity and patience, fill me with despair at my own failures, despair too at my fate, which is to serve a function for which I was not fitted. And I am weak sometimes from held-in rage. There are times when I feel only death will free us from one another, when I envy the barren woman who has the luxury of her regrets but lives a life of privacy and freedom.*

And yet at other times I am melted with the sense of their helpless, charming and quite irresistible beauty—their ability to

* The term "barren woman" was easy for me to use, unexamined, fifteen years ago. As should be clear throughout this book, it seems to me now a

go on loving and trusting—their staunchness and decency and unselfconsciousness. *I love them.* But it's in the enormity and inevitability of this love that the sufferings lie.

April 1961
A blissful love for my children engulfs me from time to time and seems almost to suffice—the aesthetic pleasure I have in these little, changing creatures, the sense of being loved, however dependently, the sense too that I'm not an utterly unnatural and shrewish mother—much though I am!

May 1965
To suffer with and for and against a child—maternally, egotistically, neurotically, sometimes with a sense of helplessness, sometimes with the illusion of learning wisdom—but always, everywhere, in body and soul, *with* that child—because that child is a piece of oneself.

To be caught up in waves of love and hate, jealousy even of the child's childhood; hope and fear for its maturity; longing to be free of responsibility, tied by every fibre of one's being.

That curious primitive reaction of protectiveness, the beast defending her cub, when anyone attacks or criticizes him—And yet no one more hard on him than I!

September 1965
Degradation of anger. Anger at a child. How shall I learn to absorb the violence and make explicit only the caring? Exhaustion of anger. Victory of will, too dearly bought—far too dearly!

March 1966
Perhaps one is a monster—an anti-woman—something driven and without recourse to the normal and appealing consolations of love, motherhood, joy in others . . .

Unexamined assumptions: First, that a "natural" mother is a person without further identity, one who can find her chief gratification in being all day with small children, living at a pace tuned to theirs; that the isolation of mothers and children together in the home must be taken for granted; that maternal love is, and should be, quite literally selfless; that children and

___

term both tendentious and meaningless, based on a view of women which sees motherhood as our only positive definition.

mothers are the "causes" of each others' suffering. I was haunted
by the stereotype of the mother whose love is "unconditional";
and by the visual and literary images of motherhood as a single-
minded identity. If I knew parts of myself existed that would
never cohere to those images, weren't those parts then abnormal, monstrous? And—as my eldest son, now aged twenty-one,
remarked on reading the above passages: "You seemed to feel
you ought to love us all the time. But there *is* no human relationship where you love the other person at every moment."
Yes, I tried to explain to him, but women—above all, mothers
—have been supposed to love that way.

From the fifties and early sixties, I remember a cycle. It
began when I had picked up a book or began trying to write
a letter, or even found myself on the telephone with someone
toward whom my voice betrayed eagerness, a rush of sympathetic energy. The child (or children) might be absorbed in
busyness, in his own dreamworld; but as soon as he felt me glid-
ing into a world which did not include him, he would come to
pull at my hand, ask for help, punch at the typewriter keys. And
I would feel his wants at such a moment as fraudulent, as an
attempt moreover to defraud me of living even for fifteen minutes as myself. My anger would rise; I would feel the futility of
any attempt to salvage myself, and also the inequality between
us: my needs always balanced against those of a child, and always losing. I could love so much better, I told myself, after
even a quarter-hour of selfishness, of peace, of detachment from
my children. A few minutes! But it was as if an invisible thread
would pull taut between us and break, to the child's sense of
inconsolable abandonment, if I moved—not even physically,
but in spirit—into a realm beyond our tightly circumscribed
life together. It was as if my placenta had begun to refuse him
oxygen. Like so many women, I waited with impatience for the
moment when their father would return from work, when for
an hour or two at least the circle drawn around mother and
children would grow looser, the intensity between us slacken,
because there was another adult in the house.

I did not understand that this circle, this magnetic field in
which we lived, was not a natural phenomenon.

Intellectually, I must have known it. But the emotion-

charged, tradition-heavy form in which I found myself cast as
the Mother seemed, then, as ineluctable as the tides. And, because of this form—this microcosm in which my children and I
formed a tiny, private emotional cluster, and in which (in bad
weather or when someone was ill) we sometimes passed days
at a time without seeing another adult except for their father—
there *was* authentic need underlying my child's invented claims
upon me when I seemed to be wandering away from him. He
was reassuring himself that warmth, tenderness, continuity,
solidity were still there for him, in my person. My singularity,
my uniqueness in the world as *his mother*—perhaps more
dimly also as Woman—evoked a need vaster than any single
human being could satisfy, except by loving continuously, un-
conditionally, from dawn to dark, and often in the middle of
the night.

2

In a living room in 1975, I spent an evening with a group of
women poets, some of whom had children. One had brought
hers along, and they slept or played in adjoining rooms. We
talked of poetry, and also of infanticide, of the case of a local
woman, the mother of eight, who had been in severe depression
since the birth of her third child, and who had recently murdered and decapitated her two youngest, on her suburban front
lawn. Several women in the group, feeling a direct connection
with her desperation, had signed a letter to the local newspaper
protesting the way her act was perceived by the press and
handled by the community mental health system. Every woman
in that room who had children, every poet, could identify with
her. We spoke of the wells of anger that her story cleft open
in us. We spoke of our own moments of murderous anger at
our children, because there was no one and nothing else on
which to discharge anger. We spoke in the sometimes tentative,
sometimes rising, sometimes bitterly witty, unrhetorical tones
and language of women who had met together over our common work, poetry, and who found another common ground in
an unacceptable, but undeniable anger. The words are being

spoken now, are being written down; the taboos are being broken, the masks of motherhood are cracking through.

For centuries no one talked of these feelings. I became a mother in the family-centered, consumer-oriented, Freudian-American world of the 1950s. My husband spoke eagerly of the children we would have; my parents-in-law awaited the birth of their grandchild. I had no idea of what *I* wanted, what *I* could or could not choose. I only knew that to have a child was to assume adult womanhood to the full, to prove myself, to be "like other women."

To be "like other women" had been a problem for me. From the age of thirteen or fourteen, I had felt I was only acting the part of a feminine creature. At the age of sixteen my fingers were almost constantly ink-stained. The lipstick and high heels of the era were difficult-to-manage disguises. In 1945 I was writing poetry seriously, and had a fantasy of going to postwar Europe as a journalist, sleeping among the ruins in bombed cities, recording the rebirth of civilization after the fall of the Nazis. But also, like every other girl I knew, I spent hours trying to apply lipstick more adroitly, straightening the wandering seams of stockings, talking about "boys." There were two different compartments, already, to my life. But writing poetry, and my fantasies of travel and self-sufficiency, seemed more real to me; I felt that as an incipient "real woman" I was a fake. Particularly was I paralyzed when I encountered young children. I think I felt men could be—wished to be—conned into thinking I was truly "feminine"; a child, I suspected, could see through me like a shot. This sense of acting a part created a curious sense of guilt, even though it was a part demanded for survival.

I have a very clear, keen memory of myself the day after I was married: I was sweeping a floor. Probably the floor did not really need to be swept; probably I simply did not know what else to do with myself. But as I swept that floor I thought: "Now I am a woman. This is an age-old action, this is what women have always done." I felt I was bending to some ancient form, too ancient to question. *This is what women have always done.*

As soon as I was visibly and clearly pregnant, I felt, for the first time in my adolescent and adult life, not-guilty. The atmosphere of approval in which I was bathed—even by strangers on the street, it seemed—was like an aura I carried with me, in which doubts, fears, misgivings, met with absolute denial. *This is what women have always done.*

Two days before my first son was born, I broke out in a rash which was tentatively diagnosed as measles, and was admitted to a hospital for contagious diseases to await the onset of labor. I felt for the first time a great deal of conscious fear, and guilt toward my unborn child, for having "failed" him with my body in this way. In rooms near mine were patients with polio; no one was allowed to enter my room except in a hospital gown and mask. If during pregnancy I had felt in any vague command of my situation, I felt now totally dependent on my obstetrician, a huge, vigorous, paternal man, abounding with optimism and assurance, and given to pinching my cheek. I had gone through a healthy pregnancy, but as if tranquilized or sleep-walking. I had taken a sewing class in which I produced an unsightly and ill-cut maternity jacket which I never wore; I had made curtains for the baby's room, collected baby clothes, blotted out as much as possible the woman I had been a few months earlier. My second book of poems was in press, but I had stopped writing poetry, and read little except household magazines and books on child-care. I felt myself perceived by the world simply as a pregnant woman, and it seemed easier, less disturbing, to perceive myself so. After my child was born the "measles" were diagnosed as an allergic reaction to pregnancy.

Within two years, I was pregnant again, and writing in a notebook:

November 1956
> Whether it's the extreme lassitude of early pregnancy or something more fundamental, I don't know; but of late I've felt, toward poetry,—both reading and writing it—nothing but boredom and indifference. Especially toward my own and that of my immediate contemporaries. When I receive a letter soliciting mss., or someone alludes to my "career", I have a

strong sense of wanting to deny all responsibility for and interest in that person who writes—or who wrote.

If there is going to be a real break in my writing life, this is as good a time for it as any. I have been dissatisfied with myself, my work, for a long time.

My husband was a sensitive, affectionate man who wanted children and who—unusual in the professional, academic world of the fifties—was willing to "help." But it was clearly understood that this "help" was an act of generosity; that *his* work, *his* professional life, was the real work in the family; in fact, this was for years not even an issue between us. I understood that my struggles as a writer were a kind of luxury, a peculiarity of mine; my work brought in almost no money: it even cost money, when I hired a household helper to allow me a few hours a week to write. "Whatever I ask he tries to give me," I wrote in March 1958, "but always the initiative has to be mine." I experienced my depressions, bursts of anger, sense of entrapment, as burdens my husband was forced to bear because he loved me; I felt grateful to be loved in spite of bringing him those burdens.

But I was struggling to bring my life into focus. I had never really given up on poetry, nor on gaining some control over my existence. The life of a Cambridge tenement backyard swarming with children, the repetitious cycles of laundry, the night-wakings, the interrupted moments of peace or of engagement with ideas, the ludicrous dinner parties at which young wives, some with advanced degrees, all seriously and intelligently dedicated to their children's welfare and their husbands' careers, attempted to reproduce the amenities of Brahmin Boston, amid French recipes and the pretense of effortlessness—above all, the ultimate lack of seriousness with which women were regarded in that world—all of this defied analysis at that time, but I *knew* I had to remake my own life. I did not then understand that we—the women of that academic community—as in so many middle-class communities of the period—were expected to fill both the part of the Victorian Lady of Leisure, the Angel in the House, and also of the Victorian cook, scullery maid, laundress, governess, and nurse. I only sensed that there were false distractions sucking at me, and I wanted desperately to strip my life down to what was essential.

June 1958
These months I've been all a tangle of irritations deepening to anger: bitterness, disillusion with society and with myself; beating out at the world, rejecting out of hand. What, if anything, has been positive? Perhaps the attempt to remake my life, to save it from mere drift and the passage of time . . .

The work that is before me is serious and difficult and not at all clear even as to plan. Discipline of mind and spirit, uniqueness of expression, ordering of daily existence, the most effective functioning of the human self—these are the chief things I wish to achieve. So far the only beginning I've been able to make is to waste less time. That is what some of the rejection has been all about.

By July of 1958 I was again pregnant. The new life of my third—and, as I determined, my last—child, was a kind of turning for me. I had learned that my body was not under my control; I had not intended to bear a third child. I knew now better than I had ever known what another pregnancy, another new infant, meant for my body and spirit. Yet, I did not think of having an abortion. In a sense, my third son was more actively chosen than either of his brothers; by the time I knew I was pregnant with him, I was not sleepwalking any more.

August 1958 (Vermont)
I write this as the early rays of the sun light up our hillside and eastern windows. Rose with [the baby] at 5:30 A.M. and have fed him and breakfasted. This is one of the few mornings on which I haven't felt terrible mental depression and physical exhaustion.

. . . I have to acknowledge to myself that I would not have chosen to have more children, that I was beginning to look to a time, not too far off, when I should again be free, no longer so physically tired, pursuing a more or less intellectual and creative life. . . . The *only* way I can develop now is through much harder, more continuous, connected work than my present life makes possible. Another child means postponing this for some years longer—and years at my age are significant, not to be tossed lightly away.

And yet, somehow, something, call it Nature or that affirming fatalism of the human creature, makes me aware of the inevitable as already part of me, not to be contended against so much as brought to bear as an additional weapon against drift, stagnation and spiritual death. (For it is really death that I have been fearing—the crumbling to death of that scarcely-born physiognomy which my whole life has been a battle to give birth to—a recognizable, autonomous self, a creation in poetry and in life.)

If more effort has to be made then I will make it. If more despair has to be lived through, I think I can anticipate it correctly and live through it.

Meanwhile, in a curious and unanticipated way, we really do welcome the birth of our child.

There was, of course, an economic as well as a spiritual margin which allowed me to think of a third child's birth not as my own death-warrant but as an "additional weapon against death." My body, despite recurrent flares of arthritis, was a healthy one; I had good prenatal care; we were not living on the edge of malnutrition; I knew that all my children would be fed, clothed, breathe fresh air; in fact it did not occur to me that it could be otherwise. But, in another sense, beyond that physical margin, I knew I was fighting for my life through, against, and with the lives of my children, though very little else was clear to me. I had been trying to give birth to myself; and in some grim, dim way I was determined to use even pregnancy and parturition in that process.

Before my third child was born I decided to have no more children, to be sterilized. (Nothing is removed from a woman's body during this operation; ovulation and menstruation continue. Yet the language suggests a cutting- or burning-away of her essential womanhood, just as the old word "barren" suggests a woman eternally empty and lacking.) My husband, although he supported my decision, asked whether I was sure it would not leave me feeling "less feminine." In order to have the operation at all, I had to present a letter, counter-signed by my husband, assuring the committee of physicians who approved such operations that I had already produced three children, and stating my reasons for having no more. Since I had had rheumatoid arthritis for some years, I could give a reason acceptable to the male panel who sat on my case; my own judgment would not have been acceptable. When I awoke from the operation, twenty-four hours after my child's birth, a young nurse looked at my chart and remarked coldly: "Had yourself spayed, did you?"

The first great birth-control crusader, Margaret Sanger, remarks that of the hundreds of women who wrote to her pleading for contraceptive information in the early part of the twentieth century, all spoke of wanting the health and strength to be better mothers to the children they already had; or of wanting to be physically affectionate to their husbands without dread of conceiving. None was refusing motherhood altogether, or asking for an easy life. These women—mostly poor, many still in their teens, all with several children—simply felt they could no longer do "right" by their families, whom they expected to go on serving and rearing. Yet there always has been, and there remains, intense fear of the suggestion that women shall have the final say as to how our bodies are to be used. It is as if the suffering of the mother, the primary identification of woman *as* the mother—were so necessary to the emotional grounding of human society that the mitigation, or removal, of that suffering, that identification, must be fought at every level, including the level of refusing to question it at all.

3

"Vous travaillez pour l'armée, madame?" (You are working for the army?), a Frenchwoman said to me early in the Vietnam war, on hearing I had three sons.

April 1965
Anger, weariness, demoralization. Sudden bouts of weeping. A sense of insufficiency to the moment and to eternity . . .

Paralyzed by the sense that there exists a mesh of relations, between e.g. my rejection and anger at [my eldest child], my sensual life, pacifism, sex (I mean in its broadest significance, not merely physical desire)—an interconnectedness which, if I could see it, make it valid, would give me back myself, make it possible to function lucidly and passionately—Yet I grope in and out among these dark webs—

I weep, and weep, and the sense of powerlessness spreads like a cancer through my being.

August 1965, 3:30 A.M.
Necessity for a more unyielding discipline of my life.
Recognize the uselessness of blind anger.
Limit society.
Use children's school hours better, for work & solitude.
Refuse to be distracted from own style of life.
Less waste.
Be harder & harder on poems.

Once in a while someone used to ask me, "Don't you ever write poems about your children?" The male poets of my generation did write poems about their children—especially their daughters. For me, poetry was where I lived as no-one's mother, where I existed as myself.

The bad and the good moments are inseparable for me. I recall the times when, suckling each of my children, I saw his eyes open full to mine, and realized each of us was fastened to the other, not only by mouth and breast, but through our mutual gaze: the depth, calm, passion, of that dark blue, maturely focused look. I recall the physical pleasure of having my full breast suckled at a time when I had no other physical pleasure in the world except the guilt-ridden pleasure of addictive eating. I remember early the sense of conflict, of a battleground none of us had chosen, of being an observer who, like it or not, was also an actor in an endless contest of wills. This was what it meant to me to have three children under the age of seven. But I recall too each child's individual body, his slenderness, wiriness, softness, grace, the beauty of little boys who have not been taught that the male body must be rigid. I remember moments of peace when for some reason it was possible to go to the bathroom alone. I remember being uprooted from already meager sleep to answer a childish nightmare, pull up a blanket, warm a consoling bottle, lead a half-asleep child to the toilet. I remember going back to bed starkly awake, brittle with anger, knowing that my broken sleep would make next day a hell, that there would be more nightmares, more need for consolation, because out of my weariness I would rage at those children for no reason they could understand. I remember thinking I would never dream again (the unconscious of the young mother—where does it entrust its messages, when dream-sleep is denied her for years?)

For many years I shrank from looking back on the first decade of my children's lives. In snapshots of the period I see a smiling young woman, in maternity clothes or bent over a half-naked baby; gradually she stops smiling, wears a distant, half-melancholy look, as if she were listening for something. In time my sons grew older, I began changing my own life, we began to talk to each other as equals. Together we lived through my leaving the marriage, and through their father's suicide. We became survivors, four distinct people with strong bonds connecting us. Because I always tried to tell them the truth, because their every new independence meant new freedom for me, because we trusted each other even when we wanted different things, they became, at a fairly young age, self-reliant and open to the unfamiliar. Something told me that if they had survived my angers, my self-reproaches, and still trusted my love and each others', they were strong. Their lives have not been, will not be, easy; but their very existences seem a gift to me, their vitality, humor, intelligence, gentleness, love of life, their separate life-currents which here and there stream into my own. I don't know how we made it from their embattled childhood and my embattled motherhood into a mutual recognition of ourselves and each other. Probably that mutual recognition, overlaid by social and traditional circumstance, was always there, from the first gaze between the mother and the infant at the breast. But I do know that for years I believed I should never have been anyone's mother, that because I felt my own needs acutely and often expressed them violently, I was Kali, Medea, the sow that devours her farrow, the unwomanly woman in flight from womanhood, a Nietzschean monster. Even today, rereading old journals, remembering, I feel grief and anger; but their objects are no longer myself and my children. I feel grief at the waste of myself in those years, anger at the mutilation and manipulation of the relationship between mother and child, which is the great original source and experience of love.

On an early spring day in the 1970s, I meet a young woman friend on the street. She has a tiny infant against her breast, in a bright cotton sling; its face is pressed against her blouse, its tiny hand clutches a piece of the cloth. "How old is she?" I ask. "Just two weeks old," the mother tells me. I am amazed to feel in myself a passionate longing to have, once again, such a small, new being clasped against my body. The baby belongs there, curled, suspended asleep between her mother's breasts, as she belonged curled in the womb. The young mother—who already has a three-year-old—speaks of how quickly one forgets the pure pleasure of having this new creature, immaculate, perfect. And I walk away from her drenched with memory, with envy. Yet I know other things: that her life is far from simple; she is a mathematician who now has two children under the age of four; she is living even now in the rhythms of other lives—not only the regular cry of the infant but her three-year-old's needs, her husband's problems. In the building where I live, women are still raising children alone, living day in and day out within their individual family units, doing the laundry, herding the tricycles to the park, waiting for the husbands to come home. There is a baby-sitting pool and a children's playroom, young fathers push prams on weekends, but child-care is still the individual responsibility of the individual woman. I envy the sensuality of having an infant of two weeks curled against one's breast; I do not envy the turmoil of the elevator full of small children, babies howling in the laundromat, the apartment in winter where pent-up seven- and eight-year-olds have one adult to look to for their frustrations, reassurances, the grounding of their lives.

4

But, it will be said, this is the human condition, this interpenetration of pain and pleasure, frustration and fulfillment. I might have told myself the same thing, fifteen or eighteen years ago. But the patriarchal institution of motherhood is not the "human condition" any more than rape, prostitution, and slavery are. (Those who speak largely of the human condition are usually those most exempt from its oppressions—whether of sex, race, or servitude.)

Motherhood—unmentioned in the histories of conquest and serfdom, wars and treaties, exploration and imperialism—has a history, it has an ideology, it is more fundamental than tribalism or nationalism. My individual, seemingly private pains as a mother, the individual, seemingly private pains of the mothers around me and before me, whatever our class or color, the regulation of women's reproductive power by men in every totalitarian system and every socialist revolution, the legal and technical control by men of contraception, fertility, abortion, obstetrics, gynecology, and extrauterine reproductive experiments—all are essential to the patriarchal system, as is the negative or suspect status of women who are not mothers.

Throughout patriarchal mythology, dream-symbolism, theology, language, two ideas flow side by side: one, that the female body is impure, corrupt, the site of discharges, bleedings, dangerous to masculinity, a source of moral and physical contamination, "the devil's gateway." On the other hand, as mother the woman is beneficent, sacred, pure, asexual, nourishing; and the physical potential for motherhood—that same body with its bleedings and mysteries—is her single destiny and justification in life. These two ideas have become deeply internalized in women, even in the most independent of us, those who seem to lead the freest lives.

In order to maintain two such notions, each in its contradictory purity, the masculine imagination has had to divide women, to see us, and force us to see ourselves, as polarized into good or evil, fertile or barren, pure or impure. The asexual Victorian angel-wife and the Victorian prostitute were institutions created by this double thinking, which had nothing to do with women's actual sensuality and everything to do with the male's subjective experience of women. The political and economic expediency of this kind of thinking is most unashamedly and dramatically to be found where sexism and racism become one.

The social historian A. W. Calhoun describes the encouragement of the rape of black women by the sons of white planters, in a deliberate effort to produce more mulatto slaves, mulattos being considered more valuable. He quotes two mid–nineteenth-century southern writers on the subject of women:

> "The heaviest part of the white racial burden in slavery was the African woman of strong sex instincts and devoid of a sexual conscience, at the white man's door, in the white man's dwelling." . . . "Under the institution of slavery, the attack against the integrity of white civilization was made by the insidious influence of the lascivious hybrid woman at the point of weakest resistance. In the uncompromising purity of the white mother and wife of the upper classes lay the one assurance of the future purity of the race."[1]

The motherhood created by rape is not only degraded; the raped woman is turned into the criminal, the *attacker*. But who brought the black woman to the white man's door, whose absence of a sexual conscience produced the financially profitable mulatto children? Is it asked whether the "pure" white mother and wife was not also raped by the white planter, since she was assumed to be devoid of "strong sexual instinct?" In the American South, as elsewhere, it was economically necessary that children be produced; the mothers, black and white, were a means to this end.

Neither the "pure" nor the "lascivious" woman, neither the so-called mistress nor the slave woman, neither the woman praised for reducing herself to a brood animal nor the woman scorned and penalized as an "old maid" or a "dyke," has had any real autonomy or selfhood to gain from this subversion of the female body (and hence of the female mind). Yet, because short-term advantages are often the only ones visible to the powerless, we, too, have played our parts in continuing this subversion.

5

Most of the literature of infant care and psychology has assumed that the process toward individuation is essentially the *child's* drama, played out against and with a parent or parents who are, for better or worse, givens. Nothing could have prepared me for the realization that I *was* a mother, one of those givens, when I knew I was still in a state of uncreation myself. That calm, sure, unambivalent woman who moved through the pages of the manuals I read seemed as unlike me as an astronaut. Nothing, to be sure, had prepared me for the intensity of relationship already existing between me and a creature I had carried in my body and now held in my arms and fed from my breasts. Throughout pregnancy and nursing, women are urged to relax, to mime the serenity of madonnas. No one mentions the psychic crisis of bearing a first child, the excitation of long-buried feelings about one's own mother, the sense of confused power and powerlessness, of being taken over on the one hand and of touching new physical and psychic potentialities on the other, a heightened sensibility which can be exhilarating, bewildering, and exhausting. No one mentions the strangeness of attraction—which can be as single-minded and overwhelming as the early days of a love affair—to a being so tiny, so dependent, so folded-in to itself—who is, and yet is not, part of oneself.

From the beginning the mother caring for her child is involved in a continually changing dialogue, crystallized in such moments as when, hearing her child's cry, she feels milk rush into her breasts; when, as the child first suckles, the uterus begins contracting and returning to its normal size, and when later, the child's mouth, caressing the nipple, creates waves of sensuality in the womb where it once lay; or when, smelling the breast even in sleep, the child starts to root and grope for the nipple.

The child gains her first sense of her own existence from the mother's responsive gestures and expressions. It's as if, in the mother's eyes, her smile, her stroking touch, the child first reads the message: *You are there!* And the mother, too, is discovering her own existence newly. She is connected with this other being, by the most mundane and the most invisible strands, in a way she can be connected with no one else except in the deep past of her infant connection with her own mother. And she, too, needs to struggle from that one-to-one intensity into new real-ization, or reaffirmation, of her being-unto-herself.

The act of suckling a child, like a sexual act, may be tense, physically painful, charged with cultural feelings of inadequacy and guilt; or, like a sexual act, it can be a physically delicious, elementally soothing experience, filled with a tender sensuality. But just as lovers have to break apart after sex and become separate individuals again, so the mother has to wean herself from the infant and the infant from herself. In psychologies of child-rearing the emphasis is placed on "letting the child go" for the child's sake. But the mother needs to let it go as much or more for her own.

Motherhood, in the sense of an intense, reciprocal relation-ship with a particular child, or children, is *one part* of female process; it is not an identity for all time. The housewife in her mid-forties may jokingly say, "I feel like someone out of a job." But in the eyes of society, once having been mothers, what are we, if not always mothers? The process of "letting-go"—though we are charged with blame if we do not—is an act of revolt against the grain of patriarchal culture. But it is not enough to let our children go; we need selves of our own to return to.

To have borne and reared a child is to have done that thing which patriarchy joins with physiology to render into the defini-tion of femaleness. But also, it can mean the experiencing of one's own body and emotions in a powerful way. We experience not only physical, fleshly changes but the feeling of a change in character. We learn, often through painful self-discipline and self-cauterization, those qualities which are supposed to be "innate" in us: patience, self-sacrifice, the willingness to repeat endlessly the small, routine chores of socializing a human being. We are also, often to our amazement, flooded with feelings both of love and violence intenser and fiercer than any we had ever known. (A well-known pacifist, also a mother, said recently on a platform: "If anyone laid a hand on *my* child, I'd murder him.")

These and similar experiences are not easily put aside. Small wonder that women gritting their teeth at the incessant de-mands of child-care still find it hard to acknowledge their children's growing independence of them; still feel they must be at home, on the *qui vive*, be that ear always tuned for the sound of emergency, of being needed. Children grow up, not in a smooth ascending curve, but jaggedly, their needs inconstant as weather. Cultural "norms" are marvelously powerless to decide, in a child of eight or ten, what gender s/he will assume on a given day, or how s/he will meet emergency, loneliness, pain, hunger. One is constantly made aware that a human existence is anything but linear, long before the labyrinth of puberty; because a human being of six is still a human being.

In a tribal or even a feudal culture a child of six would have serious obligations; ours have none. But also, the woman at home with children is not believed to be doing serious work; she is just supposed to be acting out of maternal instinct, doing chores a man would never take on, largely uncritical of the meaning of what she does. So child and mother alike are depreciated, because only grown men and women in the paid labor force are supposed to be "productive."

The power-relations between mother and child are often simply a reflection of power-relations in patriarchal society: "You will do this because I know what is good for you" is difficult to distinguish from "You will do this because I can *make* you." Powerless women have always used mothering as a channel—narrow but deep—for their own human will to power, their need to return upon the world what it has visited on them. The child dragged by the arm across the room to be washed, the child cajoled, bullied, and bribed into taking "one more bite" of a detested food, is more than just a child which must be reared according to cultural traditions of "good mothering." S/he is a piece of reality, of the world, which can be acted on, even modified, by a woman restricted from acting on anything else except inert materials like dust and food.

6

When I try to return to the body of the young woman of twenty-six, pregnant for the first time, who fled from the physical knowledge of her pregnancy and at the same time from her intellect and vocation, I realize that I was effectively alien-

ated from my real body and my real spirit by the institution—
not the fact—of motherhood. This institution—the foundation
of human society as we know it—allowed me only certain views,
certain expectations, whether embodied in the booklet in my
obstetrician's waiting room, the novels I had read, my mother-
in-law's approval, my memories of my own mother, the Sistine
Madonna or she of the Michelangelo *Pietà*, the floating notion
that a woman pregnant is a woman calm in her fulfillment or,
simply, a woman waiting. Women have always been seen as
waiting: waiting to be asked, waiting for our menses, in fear
lest they do or do not come, waiting for men to come home
from wars, or from work, waiting for children to grow up, or
for the birth of a new child, or for menopause.

In my own pregnancy I dealt with this waiting, this female
fate, by denying every active, powerful aspect of myself. I became dissociated both from my immediate, present, bodily experience and from my reading, thinking, writing life. Like a
traveler in an airport where her plane is several hours delayed,
who leafs through magazines she would never ordinarily read,
surveys shops whose contents do not interest her, I committed
myself to an outward serenity and a profound inner boredom. If
boredom is simply a mask for anxiety, then I had learned, as a
woman, to be supremely bored rather than to examine the anxiety underlying my Sistine tranquility. My body, finally truth-
ful, paid me back in the end: I was allergic to pregnancy.

I have come to believe, as will be clear throughout this book,
that female biology—the diffuse, intense sensuality radiating
out from clitoris, breasts, uterus, vagina; the lunar cycles of
menstruation; the gestation and fruition of life which can take
place in the female body—has far more radical implications
than we have yet come to appreciate. Patriarchal thought has
limited female biology to its own narrow specifications. The
feminist vision has recoiled from female biology for these reasons; it will, I believe, come to view our physicality as a resource, rather than a destiny. In order to live a fully human
life we require not only *control* of our bodies (though control
is a prerequisite); we must touch the unity and resonance of
our physicality, our bond with the natural order, the corporeal
ground of our intelligence.

The ancient, continuing envy, awe, and dread of the male for the female capacity to create life has repeatedly taken the form of hatred for every other female aspect of creativity. Not only have women been told to stick to motherhood, but we have been told that our intellectual or aesthetic creations were inappropriate, inconsequential, or scandalous, an attempt to become "like men," or to escape from the "real" tasks of adult womanhood: marriage and childbearing. To "think like a man" has been both praise and prison for women trying to escape the body-trap. No wonder that many intellectual and creative women have insisted that they were "human beings" first and women only incidentally, have minimized their physicality and their bonds with other women. The body has been made so problematic for women that it has often seemed easier to shrug it off and travel as a disembodied spirit.

But this reaction against the body is now coming into synthesis with new inquiries into the actual—as opposed to the culturally warped—power inherent in female biology, however we choose to use it, and by no means limited to the maternal function.

My own story, which is woven throughout this book, is only one story. What I carried away in the end was a determination to heal—insofar as an individual woman can, and as much as possible with other women—the separation between mind and body; never again to lose myself both psychically and physically in that way. Slowly I came to understand the paradox contained in "my" experience of motherhood; that, although different from many other women's experiences it was not unique; and that only in shedding the illusion of my uniqueness could I hope, as a woman, to have any authentic life at all.

II   THE "SACRED CALLING"

One of the letters quoted in Margaret Sanger's *Motherhood in Bondage* (1928) comes from a woman seeking birth-control advice so that she can have intercourse with her husband without fear, and thus carry out her duties both as mother and wife: "I am not passionate," she writes, "but try to treat the sexual embrace the way I should, be natural and play the part, for you know, it's so different a life from what all girls expect."[1] The history of institutionalized motherhood and of institutionalized heterosexual relations (in this case, marriage), converge in these words from an ordinary woman of half a century ago, who sought only to fulfill the requirements of both institutions, "be natural and play the part"—that impossible contradiction demanded of women. What strategy handed from ashamed mother to daughter, what fear of losing love, home, desirability as a woman, taught her—taught us all—to fake orgasm? "What all girls expect"—is that, was it for her, more than what the institution had promised her in the form of romance, of transcendent experience? Had she some knowledge of her own needs, for tenderness, perhaps, for being touched in certain ways, for being treated as more than a body for sex and procreation? What gave her the courage to write to Margaret Sanger, to try to get some modest control over the use of her body—The needs of her existing children? Her husband's demands? The dim, simmering voice of self? We may assume all three. For generations of women have asserted their courage

on behalf of their own children and men, then on behalf of
strangers, and finally for themselves.

The institution of motherhood is not identical with bearing
and caring for children, any more than the institution of heterosexuality is identical with intimacy and sexual love. Both create
the prescriptions and the conditions in which choices are made
or blocked; they are not "reality" but they have shaped the
circumstances of our lives. The new scholars of women's history have begun to discover that, in any case, the social institutions and prescriptions for behavior created by men have not
necessarily accounted for the real lives of women. Yet any institution which expresses itself so universally ends by profoundly
affecting our experience, even the language we use to describe it.
The experience of maternity and the experience of sexuality
have both been channeled to serve male interests; behavior
which threatens the institutions, such as illegitimacy, abortion,
lesbianism, is considered deviant or criminal.

Institutionalized heterosexuality told women for centuries
that we were dangerous, unchaste, the embodiment of carnal
lust; then that we were "not passionate," frigid, sexually passive; today it prescribes the "sensuous," "sexually liberated"
woman in the West, the dedicated revolutionary ascetic in
China; and everywhere it denies the reality of women's love for
women. Institutionalized motherhood demands of women maternal "instinct" rather than intelligence, selflessness rather than
self-realization, relation to others rather than the creation of
self. Motherhood is "sacred" so long as its offspring are "legitimate"—that is, as long as the child bears the name of a father
who legally controls the mother. It is "woman's highest and
holiest mission," according to a socialist tract of 1914;[2] and a
racist southern historian of 1910 tells us that "woman is the
embodied home, and the home is the basis of all institutions,
the buttress of society."[3]

A more recent version of the argument comes from the
British critic Stuart Hampshire, who equates the "liberated
woman" of today with Ibsen's panic-driven, suicidal heroine
Hedda Gabler (who also refuses motherhood), in the following
melancholy prophecy:

An entirely enlightened mind, just recently conscious of its strength and under-employed, finally corrodes and bleaches all the material of which respect is made—observances, memories of a shared past, moral resolutions for the future: no stain of weak and ordinary sentiment will remain, no differentiation of feeling and therefore no point of attachment. Why carry on the family, and therefore why carry on the race? Only a feminine skepticism, newly aroused, can be so totally subversive.[4]

Patriarchy would seem to require, not only that women shall assume the major burden of pain and self-denial for the furtherance of the species, but that a majority of that species—women—shall remain essentially unquestioning and unenlightened. On this "underemployment" of female consciousness depend the morality and the emotional life of the human family. Like his predecessors of fifty and a hundred and more years ago, Hampshire sees society as threatened when women begin to choose the terms of their lives. Patriarchy could not survive without motherhood and heterosexuality in their institutional forms; therefore they have to be treated as axioms, as "nature" itself, not open to question except where, from time to time and place to place, "alternate life-styles" for certain individuals are tolerated.

2

The "sacred calling" has had, of course, an altogether pragmatic reality. In the American colonies an ordinary family consisted of from twelve to twenty-five children. An "old maid," who might be all of twenty-five years of age, was treated with reproach if not derision; she had no way of surviving economically, and was usually compelled to board with her kin and help with the household and children.[5] No other "calling" was open to her. An English working-woman whose childhood was lived in the 1850s and 1860s writes that "I was my mother's seventh child, and seven more were born after me—fourteen in all—which made my mother a perfect slave. Generally speaking, she was either expecting a baby to be born or had one at the breast. At the time there were eight of us the eldest was not big enough to get ready to go to school without help."[6] Under American slavery,

> . . . it was common for planters to command women and girls to have children. On a Carolina plantation of about 100 slaves the owner threatened to flog all of the women because they did not breed. They told him they could not while they had to work in the rice ditches (in one or two feet of water). After swearing and threatening he told them to tell the overseer's wife when they got in that way and he would put them on the land to work.[7]

Both the white pioneer mother and the black female slave, worked daily as a fully productive part of the economy. Black women often worked the fields with their children strapped to their backs. Historically, women have borne and raised children while doing their share of necessary productive labor, as a matter of course. Yet by the nineteenth century the voices rise against the idea of the "working mother," and in praise of "the mother at home." These voices reach a crescendo just as technology begins to reduce the sheer level of physical hardship in general, and as the size of families begins to decline. In the last century and a half, the idea of full-time, exclusive motherhood takes root, and the "home" becomes a religious obsession.

By the 1830s, in America, the male institutional voice (in this case that of the American Tract Society) was intoning:

> Mothers have as powerful an influence over the welfare of future generations, *as all other earthly causes combined*. . . . When our land is filled with pious and patriotic mothers, then will it be filled with virtuous and patriotic men. The world's redeeming influence, under the blessing of the Holy Spirit, must come from a mother's lips. *She who was first in the transgression, must yet be the principal earthly instrument in the restoration.* It is maternal influence, after all, which must be the great agent in the hands of God, in bringing back our guilty race to duty and happiness. (Emphasis mine.)

The mother bears the weight of Eve's transgression (is, thus, the first offender, the polluted one, the polluter) yet precisely because of this she is expected to carry the burden of male salvation. Lest she fail, there are horrible examples to warn her:

> It was the mother of Byron who laid the foundation of his preeminence in guilt. . . . If the crimes of the poet deserve the execration of the world, the world cannot forget that it was the mother who fostered in his youthful heart those passions which made the son a curse to his fellow-man.[8]

But female voices, also, swell the chorus. Maria McIntosh, in 1850, describes the ideal wife and mother:

> Her husband cannot look on her . . . without reading in the serene expression of her face, the Divine beatitude, "Blessed are the pure in heart". Her children revere her as the earthly type of perfect love. They learn even more from her example than from her precept, that they are to live, not in themselves, but to their fellow-creatures, and to the God in them. . . . She has taught them to love their country and devote themselves to its advancement . . .[9]

Certainly the mother serves the interests of patriarchy: she exemplifies in one person religion, social conscience, and nationalism. Institutional motherhood revives and renews all other institutions.

The nineteenth-century "mother at home" seems, however, to have suffered from certain familiar evil traits, such as ill-temper.

> . . . can a mother expect to govern her child when she cannot govern herself? . . . She must learn to control herself, to subdue her own passions; she must set her children an example of meekness and of equanimity. . . . Let a mother feel grieved, and manifest her grief when her child does wrong; let her, with calmness and reflection, use the discipline which the case requires; but never let her manifest irritated feeling, or give utterance to an angry expression.[10]

This from the male expert. *The Mother's Book* (1831), by Lydia Maria Child, advises:

> Do you say it is impossible always to govern one's feelings? There is one method, a never-failing one—prayer. . . . You will say, perhaps, that you have not leisure to pray every time

your temper is provoked, or your heart is grieved.—It requires
no time.—The inward ejaculation of "Lord, help me to over-
come this temptation" may be made in any place and amid any
employments; and, if uttered in humble sincerity, the voice
that said to the raging waters, "Peace! Be still!" will restore
quiet to your troubled soul.[11]

Such advice to mothers gives us some sense of how female
anger in general has been perceived. In *Little Women*, Marmee
tells Jo, the daughter with an "Apollyon" of a "temper":

> I am angry nearly every day of my life, Jo; but I have learned
> not to show it; and I still hope to learn not to feel it, though it
> may take me another forty years to do so.[12]

I recall similar indoctrination in my own girlhood: my "temper" was a dark, wicked blotch in me, not a response to events
in the outer world. My childhood anger was often alluded to
as a "tantrum," by which I understood the adult world to mean
some kind of possession, as by a devil. Later, as a young mother,
I remember feeling guilt that my explosions of anger were a
"bad example" for my children, as if they, too, should be taught
that "temper" is a defect of character, having nothing to do
with what happens in the world outside one's flaming skin.
Mother-love is supposed to be continuous, unconditional. Love
and anger cannot coexist. Female anger threatens the institution of motherhood.

3

The nineteenth- and twentieth-century ideal of the mother and
children immured together in the home, the specialization of
motherhood for women, the separation of the home from the
"man's world" of wage-earning, struggle, ambition, aggression,
power, of the "domestic" from the "public" or the "political"—
all this is a late-arrived development in human history. But the
force both of the ideal and of the reality is so great that, clearly,
it serves no single, simple purpose.

How did this notion begin? And what purpose does it serve?
From earliest settled life until the growth of factories as

centers of production, the home was not a refuge, a place for leisure and retreat from the cruelty of the "outside world"; it was a part of the world, a center of work, a subsistence unit. In it women, men, and children as early as they were able, carried on an endless, seasonal activity of raising, preparing, and processing food, processing skins, reeds, clay, dyes, fats, herbs, producing textiles and clothing, brewing, making soap and candles, doctoring and nursing, passing on these skills and crafts to younger people. A woman was rarely if ever alone with nothing but the needs of a child or children to see to.* Women and children were part of an actively busy social cluster. Work was hard, laborious, often physically exhausting, but it was diversified and usually communal. Mortality from childbirth and pregnancy and the loss of infant lives was extremely high, the lifespan of women brief, and it would be naive to romanticize an existence constantly threatened by malnutrition, famine, and disease. But motherhood and the keeping of the home as a private refuge were not, could not be, the central occupation of women, nor were mother and child circumscribed into an isolated relationship.

On the Wisconsin frontier, pioneer mothers were innkeepers, schoolteachers, pharmacists, running a home as a subsistence unit with perhaps ten to fifteen children, taking in passing travelers and feeding and lodging them. The mother "collected wild plants, berries, barks, flowers and roots. . . . These she

---

* Agnes Smedley, writing of her grandmother at the turn of the century, sketches a vigorous, powerful woman involved in productive work:

> She milked the cows each morning and night with the sweeping strength and movements of a man. She carried pails of skimmed milk and slopped the hogs; when she kneaded bread for baking it whistled and snapped under her hands, and her arms worked like steam pistons. She awoke the men at dawn and she told them when to go upstairs at night. She directed the picking of fruit—apples, pears, peaches, berries of every kind, and she taught her girls how to can, preserve and dry them for the winter. In the autumn she directed the slaughtering of beef and pork, and then smoked the meat in the smokehouse. When the sugar cane ripened in the summer she saw it cut, and superintended the making of molasses in the long, low sugar cane mill at the foot of the hill.

This woman had five children of her own, and eight of her husband's from a prior marriage. (*Daughter of Earth* [Old Westbury, N.Y.: Feminist Press, 1973], pp. 18–19.)

. . . dried and labeled . . . to be used upon short notice. . . .
At times she was a surgeon . . . and fitted and bound together
fingers, hanging on shreds; or removed a rusty spike from a
foot, washed the wound . . . and saved the injured member."[13]
The real, depleting burdens of motherhood were physical: the
toll of continual pregnancies, the drain of constant childbearing
and nursing.

The nineteenth century saw crucial changes in Western assumptions about the home, work, women, and women's relationship to productivity. The earliest factories were actually the
homes of agricultural workers who began producing textiles,
iron, glass, and other commodities for sale to a middleman, who
might supply the raw materials as well as the market for the
finished goods.[14] Women had worked alongside men even at
the forges, had had almost a monopoly of the brewing trade,
and the textile industry in particular had always depended on
women; as early as the fourteenth century in England women
had woven not only for the home but outside it.

Gradually those women who still worked at hand-spinning
or weaving in the home were driven into the mills by the competition of power-spinning machines. There were no laws to
limit the hours of labor; a woman worked for twelve hours, then
returned to take up the burdens of her household. By 1844 a
British factory inspector could report that "a vast majority of
the persons employed at night and for long periods during the
day are females; their labour is cheaper and they are more
easily induced to undergo severe bodily fatigue than men."[15]

These same women left children at home; sometimes in the
care of a six- or seven-year-old daughter, a grandmother, or a
neighbor's hired child. Sometimes an older woman would keep
infants and young children in her house for a fee; instead of
breast-milk the unweaned babies were fed watery gruel or
"pap," or the mother, if she could afford it, was forced to buy
cow's milk for her child. The children were dosed with laudanum to keep them quiet. The severance of the sphere of work
from the sphere of child-raising thus immediately created disadvantage and hardship for both child and mother.

These women worked from necessity, to supplement a husband's inadequate or nonexistent wages; and because they were

paid less, their employment was seen as threatening to male workers. Women's work was clearly subversive to "the home" and to patriarchal marriage; not only might a man find himself economically dependent on his wife's earnings, but it would conceivably even be possible for women to dispense with marriage from an economic point of view.* These two forces—the humanitarian concern for child welfare and the fear for patriarchal values—converged to provide pressure which led to legislation controlling children's and women's labor, and the assertion that "the home, its cares and employments, is the woman's true sphere."

The home thus defined had never before existed. It was a creation of the Industrial Revolution, an ideal invested with the power of something God-given, and its power *as an idea* remains unexpunged today. For the first time, the productivity of women (apart from reproductivity) was seen as "a waste of time, a waste of property, a waste of morals and a waste of health and life." Women were warned that their absence from home did not only mean the neglect of their children; if they failed to create the comforts of the nest, their men would be off to the alehouse. The welfare of men and children was the true mission of women. Since men had no mission to care for children or keep house, the solution was to get the women out of the factories.

As public opinion became aroused over the fate of children whose mothers worked in the mills, some efforts were made to set up nurseries; but in Victorian and Edwardian England, as in twentieth-century America, state-supported child-care was opposed on the grounds that it would violate "the sanctity of the domestic hearth and the decent seclusion of private life. . . . The family is the unit upon which a constitutional Government has been raised which is the admiration and envy of mankind. Hitherto, whatever the laws have touched, they have not dared invade this sacred precinct; and the husband and

---

* The social historian A. W. Calhoun suggests that in America the factory opened the way to a new economic independence for women which they had never had in the colonial period or the opening of the frontier. The need to keep the family patriarchal was at least one force behind the enactment of child-labor laws and of laws restricting the hours and conditions of work for women.

wife, however poor, returning home from whatsoever occupation or harassing engagements, have *there* found *their* dominion, *their* repose, *their* compensation for many a care."[16]

In 1915 the Women's Cooperative Guild in Britain published a volume of letters written by the wives of manual laborers about their lives as mothers and workers in the home. These lives stood as far as possible in contradiction to the ideal of the home as a protected place apart from the brutal realities of work and struggle. The average woman had from five to eleven children with several miscarriages, most of them with no prenatal care and inadequate diet. "At the time when she ought to be well fed she stints herself in order to save; for in a working class home if there is saving to be done, it is not the husband and children, but the mother who makes her meal off the scraps which remain over, or 'plays with meatless bones.' "[17] The anxiety and physical depletion of incessant childbearing is a theme which runs throughout these letters. Many—against their principles, and often facing a husband's opposition—took drugs to bring on abortion, which were usually ineffective and on which the sickliness of the forthcoming child was blamed. But along with the ill-health, mental strain, and exhaustion of which the women write, go an extraordinary resiliency of spirit, the will to make do, and an active sense of the injustice of their situation.

> In my early motherhood I took it for granted that women had to suffer at these times, and it was best to behave and not make a fuss. . . . I do not know which is the worst—childbearing with anxiety and strain of mind and body to make ends meet, with the thought of another one to share the already small allowance, or getting through the confinement fairly well, and getting about household duties too soon, and bringing on other ailments which make life and everything a burden.[18]

Many wrote of the damage done by ignorance, the young woman's total lack of preparation for marriage and pregnancy; and even more of the insensitivity of husbands demanding sex throughout pregnancy or immediately after delivery:

> During the time of pregnancy, the male beast keeps entirely from the female: not so with the woman; she is the prey of a

man just the same as though she was not pregnant. . . . If a woman does not feel well she must not say so, as a man has such a lot of ways of punishing a woman if she does not give in to him.[19]

I do not blame my husband for this birth. [The writer had had seven children and two miscarriages.] He had waited patiently for ten months because I was ill, and thinking the time was safe, I submitted as a duty, knowing there is much unfaithfulness on the part of the husband where families are limited. . . . It is quite time this question of maternity was taken up, and we must let the men know we are human beings with ideals, and aspire to something higher than to be mere objects on which they can satisfy themselves.[20]

The women were not only pregnant for much of their lives, but doing heavy labor: scrubbing floors, hauling basins of wash, ironing, cooking over coal and wood fires which had to be fed and tended. One woman, against her doctor's orders, did her ironing and kneading in bed while recovering from a miscarriage.[21] Despite their resentment of the husbands' sexual demands and opposition to abortion, the women tried to spare their men, who had worked hard all day, from further strain in the home:

I dare not let my husband in his precarious condition hear a cry of pain from me, and travail pain cannot always be stifled; and here again the doctor helped me by giving me a sleeping draught to administer him as soon as I felt the pangs of childbirth. Hence he slept in one room while I travailed in the other, and brought forth the liveliest boy that ever gladdened a mother's heart.[22]

But there was no homecoming from work for the women.

Within the home or outside it, reality has always been at odds with the ideal. In 1860 in America a million women were employed; by the end of the Civil War there were 75,000 working-women in New York City alone. In 1973 the United States Census reported more than six million children under the age of six whose mothers worked full time outside the home.[23] Without free, universal, child-care, any woman who has ever had to contrive and improvise in order to leave her children daily and earn a living can imagine the weight of anxiety, guilt, uncertainty, the financial burden, the actual emergencies which these statistics imply. The image of the mother in the home, however unrealistic, has haunted and reproached the lives of wage-earning mothers. But it has also become, and for men as well as women, a dangerous archetype: the Mother, source of angelic love and forgiveness in a world increasingly ruthless and impersonal; the feminine, leavening, emotional element in a society ruled by male logic and male claims to "objective," "rational" judgment; the symbol and residue of moral values and tenderness in a world of wars, brutal competition, and contempt for human weakness.

4

The physical and psychic weight of responsibility on the woman with children is by far the heaviest of social burdens. It cannot be compared with slavery or sweated labor because the emotional bonds between a woman and her children make her vulnerable in ways which the forced laborer does not know; he can hate and fear his boss or master, loathe the toil; dream of revolt or of becoming a boss; the woman with children is a prey to far more complicated, subversive feelings. Love and anger *can* exist concurrently; anger at the conditions of motherhood can become translated into anger at the child, along with the fear that we are not "loving"; grief at all we cannot do for our children in a society so inadequate to meet human needs becomes translated into guilt and self-laceration. This "powerless responsibility" as one group of women has termed it, is a heavier burden even than providing a living—which so many mothers have done, and do, simultaneously with mothering— because it is recognized in some quarters, at least, that economic forces, political oppression, lie behind poverty and unemployment; but the mother's very character, her status as a woman, are in question if she has "failed" her children.

Whatever the known facts,* it is still assumed that the mother is "with the child." It is she, finally, who is held accountable for her children's health, the clothes they wear, their behavior at school, their intelligence and general development. Even when she is the sole provider for a fatherless family, she and no one else bears the guilt for a child who must spend the day in a shoddy nursery or an abusive school system. Even when she herself is trying to cope with an environment beyond her control—malnutrition, rats, lead-paint poisoning, the drug traffic, racism—in the eyes of society the mother *is* the child's environment. The worker can unionize, go out on strike; mothers are divided from each other in homes, tied to their children by compassionate bonds; our wildcat strikes have most often taken the form of physical or mental breakdown.

For mothers, the privatization of the home has meant not only an increase in powerlessness, but a desperate loneliness. A group of East London women talked with Hannah Gavron of the difference between trying to raise children in a street of row houses and in the new high-rise flats of postwar London: the loss of neighborhood, of stoop life, of a common pavement where children could be watched at play by many pairs of eyes.[24] In Cambridge, Massachusetts in the 1950s, some married graduate students lived in housing built on the plan of the "lane" or row-house street, where children played in a common court, a mother could deliver her child to a neighbor for an hour, children filtered in and out of each others' houses, and mothers, too, enjoyed a casual, unscheduled companionship with each other. With the next step upward in academic status, came the move to the suburbs, to the smaller, then the larger, private house, the isolation of "the home" from other homes increasing with the husband's material success. The working-class mothers in their new flats and the academic wives in their new affluence all lost something: they became, to a more extreme degree, house-bound, isolated women.

* Twenty-six million children of wage-earning mothers, 8 million in female-headed households in the United States by the mid-1970s (Alice Rossi, "Children and Work in the Lives of Women," a paper delivered at the University of Arizona, February 7, 1976).

Lee Sanders Comer, a British Marxist-feminist, reiterates the classic Marxist critique of the nuclear family—the small, privatized unit of a woman, a man, and their children. In this division of labor the man is the chief or the sole wage-earner, and the woman's role is that of housewife, mother, consumer of goods, and emotional support of men and children. The "family" really means "the mother," who carries the major share of child-rearing, and who also absorbs the frustrations and rage her husband may bring home from work (often in the form of domestic violence). Her own anger becomes illegitimate, since her job is to provide him with the compassion and comfort he needs at home in order to return daily to the factory or the mine pit. Comer sees this division of labor as demanded by capitalism. But why should capitalism *in and of itself* require that women specialize in this role of emotional salvager, or that women and never men rear children and take care of the home? How much does this really have to do with capitalism, and how much with the system which, as Eli Zaretsky points out, pre-dated capitalism and has survived under socialism—patriarchy?[25]

The dependency of the male child on a woman in the first place, the spectacle of women producing new life from their bodies, milk from their breasts, the *necessity* of women for men —emotionally and as reproducers of life—these are elements we must recognize in any attempt to change the institutions that have germinated from them. Under patriarchal socialism we find the institution of motherhood revised and reformed in certain ways which permit women to serve (as we have actually served through most of our history) *both* as the producers and nurturers of children *and* as the full-time workers demanded by a developing economy. Child-care centers, youth camps, schools, facilitate but do not truly radicalize the familiar "double role" of working women; in no socialist country does the breakdown of the division of labor extend to bringing large numbers of men into child-care. Under Marxist or Maoist socialism, both motherhood and heterosexuality are still institutionalized; heterosexual marriage and the family are still viewed as the "normal" situation for human beings and the building-blocks of the new society. Lesbianism is announced to be non-existent in China, while in Cuba homosexuals are treated as political criminals. Birth control may or may not be available to women, depending on economic, military, and demographic pressures; in China women are pressured to become experimental subjects for new methods of birth control "for the revolution."[26] There is nothing revolutionary whatsoever about the control of women's bodies by men. The woman's body is the terrain on which patriarchy is erected.

III THE KINGDOM
OF THE FATHERS

For the first time in history, a pervasive recognition is developing that the patriarchal system cannot answer for itself; that it is not inevitable; that it is transitory; and that the cross-cultural, global domination of women by men can no longer be either denied or defended. When we acknowledge this, we tear open the relationship at the core of all power-relationships, a tangle of lust, violence, possession, fear, conscious longing, unconscious hostility, sentiment, rationalization: the sexual understructure of social and political forms. For the first time we are in a position to look around us at the Kingdom of the Fathers and take its measure. What we see is the one system which recorded civilization has never actively challenged, and which has been so universal as to seem a law of nature.*

* Jane Harrison in 1912, Helen Diner in the 1920s, Virginia Woolf in 1938, all indicated, questioned, and challenged the prevalence of patriarchal values. Simone de Beauvoir, in 1949, stated categorically that "this has always been a man's world"; but her discussion of the widest implications of this is largely by inference. The first extensive analysis of patriarchy in contemporary American feminist literature is that of Kate Millett in *Sexual Politics* (1970). An even more detailed and widely ramified treatment is found throughout Mary Daly's *Beyond God the Father: Toward a Philosophy of Women's Liberation* (1973). Daly depicts at length the patriarchal bias which saturates all culture as an unacknowledged assumption. The earlier writings of men like J. J. Bachofen, Robert Briffault, Frederick Engels, Erich Neumann, among others, though useful as preliminary steps in identifying the phenomenon and in suggesting that the patriarchal family is not an inevitable "fact of nature," still stop short of recognizing the omnipresence of patriarchal bias as it affects even the

The Kingdom of the Fathers   57

Patriarchy is the power of the fathers: a familial-social, ideo-logical, political system in which men—by force, direct pres-sure, or through ritual, tradition, law, and language, customs, etiquette, education, and the division of labor, determine what part women shall or shall not play, and in which the female is everywhere subsumed under the male. It does not necessarily imply that no woman has power, or that all women in a given culture may not have certain powers. Among the matrilineal Crow, for example, women take major honorific roles in cere-mony and festival, but are debarred from social contacts and sacred objects during menstruation. Where women and men alike share a particular cultural phenomenon, it implies quite different things according to gender. "Where men wear veils—as among the North African Tuareg—this remoteness serves to increase the status and power of an individual, but it hardly does so for women in purdah." "Ultimately the line is drawn," as it is drawn, albeit differently, in every culture.[1]

Nor does patriarchy imply a direct survival of the father's power over the son, although this power-relationship was once culturally unquestioned, as for example under feudalism, or in the Victorian family. The German psychoanalyst Alexander Mitscherlich traces the decline of this father-son relationship under the pressures of industrialization, mass production, and the specialization of labor: as "work" moves outside the home and society becomes more complex and fragmented the father becomes a figure largely absent from the family, one who has lost the "substance" of his old practical authority. Yet, as Mitscherlich points out, "the patriarchal structural components in our society are closely associated with magical thought. It assumes the omnipotence-impotence relationship between fa-ther and son, God and man, ruler and ruled, to be the natural principle of social organization." This omnipotence-impotence relationship exists above all between men and women; and edu-cation, social organization, and our own "magical thought" still bear the imprint of that paternalistic image.[2]

The power of the fathers has been difficult to grasp because it

categories in which we think, and which has made of even the most edu-cated and privileged woman an outsider, a nonparticipant, in the molding of culture.

permeates everything, even the language in which we try to describe it. It is diffuse and concrete; symbolic and literal; universal, and expressed with local variations which obscure its universality. Under patriarchy, I may live in *purdah* or drive a truck; I may raise my children on a *kibbutz* or be the sole breadwinner for a fatherless family or participate in a demonstration against abortion legislation with my baby on my back; I may work as a "barefoot doctor" in a village commune in the People's Republic of China, or make my life on a lesbian commune in New England; I may become a hereditary or elected head of state or wash the underwear of a millionaire's wife; I may serve my husband his early-morning coffee within the clay walls of a Berber village or march in an academic procession; whatever my status or situation, my derived economic class, or my sexual preference, I live under the power of the fathers, and I have access only to so much of privilege or influence as the patriarchy is willing to accede to me, and only for so long as I will pay the price for male approval. And this power goes much further than laws and customs; in the words of the sociologist Brigitte Berger, "until now a primarily masculine intellect and spirit have dominated in the interpretation of society and culture—whether this interpretation is carried out by males or females . . . fundamentally masculine assumptions have shaped our whole moral and intellectual history."[3]

Matrilineal societies—in which kinship is traced and property transmitted through the mother's line—or matrilocal societies—where the husband moves into the house or village of the wife's mother—exist as variations on the more familiar western pattern of the patriarchal family which is also patrinomial, patrilineal, and patrilocal, and in which, without the father's name, a child is "illegitimate." But these variations merely represent different ways of channeling position and property to the male; they may confer more status and dignity on women and reduce the likelihood of polygamy; but they are not to be confused with "matriarchy." Nor, as Angela Davis has noted, can a black woman who is the head of her household be termed a "matriarch" while she is powerless and oppressed in the larger society.[4]

In matrilineal descent groups, women are responsible for the

care of children, and every child is the primary responsibility
of a particular woman even where other women share its care;
adult men have authority over women and children; and descent-
group exogamy (marrying out of the maternal family) is required. David Schneider makes the relative power of men and
women extremely clear: women and children are under male
authority "except perhaps for specially qualifying conditions applicable to a very few women of the society. Positions of highest
authority within the matrilineal descent group will . . . ordinarily be vested in statuses occupied by men."[5]

The advantages to women of a matrilineal over a patrilineal
order are actually slight. The emotional bonds between a mother
and her children are subject to the strain of the father's kinship
group pulling the child away from the maternal descent group;
particularly in the case of sons, "economic cooperation and the
transfer of property between father and child" has a compelling
effect in weakening the emotional and psychological authority
of the mother. The reverse is not true in patrilineal societies
because the mother, however strongly bonded with her children
emotionally, has no power beyond that relationship which
might challenge the power of father-right (descent and inheritance in the male line).[6]

The terms "matriarchy," "mother-right," and "gynocracy" or
"gynarchy" tend to be used imprecisely, often interchangeably.
Robert Briffault* goes to some pains to show that matriarchy
in primitive societies was not simply patriarchy with a different
sex in authority; he reserves the term "gynocracy" for a situation in which women would have economic domination and
control through property. He points out that the matriarchal elements in any society have had a *functional* origin—i.e., the
maternal function of gestating, bearing, nurturing, and educating children; and that with this function in early society went a
great deal of activity and authority which is now relegated to
the male sphere outside the family. Briffault's matriarchal society is one in which female creative power is pervasive, and
women have organic authority, rather than one in which the
woman establishes and maintains domination and control over

---

* *The Mothers* (1927); for a further discussion of Briffault's work, see
Chapter IV.

the man, as the man over the woman in patriarchy. There would be, according to Briffault, a kind of free consent to the authority of woman in a matriarchal society, because of her involvement with the essential practical and magical activity of that society. He thus sees matriarchy as organic by nature: because of the integration of agriculture, craft, invention, into the life centered around the mother and her children, women would be involved in a variety of creative and productive roles.* Patriarchy, in Briffault's view, develops when men revolt against this organic order, by establishing economic domination and by taking over magical powers previously considered the domain of women. "Gynocracy," like patriarchy, would thus mean a holding of power through force or economic pressure, and could only exist with the advent of private ownership and the economic advantage of one group over another.[7]

At the core of patriarchy is the individual family unit which originated with the idea of property and the desire to see one's property transmitted to one's biological descendants. Simone de Beauvoir connects this desire with the longing for immortality —in a profound sense, she says, "the owner transfers, alienates, his existence into his property; he cares more for it than for his very life; it overflows the narrow limits of his mortal lifetime, and continues to exist beyond the body's dissolution—the earthly and material incorporation of the immortal soul. But this survival can only come about if the property remains in the hands of its owner; it can be his beyond death only if it belongs to individuals in whom he sees himself projected, who are *his*."[8] A crucial moment in human consciousness, then, arrives when man discovers that it is he himself, not the moon or the spring rains or the spirits of the dead, who impregnates the woman; that the child she carries and gives birth to is *his* child, who can make *him* immortal, both mystically, by propitiating the gods with prayers and sacrifices when he is dead, and concretely, by receiving the patrimony from him. At this crossroads of

* See Kate Millett, *Sexual Politics* (New York: Doubleday, 1970): "One might . . . include the caveat that such a social order need not imply the domination of one sex which the term 'matriarchy' would, by its semantic analogue to patriarchy, infer. Given the simpler scale of life and the fact that female-centered fertility religion might be offset by male physical strength, pre-patriarchy might have been fairly egalitarian" (p. 28).

sexual possession, property ownership, and the desire to transcend death, developed the institution we know: the present-day patriarchal family with its supernaturalizing of the penis, its division of labor by gender, its emotional, physical, and material possessiveness, its ideal of monogamous marriage until death (and its severe penalties for adultery by the wife), the "illegitimacy" of a child born outside wedlock, the economic dependency of women, the unpaid domestic services of the wife, the obedience of women and children to male authority, the imprinting and continuation of heterosexual roles.

Again: some combination or aspect of patriarchal values prevails, whether in an Orthodox Jewish family where the wife mediates with the outer world and earns a living to enable the husband to study Torah; or for the upper-class European or Oriental couple, both professionals, who employ servants for domestic work and a governess for the children. They prevail even where women are the nominal "heads of households." For, much as she may act as the coequal provider or so-called matriarch within her own family, every mother must deliver her children over within a few years of their birth to the patriarchal system of education, of law, of religion, of sexual codes; she is, in fact, *expected* to prepare them to enter that system without rebelliousness or "maladjustment" and to perpetuate it in their own adult lives. Patriarchy depends on the mother to act as a conservative influence, imprinting future adults with patriarchal values even in those early years when the mother-child relationship might seem most individual and private; it has also assured through ritual and tradition that the mother shall cease, at a certain point, to hold the child—in particular the son—in her orbit. Certainly it has created images of the archetypal Mother which reinforce the conservatism of motherhood and convert it to an energy for the renewal of male power.

Of these images, and their implications for the whole spectrum of human relations, there is still much unsaid. Women have *been* both mothers and daughters, but have written little on the subject; the vast majority of literary and visual images of motherhood comes to us filtered through a collective or individual male consciousness. As soon as a woman knows that a child is growing in her body, she falls under the power of theories, ideals, archetypes, descriptions of her new existence, almost none of which have come from other women (though other women may transmit them) and all of which have floated invisibly about her since she first perceived herself to be female and therefore potentially a mother. We need to know what, out of all that welter of image-making and thought-spinning, is worth salvaging, if only to understand better an idea so crucial in history, a condition which has been wrested from the mothers themselves to buttress the power of the fathers.

2

Women are beginning to ask certain questions which, as the feminist philosopher Mary Daly observes, patriarchal method has declared nonquestions. The dominant male culture, in separating man as knower from both woman and from nature as the objects of knowledge,[8] evolved certain intellectual polarities which still have the power to blind our imaginations. Any deviance from a quality valued by that culture can be dismissed as negative: where "rationality" is posited as sanity, legitimate method, "real thinking," any alternative, intuitive, supersensory, or poetic knowledge is labeled "irrational." If we listen well to the connotations of "irrational" they are highly charged: we hear overtones of "hysteria" (that disease once supposed to arise in the womb), of "madness" (the *absence* of a certain type of thinking to which all "rational men" subscribe), and of randomness, chaotic *absence* of form. Thus no attempt need be made to discover a form or a language or a pattern foreign to those which technical reason has already recognized. Moreover, the term "rational" relegates to its opposite term all that it refuses to deal with, and thus ends by assuming itself to be purified of the nonrational, rather than searching to identify and assimilate its own surreal or nonlinear elements. This single error may have mutilated patriarchal thinking—especially scientific and philosophic thinking—more than we yet understand.

Perhaps an even more fundamental split is that which divides the "inner" from the "outer." A concise description of this way of perceiving can be found in Freud's essay "On Negation":

> Expressed in the language of the oldest, that is, of the oral instinctual impulses, the alternative runs thus: "I should like to eat that, or I should like to spit it out," or, carried a stage further, "I should like to take this into me and keep that outside of me." That is to say: it is to be either *inside* me or *outside* me. . . . From [the point of view of the original pleasure-ego] what is bad, what is alien to the ego, and what is external are, to begin with, identical.[10]

As the inhabitant of a female body, this description gives me pause. The boundaries of the ego seem to me much less crudely definable than the words "inner" and "outer" suggest. I do not perceive myself as a walled city into which certain emissaries are received and from which others are excluded. The question is much more various and complicated. A woman may be raped—penetrated vaginally against her will by the penis or forced to take it into her mouth, in which case it is certainly experienced as alien invader—or, in heterosexual love-making, she may accept the penis or take it in her hand and insert it in her vagina. In love-making which is not simply "fucking" there is, often, a strong sense of *inter*penetration, of feeling the melting of the walls of flesh, as physical and emotional longing deliver the one person into the other, blurring the boundary between body and body. The identification with another woman's orgasm as if it were one's own is one of the most intense interpersonal experiences: nothing is either "inside" me or "outside" at such moments. Even in autoeroticism, the clitoris which is more or less external delivers its throbbing signals to the vagina and all the way into the uterus which cannot be seen or touched.

Nor, in pregnancy, did I experience the embryo as decisively internal in Freud's terms, but rather, as something inside and of me, yet becoming hourly and daily more separate, on its way to becoming separate from me and of-itself. In early pregnancy the stirring of the fetus felt like ghostly tremors of my own body, later like the movements of a being imprisoned in me; but both sensations were *my* sensations, contributing to my own sense of physical and psychic space.

Without doubt, in certain situations the child in one's body can only feel like a foreign body introduced from without: an alien. (However, in her monograph, *Maternal Emotions*, Niles Newton cites studies of vomiting during pregnancy which suggest that it is related not to aversion to the pregnancy itself but to the conditions of conception—frequent undesired sex and the absence of orgasm.[11]) Yet even women who have been raped seem often to assimilate that germ of being, created in violence, not as something introduced from without but as nascent from within. The embryo is, of course, both. We ovulate whether or not the ovum is to encounter a sperm. The child that I carry for nine months can be defined *neither* as me or as not-me. Far from existing in the mode of "inner space," women are powerfully and vulnerably attuned both to "inner" and "outer" because for us the two are continuous, not polar.

The rejection of the dualism, of the positive-negative polarities between which most of our intellectual training has taken place, has been an undercurrent of feminist thought.[12] And, rejecting them, we reaffirm the existence of all those who have through the centuries been negatively defined: not only women, but the "untouchable," the "unmanly," the "nonwhite," the "illiterate": the "invisible." Which forces us to confront the problem of the essential dichotomy: power/powerlessness.

Power is both a primal word and a primal relationship under patriarchy. Through control of the mother, the man assures himself of possession of his children; through control of his children he insures the disposition of his patrimony and the safe passage of his soul after death. It would seem therefore that from very ancient times the identity, the very personality, of the man depends on power, and on power in a certain, specific sense: that of *power over others*, beginning with a woman and her children. The ownership of human beings proliferates: from primitive or arranged marriage through contractual marriage-with-dowry through more recent marriage "for love" but involving the economic dependency of the wife, through the feudal system, through slavery and serfdom. The powerful (mostly male) make decisions for the powerless: the well for the sick, the middle-aged for the aging, the "sane" for the "mad," the educated for the illiterate, the influential for the marginal.

However the man may first have obtained *power over* the woman as mother, this power has become diffused through our society in terms of that first sexual enslavement. Each colonized people is defined by its conqueror as weak, feminine, incapable of self-government, ignorant, uncultured, effete, irrational, in need of civilizing. On the other hand it may also be savored as mystical, physical, in deep contact with the earth—all attributes of the primordial Mother. But to say that the conquered are seen in this way does not mean that they have been truly *seen*.

To hold power over others means that the powerful is permitted a kind of short-cut through the complexity of human personality. He does not have to enter intuitively into the souls of the powerless, or to hear what they are saying in their many languages, including the language of silence. Colonialism exists by virtue of this short-cut—how else could so few live among so many and understand so little?

Much has been written about the effect of this condition upon the psyche of the powerless, all of it applicable to women, though the writers have been male, and sexist.[13] Powerlessness can lead to lassitude, self-negation, guilt, and depression; it can also generate a kind of psychological keenness, a shrewdness, an alert and practiced observation of the oppressor—"psyching-out" developed into a survival tool. Because the powerful can always depend on the short-cut of authority or force to effect his will, he has no apparent need for such insights, and, in fact, it can be dangerous for him to explore too closely into the mind of the powerless. Southern whites maintained well into the years of black civil-rights struggle that "our Negroes" were really satisfied with their condition. In similar vein, a complacent husband will announce that *his* wife is a "liberated woman," while male psychoanalysts and philosophers weave fanciful and uncorroborated theories about women.[14] The powerful person would seem to have a good deal at stake in suppressing or denying his awareness of the personal reality of others; power seems to engender a kind of willed ignorance, a moral stupidity, about the inwardness of others, hence of oneself. This quality has variously been described as "detachment," "objectivity," "sanity"—as if the recognition of another's being would open the floodgates to panic and hysteria. E. M. Forster personifies this quality in his novel *Howards End* (1910), in the characters of the industrialist Mr. Wilcox and his son, for whom the personal is both trivial and dangerous:

> . . . there was one quality in Henry for which [his wife] was never prepared, however much she reminded herself of it: his obtuseness. He simply did not notice things, and there was no more to be said . . . he never noticed the lights and shades that exist in the greyest conversation, the finger-posts, the milestones, the collisions, the illimitable views. Once . . . she scolded him about it. He was puzzled, but replied with a laugh: "My motto is Concentrate. I've no intention of frittering away my strength on that kind of thing." "It isn't frittering away the strength," she protested. "It's enlarging the space in which you may be strong." He answered, "You're a clever little woman, but my motto's Concentrate."[15]

Mr. Wilcox is powerful as one member of a moneyed, imperialist male establishment, the pre–World War I England already losing itself to urban sprawl, speculative capitalism, and a peculiarly abstract type of class relationship. The class oppression in the novel is inextricable from male contempt and condescension toward women, of which Wilcox and his son provide innumerable examples. He is also powerful as the head of household, the dictator of family principle, who is not above suppressing his first wife's deathbed letter in the name of keeping her property in the family. His son—also in the name of protecting family honor and property—commits manslaughter. Lies, force, but above all a profound disavowal of the claims of human personality, characterize the Wilcox world. Margaret, who becomes Mr. Wilcox's second wife, and her sister Helen, correctly perceive these men as hollow, as concealing an inner "chaos and emptiness." Yet this male power is derived from the power of an ideology: a structure internalized in the form of tradition and even of religion.

Monotheism posits a god whose essential attribute is that he (*sic*) is *all-powerful:* He can raze Babylon or Nineveh, bring plague and fire to Egypt, and part the sea. But his power is most devastatingly that of an *idea* in people's minds, which leads them to obey him out of fear of punishment, and to reject other (often female) deities because they are convinced that in any contest *he* will be victorious. He calls himself "Father"—but we must remember that a father is simply a male who has possession and control of a female (or more than one) and her offspring. It is not from God the Father that we derive the idea of paternal authority; it is out of the struggle for paternal control of the family that God the Father is created. His word is law and the idea of his power becomes more important than any demonstration of it; it becomes internalized as "conscience," "tradition," "the moral law within."

The idea of power thus becomes the power of an idea, which saturates all other notions of power. In both East and West, sexual love is imagined as power *over* someone, or the falling *under* someone else's power. Arabic tradition has it that to fall in love is to have fallen under the power of witchcraft.[16] The Occidental lover is similarly "bewitched" or "fascinated"— i.e., *bound:* powerless. Once more, responsibility toward the other, genuine knowledge of the other as person, is unnecessary. The language of patriarchal power insists on a dichotomy: for one person to have power, others—or another—must be powerless.

Thus, as women begin to claim full humanity, a primary question concerns the meaning of power. In the move from powerlessness, toward what are we moving? The one aspect in which most women have felt their own power in the patriarchal sense—authority over and control of another—has been motherhood; and even this aspect, as we shall see, has been wrenched and manipulated to male control.

Ancient motherhood was filled with a *mana* (supernatural force) which has been explored in the work of such writers as Joseph Campbell and Erich Neumann. Yet the helplessness of the child confers a certain narrow kind of power on the mother everywhere—a power she may not desire, but also often a power which may compensate to her for her powerlessness everywhere else. The power of the mother is, first of all, to give or withhold nourishment and warmth, to give or withhold survival itself.* Nowhere else (except in rare and exceptional cases, e.g., an absolute ruler like Catherine de' Medici, or a

* I have never read a child-rearing manual that made this point, or that raised the question of infanticide.

woman guard in a concentration camp) does a woman possess
such literal power over life and death.* And it is at this moment that her life is most closely bound to the child's, for
better or worse, and when the child, for better or worse, is receiving its earliest impressions. In de Beauvoir's words, "It was
as Mother that woman was fearsome; it is in maternity that
she must be transfigured and enslaved."[17] The idea of maternal
power has been domesticated. In transfiguring and enslaving
woman, the womb—the ultimate source of this power—has historically been turned against us and itself made into a source
of powerlessness.

3

Outside of the mother's brief power over the child—subject to
male interference—women have experienced "power over" in
two forms, both of them negative. The first is men's power
over us—whether physical, economic, or institutional—along
with the spectacle of their bloody struggles for power over other
men, their implicit sacrifice of human relationships and emotional values in the quest for dominance. Like other dominated
people, we have learned to manipulate and seduce, or to internalize men's will and make it ours, and men have sometimes
characterized this as "power" in us; but it is nothing more than
the child's or courtesan's "power" to wheedle and the dependent's "power" to disguise her feelings—even from herself—in
order to obtain favors, or literally to survive.

The possibility of "power" for women has historically been
befogged by sentimentality and mystification. When the
Grimké sisters began to speak before antislavery societies in the
1830s, they were breaking with a convention that forbade

* Anton Chekhov describes in his story, "Sleepy", the process by which a
young nursemaid who has not slept for days is driven to strangle the child she is
nursing. It is a story of human torture, the crying of the baby is akin to the
sleep-deprivation techniques of brainwashing. Yet even Chekhov, whose
human honesty was great, makes the infanticide not the child's mother but a
serf. It is probable that in his medical practice in early nineteenth-century
Russia he encountered many instances of maternal infanticide.

women to appear on public platforms. A pastoral letter from the Congregational Church was issued against them, saying:

> The appropriate duties and influence of women are clearly stated in the New Testament. Those duties and that influence are unobtrusive and private, but *the sources of mighty power.* When the mild, dependent, softening influence upon the sternness of man's opinion is fully exercised, society feels the effect of it in a thousand forms. *The power of woman is her dependence,* flowing from the consciousness of that weakness which God has given her for her protection. But when she assumes the place and tone of man as a public reformer . . . she yields *the power which God has given her for her protection,* and her character becomes unnatural . . . (Emphasis mine.) [18]

It was as if in answer to such sentiments that Olive Schreiner, in her novel, *The Story of an African Farm* (1883), made her heroine Lyndall burst forth in response to her friend Waldo's remark that "some women have power":

> "Power! Did you ever hear of men being asked whether other souls should have power or not? It is born in them. You may dam up the fountain of water and make it a stagnant marsh, or you may let it run free and do its work; but *you* cannot say whether or not it shall be there; *it is there.* And it will act, if not openly for good, then covertly for evil; but it will act. . . . Power!" she said suddenly, smiting her little hand upon the rail. "Yes, we have power; and since we are not to expend it in tunnelling mountains, nor healing diseases, nor making laws, nor money, nor on any extraneous object, we expend it on *you.* You are our goods, our merchandise, our material for operating on. . . . We are not to study law, nor science, nor art; so we study you. There is never a nerve or fibre in your man's nature but we know it . . ." [19]

For a moment, in this passage, Olive Schreiner brushes against a somewhat different definition of power—but only for a moment. Her Lyndall is a woman of intense energy, longing for education and for "extraneous objects" in the form of ideas into which to pour that energy. And she experiences herself as potentially malign, if that energy is to be denied any outlet except the "appropriate duties and influence of women." For cen-

turies women have felt their active, creative impulses as a kind
of demonic possession. But no less have men identified and
punished such impulses as demonic: the case of Anne Hutchinson being merely one example.[20]

Besides men's power over us, and our own discernment of
something denied and aborted in us, women have also felt
man's *powerfulness* in the root sense of the word (*posse, potere,*
or *pouvoir*—to be able, to be capable)—expressed in the creations of his mind. In the torsion of a piece of music or the
spatial harmony of a building, in the drenching light of a
painting, the unity and force of an intellectual structure, we
have experienced that *powerfulness* as the expressive energy of
an ego which, unlike ours, was licensed to direct itself outward
upon the world. If we have experienced man's brute battle for
power as a terror, often visited directly on ourselves and our
children, we have also known this other powerfulness, not our
own, set before us as a measure of human aspiration. And we
have often longed to ally ourselves with that kind of power. (In
a high-school yearbook of my generation one of the most brilliant students listed as her ambition: "To be married to a
great man.") To have some link with male power has been
the closest that most of us could come to sharing in power directly; to have no link with any form of male power, however
petty and corrupt, has meant that we lived unprotected and
vulnerable indeed. The idea of power has, for most women,
been inextricably linked with maleness, or the use of force; most
often with both.

But we have also experienced, more intuitively and unconsciously, men's fantasies of our power, fantasies rooted far back
in infancy, and in some mythogenetic zone of history. Whatever their origins, for most women these male fantasies, because so obliquely expressed, have been obscured from view.
What we did see, for centuries, was the hatred of overt strength
in women, the definition of strong independent women as freaks
of nature, as unsexed, frigid, castrating, perverted, dangerous;
the fear of the maternal woman as "controlling," the preference
for dependent, malleable, "feminine" women.* But that *all*

* Margaret Mead suggests that the opening of the American frontier required that a different kind of valuation be placed on female qualities and

women might at some profound level be the objects of men's fear and hatred has only slowly begun to melt into our awareness through the writings of some post-Freudians,[21] and it is still an insight which women resist. As Karen Horney remarks:

> Is it not really remarkable (we ask ourselves in amazement) when one considers the overwhelming mass of this transparent material, that so little recognition and attention are paid to the fact of men's secret dread of women? It is almost more remarkable that women themselves have so long been able to overlook it . . .[22]

She suggests that behind women's obliviousness of this male dread lie "anxiety and the impairment of self-respect." Anxiety there certainly is; the anxiety of the objectified who realizes that however much she may *wish* to render herself pleasing and non-threatening, she will still to some degree partake of the feared aspect of Woman, an abstraction which she feels has nothing to do with her. Since politically and socially men do wield immense power over women, it is unnerving to realize that your mate or employer may also fear you. And if a woman hopes to find, not a master but a brother, a lover, an equal, how is she to meet this dread? If it brings to her intimations of a power inherent in her sex, that power is perceived as hostile, destructive, controlling, malign; and the very idea of power is poisoned for her. We shall have return to this fear of women; for the present it must be repeated that women's primary experience of power till now has been triply negative: we have experienced men's power as oppression; we have experienced our own vitality and independence as somehow threatening to men; and, even when behaving with "feminine" passivity, we have been made aware of masculine fantasies of our potential destructiveness.

The resurgence of interest in the work of J. J. Bachofen,

---

that "strong women, women with character and determination, in fact women with guts, became more and more acceptable" (*Male and Female* [New York: Morrow, 1975], p. 225). However, she acknowledges that women were still expected to be capable of "pleasing men"; and as the West was opened and a new leisure class began to establish itself in the cities, the "strong" female of the frontier declined in value, as Thorstein Veblen and Emily James Putnam (*The Lady*, 1910) make abundantly clear.

Robert Briffault, Joseph Campbell, Robert Graves, Helen Diner, Jane Harrison, the response generated by E. G. Davis's *The First Sex*, essays in feminist theory such as Jane Alpert's "Mother-Right," have been in part a search for vindication of the belief that patriarchy is in some ways a degeneration, that women exerting power would use it differently from men: nonpossessively, nonviolently, nondestructively. A "matriarchal controversy" has arisen directly from this quest, and has served as a catalyst for reexamining the reaction against "biology" which was necessarily an early stage in feminist thought.

Two widely read women theorists, Helen Diner (first published in Germany in the late 1920s) and Elizabeth Gould Davis (writing in the 1970s) both drew heavily on earlier writers, notably J. J. Bachofen and Robert Briffault, to argue that woman's physiology was the original source of her prepatriarchal power, both in making her the source of life itself, and in associating her more deeply than man with natural cycles and processes. All these writers envisioned a prehistoric civilization centered around the female, both as mother and head of family, and as deity—the Great Goddess who appears throughout early mythology, as Tiamat, Rhea, Isis, Ishtar, Astarte, Cybele, Demeter, Diana of Ephesus, and by many other names: the eternal giver of life and embodiment of the natural order, including death.

For Diner and Davis, Woman as Mother naturally led to gynarchy: to societies headed by and marked with profound reverence for women. Other writers, including Simone de Beauvoir and Shulamith Firestone, deny that either a "matriarchal" or "gynocratic" order ever existed, and perceive women's maternal function as, quite simply and precisely, the root of our oppression. Whatever the conclusion drawn, there is an inescapable correlation between the idea of motherhood and the idea of power.

The sociologist Philip Slater, for example, sees real evidence for an early matriarchal culture in Greece, supplanted by patriarchy in later times, although he hesitates to assume a like transition from matriarchal to patriarchal power in other cultures, since "the *ontogenetic* experience of primeval matriarchy is universal, and may provide the source of much of this tradition" in mythology and folklore. In other words (and this was Freud's view) each woman and each man has once, in earliest infancy, lived under the power of the mother, and this fact alone could account for the recurrence of dreams, legends, myths, of an archetypal powerful Woman, or of a golden age ruled by women.[23] Whether such an age, even if less than golden, ever existed anywhere, or whether we all carry in our earliest imprintings the memory of, or the longing for, an individual past relationship to a female body, larger and stronger than our own, and to female warmth, nurture, and tenderness, there is a new concern for the *possibilities* inherent in beneficent female power, as a mode which is absent from the society at large, and which, even in the private sphere, women have exercised under terrible constraints.[24]

4

The history of patriarchy is yet to be written—I do not mean the history of men, but of an idea which arose, prospered, had its particular type of expression, and which has proven self-destructive. But there are four or five movements of recent history which seem to intersect here. One is the so-called sexual revolution of the sixties—briefly believed to be congruent with the liberation of women. The "pill," it was believed by some, would release women from the fear of pregnancy, hence from the double standard, and would make us sexually coequal with men. For many reasons, this proved a myth; it did not mean that we were free to discover our own sexuality, but rather that we were expected to behave according to male notions of female sexuality, as surely as any Victorian wife, though the notions themselves had changed. And the "pill" itself is a mechanistic and patriarchal device, recently proven to have deadly side-effects.[25] But the liberalization of sexual attitudes, the increase in pre- and extramarital sex, the growing divorce rate, and the acknowledgedly threadbare texture of the nuclear family, did lead toward a new recognition of the contradictions between patriarchal theory and practice.*

* A classic contradiction is the prevalence of rape, which is estimated to be the most frequently committed violent crime in America today. As one

Also relevant are the movements for ecology and zero population growth. These have arisen, to be sure, not from any primary concern for women, but from pressures generated by the wastefulness of technological society and the misallocation and monopoly of resources on the planet, which are usually referred to as the problems of famine and overpopulation. In the ecological analysis there has been some fresh examination of the values of technologically oriented society, recognition not only of its capricious unthrift and short-sighted profiteering, but of the increasing disappearance of certain values such as intimacy, protectiveness toward the living, respect for variety and variation, and for natural processes. To some extent this analysis might be seen as a reassertion of prepatriarchal values. However, these movements do aim, among other things, at a reduction of the birth rate; and they are presumably prepared to achieve this, if expedient, by propaganda aimed at evoking guilt in women who wish to become biological mothers.

Moreover, the control by women of our bodies has never been recognized as a primary issue in these movements. A report by a British feminist on the International World Population Conference at Bucharest in 1974 notes that:

> Despite lip-service to the idea that couples and families (*never* women) should have the right to determine the number and spacing of their children, in no case is this right seen as more important than the requirements of the economy. A brief look at the history of the developed countries—both capitalist and socialist—over the past 50 years will confirm that it is always women who are expected to adjust their fertility to the need for labor or cannon-fodder, never the economy which must adapt to an increasing or decreasing birthrate.[26]

---

writer points out, rape illuminates the sexual schizophrenia of the society in which "the masculine man is . . . expected to prove his mettle as a protector of women," while rape is also a measure of virility (Susan Griffin, "Rape: The All-American Crime," in Jo Freeman, ed., *Women: A Feminist Perspective* [Palo Alto, Calif.: Mayfield, 1975]). But it is more than simply an all-American crime. From the Book of Numbers (31: 14–36), which describes the rape of 32,000 Midianite women by order of Moses, to the recent rape by Pakistani soldiers of 200,000 women of Bangladesh, rape remains the great unpunished war crime in every culture. As a crime of violence committed by a man against his wife, it is not even legally recognized.

In contrast, the black nationalist movement has declared that birth control and abortion are "genocidal" and that black women should feel guilty if they do *not* provide children to carry on the black struggle for survival. Black women have increasingly rejected this rhetoric, however, and have criticized "the irresponsible, poorly thought-out call to young girls, on-the-margin scufflers, every Sister at large to abandon the pill that gives her certain decisive power, a power that for a great many of us is all we know, given the setup in this country and in our culture."[27] (This was of course written before the lethal side-effects of the pill were publicly acknowledged.) Janis Morris, community organizer and mother, states that "the Black woman has got to consider what is best for the child during pregnancy and after birth, and too often she has to bear all the responsibility alone. So frankly, when the sister tells a brother 'I'm not going to have this baby,' it ain't nobody's business but her own."[28]

None of these movements, for or against the limitation of births, has the condition of women at heart as a root of insight; all are prepared to dictate to women—as patriarchy has always dictated—whether or not and under what circumstances to "produce" children.* As the sociologist Jessie Bernard puts it:

> It was not until the late 1960's that motherhood became a serious political issue in our country. Like so many other issues, it came not in clear-cut, carefully thought-through form but in a murky conglomerate of ecology, environmental protection, and a "welfare mess". It took an "antinatalist" slant. The problem posed was how to stop women from having so many babies. Ecologists frightened us with images of millions suffocating for

* And more than dictate. The involuntary sterilization of poor women on welfare in federally financed clinics was publicized widely when the Southern Poverty Law Center brought suit on behalf of the Relf sisters, aged twelve and fourteen, sterilized under a federal program, in Montgomery, Alabama. Neither of the young women had ever been pregnant. Barbara Segal reports that "In China . . . women are not given birth control information until after they are married. It has also been reported that in certain areas women are offered incentives such as clothing and so-called 'transportation costs' if they will be sterilized" (*Off Our Backs*, Vol. 5, No. 1, p. 11). See also Carl Djerassi, "Some Observations on Current Fertility Control in China," *The China Quarterly*, No. 57 (January–March 1974), pp. 40–60.

lack of oxygen and hostile reformers with images of women—
especially black women—having babies in order to remain on
welfare rolls. The first group directed their attack against
middle-class women, the second, against welfare women.[29]

A third strand in this historical pattern is technological; the
genetic revolution, now in progress in laboratories, which has
already developed the "sperm bank" and artificial insemination,
and is now at work on "cloning" or the controlled reproduction
of selected types through the growing, in a matrix, of cell nuclei
transplants from a single "parent," to create a series of geneti-
cally identical offspring. Shulamith Firestone, an enthusiastic
believer in replacing biological with artificial motherhood, has
observed that the possibilities are terrifying if we envision the
choice of human types, gender, and capacities being controlled
by patriarchy.[30] On the other hand, if biological motherhood
can become a real choice (as distinct from being forcibly prescribed or rendered obsolete by fiat) then the concept of woman
as womb, and of "biological destiny" becomes harder to defend.
And these concepts have buttressed the structure of patriarchy
from the first.

5

In the mid-fifties, a few scattered male writers such as Denis de
Rougemont and Erich Neumann had begun to identify the
denial of what Neumann called "the feminine" in civilization
with the roots of inhumanity and self-destructiveness, and to
call for a renewal of "the feminine principle."[31] In *The Flight
from Woman*, Karl Stern, a Jewish Freudian analyst turned
Catholic, sees the scientific mode of knowledge beginning with
Descartes as a rejection of the "feminine" mode of knowledge
associated with intuition, spirituality, and poetry; and announces
"the mystery of Androgyny . . . manifest in the historical crisis" of the present.[32]* More recently writers ranging from the

---

* "Androgyny" has recently become a "good" word (like "motherhood"
itself!) implying many things to many people, from bisexuality to a vague
freedom from imposed sexual roles. Rarely has the use of the term been
accompanied by any political critique. Carolyn Heilbrun argues in her
Toward a Recognition of Androgyny that an "androgynous" undercurrent
runs throughout Western humanism, which if recognized would help us

philosopher Herbert Marcuse to the poet Robert Bly, have suggested that a return to the "feminine" (Marcuse calls it "the femalization of man") is the next stage in the development of the species.[33] This "feminine principle," however, like "androgyny," remains for such writers elusive and abstract and seems to have, for them, little connection with the rising expectations and consciousness of actual women. In fact, Marcuse and Bly might be likened to the Saint-Simonians and Shelley, who likewise insisted theoretically on the importance of the feminine, yet who betrayed much of the time their unconscious patriarchal parochialism.[34]

Philip Slater perceives women as the peripheral members of the society, therefore "in a better position to liberate [it] emotionally"—whatever this may mean, since he discounts the likelihood that women will actually rise up against patriarchal values. In his discussion of the "concept of the tyrannical father" in the American unconscious—displaced, as he notes, from the actual father onto some abstract authority, fantasy-father, or technology itself—he implies that patriarchy is the real name of the system he is describing, and which is ultimately dangerous to human existence—a conclusion he would be reluctant to draw.[35]

None of these writers mention the possibility that a "return to the feminine" may actually involve pain and dread, and hence active resistance, on the part of men. We do not find in their work any such powerful analysis of the nature and extent of patriarchy as in Firestone, Millett, and Daly; but we do

---

to free ourselves and society from the role-playing and division of labor required under patriarchy. Other writers have criticized the reactionary associations of "androgyny"; as Catherine Stimpson points out, "the androgyne still fundamentally thinks in terms of 'feminine' and 'masculine.' It fails to conceptualize the world and to organize phenomena in a new way that leaves 'feminine' and 'masculine' behind" (Catherine R. Stimpson, "The Androgyne and the Homosexual," *Women's Studies*, Vol. 2 [1974], pp. 237–48). See also Cynthia Secor, "Androgyny: An Early Reappraisal"; Daniel A. Harris, "Androgyny: The Sexist Myth in Disguise"; Barbara Charlesworth Gelpi, "The Politics of Androgyny," in the same issue; and Janice Raymond, "The Illusion of Androgyny," *Quest: A Feminist Quarterly*, Vol. 2, No. 1 (Summer 1975). Finally, the very structure of the word replicates the sexual dichotomy and the priority of *andros* (male) over *gyne* (female). In a truly postandrogynous society the term "androgyne" would have no meaning.

find corroboration of a sense that patriarchy, in degrading and oppressing its daughters, has also at some less overt level failed its sons.

Such a sense—though unperceived as such—fluttered, at least, in the "Movement" of the 1960s, despite the profound sexism underlying its apparent rejection of racist violence and the Vietnam war. Men who refused to serve in the armed forces, and who underwent imprisonment or exile as the penalty for their decisions, demonstrated a revulsion against the patriarchal stereotypes of authoritarianism, militarism, nationalism, "being a man." (The "counter-culture" style of unisex clothing, male self-adornment, gentler manners, long hair, was a more superficial token. Much might be written on the various costumes in which male privilege and male supremacism have masked, as well as advertised, themselves in our time.) The peace movement, sexist as it was ("CHICKS SAY YES TO MEN WHO SAY NO"), expressed disenchantment with the values of violence, super-technology, and imperialism. The student radicalism of the sixties commonly met with the charge that these young people were in revolt against their fathers, "acting-out" their Oedipal rage; in fact the "counter-culture" (most of it, to be sure, soon absorbed into the omnivorous Culture) did for awhile constitute an unconscious critique of the authority-through-role or through force which has characterized patriarchy. There was a fleeting revolt against authoritarian education; the teacher was for the first time asked to justify himself as a human being rather than a role; obedience was seen as the reverse of learning. This questioning of the power-relationship in education often took on an aggressive, anti-intellectual, and destructive style, thoroughly masculinist in its dehumanization of the individual teacher facing the classroom. Yet it, too, sprang from some kind of instinctual resistance to the dehumanization of the student in the learning process, the sense of being "merely a number" or a bank in which information is deposited.

But these tendrils of antimasculinism straggled forth quite innocent of any antimasculinist theory, and easily submerged under the macho ethic of SDS and Weathermen, with their sexual exploitation of women and their inherited theories of patriarchal revolution; or under the male homophile movement.

In the mid-1970s a reaction has made itself felt in the form of what Susan Sontag has perceived as an eroticization of Nazism, a cult of fascist aesthetics.* It is no accident, I think, that this fascination with the regalia of stormtroopers has arisen along with a pervasively changing consciousness and a new self-definition on the part of women. Nazism had a clear and unmistakable political formula for women and where they belonged: mothers of men, *kinder, kirche, kuche*. It glorified as no other twentieth-century system has done, the healthy body of the racially "pure" woman as an incubator of sons and heroes.

6

The mid–twentieth-century wave of feminism has gone further and asked more than its predecessors. Like patriarchy itself, the extent and influence of the antipatriarchal women's movement is difficult to grasp. It is not defined by specific organizations, groupings, or factions, though these exist in abundance. It exists in many stages of development throughout the world, at the most local, pragmatic levels, as a network of formal and informal communications, as a growing body of analysis and theory, and as a profound moral, psychic, and philosophic revaluation of what it means to be "human." For a movement which has existed in its present form less than a decade, it has already brought forth decisive shifts of value, relation, and identity among women of all ages and economic levels, many of whom would not call themselves feminists. It has opened a new range of choices to women, many of which seem private and inconsequential yet each of which, multiplied by the thousands, has helped create a new climate of perception. Elizabeth Oakes-Smith, an early–nineteenth-century suffragist, writer, and preacher, had demanded in 1852: "Do we really understand that we aim at nothing less than an entire subversion of the present

* "Much of the imagery of far-out sex has been placed under the sign of Nazism. More or less Nazi costumes with boots, leather, chains, Iron Crosses on gleaming torsos, swastikas, have become, along with meat hooks and heavy motorcycles, the secret and most lucrative paraphernalia of eroticism" ("Fascinating Fascism," *New York Review of Books*, February 6, 1975, p. 29).

state of society, a dissolution of the whole existing social compact?" By 1970, Shulamith Firestone was responding: "Rather than concentrating the female principle into a 'private' retreat . . . we want to rediffuse it—for the first time creating society from the bottom up." And Mary Daly continued, in 1973: "Only radical feminism can act as the 'final cause', because of all revolutionary causes it alone opens up human consciousness adequately to the desire for non-hierarchal, nonoppressive society revealing sexism as the basic model and source of oppression."*

Where the two powerful shapers of contemporary Western thought, Marx and Freud, had completed—as if by some tacit collaboration—the centuries' process of dichotomizing "man" into mind/body, psychological/political, Simone de Beauvoir, in 1949, was bringing a phenomenological approach to bear on "discovering woman":

> So . . . we reject for the same reasons both the sexual monism of Freud and the economic monism of Engels. A psychoanalyst will interpret all social claims of women as phenomena of the "masculine protest"; for the Marxist, on the contrary, her sexuality only expresses her economic situation in more or less complex, roundabout fashion. But the categories of "clitorid" and "vaginal", like the categories of "bourgeois" or "proletarian" are equally inadequate to encompass a concrete woman. Underlying all individual drama, as it underlies the economic history of mankind, there is an existential foundation that alone enables us to understand in its unity that particular form of being which we call a human life.[36]

Masculine intellectual systems are inadequate because they lack the wholeness that female consciousness, excluded from contributing to them, could provide. In taking the "otherness" of

* "I hope my use of 'final cause' is clear: In 'tradition' the final cause is 'first', it is motivating purpose, an insight which elicits seeking, movement. It is 'first in the order of intention', opening the subject to action. She may not know all of the directions and implications of the action. . . . So to say the Women's Movement is the final cause is to mean it sets many-dimensional movements in motion, e.g. liberation of children, of the aged, of the racially oppressed. To say this is to see a priority for the women's movement as catalyst, as *the* necessary catalyst—hardly to see it as a self-enclosed system" (Personal communication, Spring 1974).

the "second" sex for granted, these systems are erected on an essential intellectual fault. Truly to liberate women, then, means to change thinking itself: to reintegrate what has been named the unconscious, the subjective, the emotional with the structural, the rational, the intellectual; to "connect the prose and the passion" in E. M. Forster's phrase; and finally to annihilate those dichotomies. In the being of a woman sold as a bride, or rejected because she is "barren" and cannot produce sons to enhance a man's status, economics and sexuality, legalism and magic, caste structure and individual fear, barter and desire, coexist inextricably; only in the outer world of patriarchal categories and patriarchal denial can they be conceived as separate.

De Beauvoir in 1949 still saw the liberation of women as but one of many liberations which would come about as the result of socialist revolution, insofar as socialism promised to do away with private property and the patriarchal family and to release women into economic equality with men. Her experience and her analysis have since taken her further.[37] But radical feminism is now speaking in terms of "feminist revolution," of a "post-androgynous" society, of creating a new kind of human being.

7

Imagine a spectrum, at one end of which is a tar-paper shack in Appalachia or rural New Hampshire, in which an eighteen-year-old mother of four is expecting her fifth child, her first menstrual period having been her last. Her legs are discolored with varicose veins, her abdominal wall permanently distended, her breasts already sagging, her teeth decaying from calcium loss: functionally illiterate, she lives from hour to hour and day to day, her nights splintered by the crying of infants, her energy drained into the survival of lives which suck on her like mouths. To get to a birth-control or prenatal clinic would be to command herself into a control of her existence which she has never had, and of which, as one of eleven children herself, she has seen no example. She has not been physically away from her children since the conception of the first child, when she was thirteen years of age. When her husband rapes her, she does not call it rape, but somewhere in her memory lingers a distant past of twelve-year-old restlessness, curiosity, physical energy, and germinating desire—even, perhaps, some vague imagination that her life might be different from her mother's. Her sense of time is vague; impossible to imagine herself as a being separate from all these lives. Once in a while she looks into the glass and sees that she is becoming her mother.

At the other end of the spectrum let us imagine a laboratory in which men—the most powerful men in history, it is said—are engaged in work of extreme delicacy and precision, preparing a new series of multiple, identical embryos from cells derived from selected human tissue. The embryos will come into consciousness with their identity already prepared, for they will have been selected to provide the patriarchy of a new generation, selected by the patriarchy of the current generation, to perpetuate its own characteristics—especially those of rational genius, the gift of abstraction, and the ability to dissociate "work" from "personal" problems and disturbances. Females are also being bred, for specific physical characteristics, and they fall into two categories. One is a body-type, or range of body-types, capable of producing erections in a range of males, not for procreation but because impotence is an increasing problem since the end of physical paternity. The other is a body-type matched with mental qualities suited for special purposes, such as "manned" space flights requiring smallness of build, adaptiveness, physical endurance, and a low level of emotive intensity or desire for interhuman relation. The new males will be free from the disturbing effects of mother-love and mother-dominance; and the new females will not suffer from sex-role frustration, since no Joan of Arc, no Elizabeth I, no Mary Wollstonecraft, no Anne Hutchinson, no Sojourner Truth, no George Eliot, no Emma Goldman, no Margaret Sanger, no Gertude Stein or Emily Dickinson has been or will be chosen for the reproduction of her "type" in quantity. Elite women, chosen by and working with men, are used not only as intellectual contributors to social engineering but also as donors of cell nuclei to insure that a token quantity of women can be produced as required. Thus, it is demonstrated that females with the proper endowment—though quantitatively much fewer—are valued as highly as males.

Neither of these two visions is fantastic. A revolution based on patriarchal socialism might abolish the tar-paper shack, but who could claim that it would abolish the engineering of society by men? For, however theoretically men may call for "women's liberation" in any social order they may devise, however much they consciously may wish for an end to sexual caste, they still live in the unacknowledged cave of their own subjectivity, their denied fears and longings; and few men can bear to confront that shadow-world. For patriarchy, however much it has failed them, however much it divides them from themselves, is still *their* order, confirming them in privilege. They are protected from seriously addressing the issues of sexual caste and institutionalized misogyny, in large part by the central ambiguity at the heart of patriarchy: the ideas of the sacredness of motherhood and the redemptive power of woman as means, contrasted with the degradation of women in the order created by men.

IV THE PRIMACY
OF THE MOTHER

Woman to primitive man is . . . at once weak and
magical, oppressed, yet feared. She is charged with
powers of childbearing denied to man, powers only
half-understood . . . forces that all over the world
seem to fill him with terror. The attitude of man to
woman, and, though perhaps in a lesser degree, of
woman to man, is still today essentially magical.

—Jane Harrison, *Themis: A Study of the
Social Origins of Greek Religion*

As women our relationship to the past has been problematical.
We have been every culture's core obsession (and repression);
we have always constituted at least one-half, and are now a
majority, of the species; yet in the written records we can barely
find ourselves. Confronted with this "Great Silence," we have
apparently had two paths to follow: the path of anatomizing
our oppression, detailing the laws and sanctions ranged against
us; and the path of searching out those women who broke
through the silence, who, though often penalized, miscon-
strued, their work neglected or banned, or though tokenized in
lonely and precarious acceptance, still embodied strength, daring, self-determination; who were, in short, exemplary.

When we survey the lost, undocumented lives of the majority
of women, the waste of women's brains and talents throughout history, the idea of a prehistoric period, when not a handful,

but most women were using their capacities to the utmost, becomes extremely seductive. And anthropology, more than history, has given license to that desire. Once it began to be recognized that human society embodies diversity as much as conformity, once non-Western societies began to be examined, not as heathen, retarded, or infantile versions of Western culture, but for their own values, it began to be possible to imagine that the patriarchal, patrilineal family of Western culture was neither as essential nor as inevitable as it had seemed. It began to be possible to imagine some universal earlier civilization in which mother-right, not father-right, prevailed; in which matrilineality and matrifocality played a part; in which women were active and admired participants in all of culture; and so to imagine a wholly different way for women to exist in the world. If we were not simply bound "by nature" to the "passive," "docile," "irrational" aspects of human personality, if it was in fact institutions and culture that determined our "nature," the victimization and abnegation demanded of "motherhood" could be seen as the inversion of a period of mother-power—of matriarchy.*

The desire for a clearly confirmed past, the search for a tradition of female power, also springs from an intense need for validation. If women were powerful once, a precedent exists; if female biology was ever once a source of power, it need not remain what it has since become: a root of powerlessness. For many women, the inconclusiveness of any historical argument, the fact that history has been written by and for men, and the belief that we need not turn to the past in order to justify the future, are reasons enough to discount past theories of matriarchy and to concentrate on the present and the future. For

---

* Along with the idea of matriarchy goes an ideal of "Amazonism"—as early as the 1920s Helen Diner called her "first feminine history of culture" *Mothers and Amazons*. Feminists have sometimes become polarized between the "matriarchal" and an "Amazonian" ideal, neither of which has, so far, much historical verification, but both of which have been potent as myths. "Matriarchal" and "Amazonian" culture are seen as opposed—not merely in Diner, or in the earlier German writer, J. J. Bachofen, on whom she bases much of her theory, but in the minds of some contemporary writers like Jill Johnston, who wants no part of "matriarchy" (seeing it as patriarchy with a different set of genitals) but who believes all women should be daughters.

others, a belief in the necessity to create ourselves anew still allows for curiosity about the artifacts of written history—not as verifiable evidence of things done, but as something like the notebooks of a dreamer, which incompletely yet often compellingly depict the obsessions, the denials, the imaginative processes, out of which s/he is still working. Believing in continuity, I myself am hard put to know where the "past" ends and the "present" begins; and far from assuming that what we call the past must teach us to be conservative, I think that for women a critical exploration backward in time can be profoundly radicalizing. But we need to be critically aware of the limitations of our sources.

Certain writers, like Elizabeth Gould Davis, have taken the existence of an ancient, Arcadian matriarchal world as a given. The source of such theory, apart from Robert Graves's *The White Goddess,* is largely the work of two men, J. J. Bachofen and Robert Briffault.* Bachofen's work had earlier been used by Helen Diner in her *Mothers and Amazons,* published in Germany in 1929, and first translated into English in 1965.† Perhaps Diner had read Bachofen in its entirety, but since she provides no notes, we must bear in mind that she may simply have used the 1926 German abridged edition. She does pay tribute, in her preface, both to Bachofen and to Briffault.

The reader of Diner or Davis is likely to receive the impression that Bachofen was a celebrant of female power, and that he perceived the "matriarchal" age not simply as a universal stage through which all cultures once passed, but as a golden age, a lost utopia, to which if the species were fortunate we might yet return. To look closely at the fragments of Bachofen translated by Manheim, however, is to receive a different impression. Like many other Victorians, Bachofen is given to sen-

---

* Bachofen's *Das Mütterrecht,* first published in Germany in 1861, exists in a partial and unsatisfactory edition in English—Ralph Manheim's 1967 translation of a German edition of selections from Bachofen's work published in 1926. The chapter on Crete, which might be expected to contain especially interesting materials, is omitted, and a fragment of Bachofen's essay, "Gräbersymbolik," is grafted onto the section on Egypt.
† This first American edition, with a somewhat patronizing foreword by Joseph Campbell, has now been superseded by the 1973 Anchor edition, with a critical introduction by Brigitte Berger.

timental generalizations about women. The feminine principle, for him, is "distinguished less by sharpness and freedom of outline than by prophetic feeling; governed more by sentiment than by thought; subject always to division of mind and the *strange, aimless striving peculiar to women* . . . hovering between frenzy and reflection, between voluptuousness and virtue." (Emphasis mine.)[1]* In the conflict between the sexes, whose cycles he attempts to trace in myth, "the realm of the idea belongs to the man, the realm of material life to the woman." "The transience of material life goes hand in hand with mother right. Father right is bound up with the immortality of a supramaterial life belonging to the regions of light."[2] The matriarchal phase is identified with agriculture, with an advance out of the tellurian (earth-derived) swamp life (which Bachofen identifies with sexual promiscuity). As such, it is a superior phase; but it is essentially a stepping-stone toward the higher phase of father-right:

> In this respect the establishment of matriarchy represents a step forward toward civilization. . . . Woman counters man's abuse of his superior strength by the dignity of her enthroned motherhood. . . . The more savage the men of this first period, the more necessary becomes the restraining force of women. . . . Matriarchy is necessary to the education of mankind *and particularly of men.* Just as the child is first disciplined by his mother, so the races of men are first disciplined by woman. The male must serve before he can govern. It is the woman's vocation to tame man's primordial strength, to guide it into benign channels. (Emphasis mine.)[3]

The idealization of Amazonism also gets short shrift from Bachofen. According to his view of the historical process, there were two phases of Amazonism in ancient times, alternating

---

* Cf. Briffault: "Women are constitutionally deficient in the qualities that mark the masculine intellect. . . . Feminine differs from masculine intelligence in kind: it is concrete, not abstract; particularizing, not generalizing." (Note that this is phrased in terms of female, not male, "deficiency.") "Women are more precocious than men, their maturity is reached earlier. There is in their growth the arrest of development, physical and mental, which goes with relative precocity. It has been said that a man learns nothing after forty; it can be said in the same broad sense that a woman learns nothing after twenty-five" (*The Mothers* [New York: Johnson Reprint, 1969], III: 507–8).

with two phases of matriarchy. The period of promiscuous
sexuality and hetaerism is linked with an Amazon phase in
which women revolt against their sexual exploitation, take arms,
and resist the physical abuses of men. But these earlier Amazons, according to the myth cited in Plutarch and interpreted
by Bachofen, are in turn defeated by the Mothers in a kind of
spiritual victory. Matriarchy is seen as the acceptance by woman
of her "natural vocation," and it is indissoluble from monogamous marriage. It is *"conjugal* matriarchy," against which
Bachofen sees Amazonism as a perversion of womanhood, an
"unnatural intensification of women's power."[4]

Demetrian matriarchy, says Bachofen, is "chaste . . .
grounded in strict order . . . a source of lofty virtues and of an
existence which, though limited in its ideas, was nevertheless
secure and well-ordered." This phase gives way to Dionysian,
or Aphroditean matriarchy, a decadent phase in which "one
extreme followed the other, showing how hard it is, at all times,
for women to observe moderation."[5] However, for all its lofty
virtues, Demetrian matriarchy is still bound up with the tellurian
swamp-grass, the material and physical, as distinct from (and
even opposed to) the "liberation" and "sublimation" of father-
right and the victory of patriarchy. For Bachofen these opposites are always in dialectical struggle; and this struggle is seen
from a purely masculine point of view: "Maternity pertains to
the physical side of man, *the only thing he shares with the
animals*; the paternal-spiritual principle belongs to him alone.
Here he breaks through the bonds of tellurism and lifts his eyes
to *the higher regions of the cosmos.*" (Emphasis mine.)[6] In
breaking the matriarchal bonds, however, man degrades and
debases woman, giving rise to a new wave of Amazonism, the
offspring of Dionysian excesses, which in turn is vanquished,
creating the patriarchy which, in this author's view, has since
enlightened the world.

In Bachofen we are dealing with several layers of expression:
the actual myths reported or embodied in sources such as Plutarch, Strabo, Herodotus, Ovid, the Greek dramatists; the ancient consciousness which produced such myths; and the nineteenth-century German masculine consciousness of Bachofen

himself, which frequently contradicts itself.* It is a little as if we were looking at the reflection of a painting in a windowpane at night. At times Bachofen's lack of clarity and precision is so frustrating that one is tempted to attribute the problem to the fragmentary nature of the excerpts in Manheim's translation.

It can at best be charitably assumed that sometimes Bachofen is expressing, not his own opinions, but the climate of opinion crystallized in the myth—for example, when he announces that woman is possessed of "an insatiable blood-thirst," as demonstrated in the story (related in Aeschylus and Apollodorus) of how the women of Lemnos massacre all but one of their men for cohabiting with Thracian women. As a support for this characterization of women (whom he sees elsewhere as chaste, the bringers of order and harmony, etc.) he cites Euripides's *Ion* and *Medea.* It is difficult to be sure when Bachofen is accepting the mythology and poetry of males as an objective description of women, and when he may be suggesting simply that this is how women have been perceived at certain times by certain males. One thing is clear: in Bachofen's own mind there is no yearning for a matriarchy of the future, and there is great ambivalence toward the idea of past matriarchy, and indeed toward the female presence.

2

Robert Briffault's three-volume work, *The Mothers,* first published in 1927, is the work of a lonely, furious, and obsessive mind. He set out to show in this book that the socializing element in human history has been "traceable to the operation of instincts that are related to the functions of the female and not to those of the male."[7] He saw the patriarchal family as essentially antisocial: "a euphemism for the individualistic male with his subordinate dependents. As a social unit the family means the individual, actuated by his most aggressively individualistic instincts; it is not the foundation, but the negation of

---

* Bachofen, trans. Ralph Manheim, *Myth, Religion, and Mother Right* (Princeton, N.J.: Princeton University Press, 1967); compare, for example, the texts on facing pages 100 and 101.

society." The real social bonds grew out of "the natural and biological dominance of the primitive mother over the group which she created, the awe attaching to her magical nature and powers." Such a social bonding emerged from "the primitive mystery of generation and the primitive sacrament of common blood and common food, bestowed upon the ideal tribe of its followers."[8]

In tracing the aspects of this natural dominance and bonding, Briffault consumed a bibliography of nearly 200 close-printed pages; his three volumes are copiously footnoted and his practice was, with scholarly compendiousness, to make no statement that should rest on merely one or two examples. The unabridged Briffault (there are two abridged editions, one edited by him, the other by G. Rattray Taylor) is a mine of lore for anyone interested in what history, legend, and anthropology were saying about women up to the time of Briffault's authorship. Whatever his conclusions, however we may wish to quarrel with them, it is difficult not to feel gratitude to a man so committed to unearthing the details and the patterns of female influence in civilization. Admittedly, when he strays far from the realm of his special genius—assimilating and condensing vast amounts of material and seeing relationships between them—he veers toward the moralistic, expounding freely at the end of his book on marriage, female intellect as it differs from male, and the necessity for women to save civilization (though without, as he puts it, "provoking" antagonism between the sexes). Yet one senses in his final chapter a profound weariness with patriarchy: "We live in a patriarchal society in which patriarchal principles have ceased to be valid. . . . Power, energy, ambition, intellect, the interests of the combative male, no more achieve the fulfillment of his being than they can of themselves build up a human society." What Briffault longs for is a movement, not back to matriarchy (a term which he used rather loosely in the end of his book, though he had defined it quite precisely in the beginning), but to "new forms of marriage" and a condition where, "in the love of the mother, in the mutual devotion of man and woman, the achievements of the organizing and constructive intellect fade into the mist."

Into the mist, perhaps, of Briffault's own vision; certainly not into the clarity of a vision which can see both intellect and maternal altruism as coexistent, because it affirms the natural capacity of women to think, to analyze, to construct, and to create and nurture more than our individual children.

3

If Bachofen was a mid–nineteenth-century German patriarchal mythographer, drawing on earlier myths and fragments of historical record, Elizabeth Gould Davis was the first contemporary feminist myth-maker. *The First Sex*, published one hundred and ten years after *Das Mütterrecht*, is at times inaccurate, biased, unprofessional—all these charges do not really dismiss it. Furthermore, Davis fails to mention or examine Oriental or precolonial African and American myths and traditions of female power, thereby limiting the scope of her work to Western Civilization with a seemingly unconscious parochialism. Her book has undoubtedly been an embarrassment to academic feminists intent on working within strictly traditional and orthodox definitions of what constitutes serious knowledge. Yet its impact has been great, beginning with the arresting implications of its title. Its scholarly deficiencies can be and have been easily enumerated;[9] Davis had, for one thing, a frustrating tendency to quote without indicating omissions, and to rearrange sentences in a quoted paragraph. "Professional" history, on the other hand, has been blindingly unscholarly where women are concerned. What Davis did was to exhume a wealth of materials—some mythic, some historical, some archeological or literary—like someone stirring a fire and rousing showers of sparks sleeping in the ashes. She assumed the role of the tribal story-teller of a conquered people, reciting legends of their past, reminding them that their mothers once were queens and goddesses, strong and courageous leaders. Out of a blend of fact and guesswork, fragments of rumor, memory, and desire, she tried to do in prose what the poet of earlier times did in epic or ballad—to call up before women a different condition than the one we have known, to prime the imagination of women living today to conceive of other modes of existence.

Davis, unlike Simone de Beauvoir or Helen Diner, exhaustively footnoted her book, creating the impression that it can be read—and criticized—like a doctoral thesis. Thus, the academic scholar finds it wanting as a piece of "professional" research, while the awakening feminist may be lured into taking its claims as Scripture was once taken—for a literal rendition of the past. (Her bibliography, however, is a document of immense value in itself.) If we approach Davis as a catalyst of memory and imagination, rather than as a documenter of unshakable fact, or a failed pedant, we can better appreciate the achievement of her book.

The myth of matriarchy pieced together by Davis will perhaps never be completely disproven or verified. But against all the works detailing woman's oppressed condition, Davis's book stands out as the first to create a counter-image—and, let it be added, one which can by no means be lightly dismissed by academic historians and anthropologists.

It is notable that while some feminist anthropologists may deny that any actual "matriarchal" period ever existed, as a universal phase of culture, they do not necessarily dismiss the *idea* of matriarchy as "crazy" or absurd. As the classical anthropologist Jane Harrison once expressed it, a myth is not something that springs "clean and clear" out of the imagination (if anything can be said to do that) but is rather a response to the environment, an interaction between the mind and its external world.[10] It expresses a need, a longing. And myth has always accumulated, accreted; the profile of the goddess or the hero is always changing, weathered by changes in external conditions. If Davis's book depicts women finally as the sole possessors of practical and spiritual vision, if she previsions a world where men are left to tinker with gadgetry of a toylike inconsequentiality while the spiritual and political order is created by women, this is a powerful and an imaginative response to the faces we see aggrandized on our TV screens, the faces of male leaders, the pure products of patriarchy, who appear less and less credible, less and less informed by any responsible vision, less and less capable of governing any community, and more and more technologically capable of degrading and destroying human life. For many women, Davis provided a genesis, though

not a resting place, for speculations about the possibility and
nature of female power: a springboard into feminist desire.

4

The question, "Was there ever true universal matriarchy?" seems
to me to blot out, in its inconclusiveness, other and perhaps
more catalytic questions about the past. I therefore use the
term *gynocentric* in speaking of periods of human culture
which have shared certain kinds of woman-centered beliefs
and woman-centered social organization. Throughout most of
the world, there is archeological evidence of a period when
Woman was venerated in several aspects, the primal one being
maternal; when Goddess-worship prevailed, and when myths
depicted strong and revered female figures. In the earliest artifacts we know, we encounter the female as primal power.

Leave aside for the moment whether those images were made
by women's or men's hands: they express an attitude toward
the female charged with awareness of her intrinsic importance,
her depth of meaning, her existence at the very center of what
is necessary and sacred.* She is beautiful in ways we have almost
forgotten, or which have become defined as ugliness. Her body
possesses mass, interior depth, inner rest, and balance. She is not
smiling; her expression is inward-looking or ecstatic, and sometimes her eyeballs seem to burn through the air. If, as very
often, there is a child at her breast, or on her lap, she is not absorbed in contemplation of him (the "Adoration of the Virgin"
with the Son as center of the world, will come later). She is not
particularly young, or rather, she is absolutely without age. She
is *for-herself* even when suckling an infant, even when, like the
image of the Ephesian Diana, she appears as a cone of many
breasts. Sometimes she is fanged, wielding a club, sometimes she
is girdled by serpents; but even in her most benign aspect the

* Some illustrative photographs of such images may be found in the early
sections of the *Larousse World Mythology*, edited by Paul Grimal; in
Paul Radin's *African Folktales and Sculpture*; in Reynold Higgins, *Minoan
and Mycenean Art*. See also (for descriptive text) E. O. James, *The Cult
of the Mother-Goddess* (New York: Praeger, 1959).

ancient Goddess is not beckoning to her worshipers. She exists, not to cajole or reassure man, but to assert herself.

Let us try to imagine for a moment what sense of herself it gave a woman to be in the presence of such images. If they did nothing else for her, they must have validated her spiritually (as our contemporary images do not), giving her back aspects of herself neither insipid nor trivial, investing her with a sense of participation in essential mysteries. No *Pietà* could do this, nor even the elegant queen of the Amarnan divine family of Egypt, in which the Sun-King stands with his hand patriarchally on his son's head, while his consort—regal as she is—remains clearly a consort. The images of the prepatriarchal goddess-cults did one thing; they told women that power, awesomeness, and centrality were theirs by nature, not by privilege or miracle; the female was primary. The male appears in earliest art, if at all, in the aspect of a child, often tiny and helpless, carried horizontally in arms, or seated in the lap of the goddess, or suckling at her breast.*

Now it can be argued that these figures—Neolithic, pre-Columbian, Cypriot, Cycladic, Minoan, predynastic Egyptian—can tell us nothing of woman's early perception of *herself*; that they are the work of men, the casting into symbolic form of man's sense of *his* relation to earth and nature. Erich Neumann, a Jungian analyst (1905–1960), inclines to this view. First of all, he sets up a triad of relationships characterized by (1) "the

* In her suggestive and closely documented book *Religious Conceptions of the Stone Age*, G. Rachel Levy discusses the types of tracings found in Neolithic caves from Siberia to southern France. She sees the female symbolism and images in many of these paintings—some linear, some fully painted and gloriously immanent with power—along with the female statuettes found in the caves, as suggesting not just a "cult of the Mother Goddess" but a later identification of the caverns with the body of a Mother of Rebirth. She points out that the cave was not simply a shelter in the secular sense, but a religious sanctuary; that its most exquisite and mysterious images are found, not in the general domestic dwelling area, but in labyrinthine corridors, difficult to reach, and clearly sacred zones. The cave itself as a whole was perceived as the body of the Mother, but within it there is also an abundance of vaginal imagery, a triangular symbol in particular, which is found at the entrance to enclosed spaces, and which seems to demarcate profane from sacred areas. Although figures of male hunters occasionally appear, they are not cult-objects; "the underlying principle [of the Aurignacian culture] was feminine."

child's relationship to its mother, who provides nourishment . . ."; (2) "an historical period in which man's dependence on the earth and nature is at its greatest"; and (3) "the
dependence of the ego and consciousness on the unconscious."[11]* Then, according to Neumann, "the Feminine, the
giver of nourishment, becomes everywhere a revered principle of
nature, on which man is dependent in pleasure and pain. *It is
from this eternal experience of man,* who is as helpless in his
dependence on nature as the infant in his dependence on his
mother, *that the mother-child figure is inspired forever anew.*"
(Emphasis mine.)[12] In other words, we again have woman reduced to bearer and nourisher, while man depicts his vision of
her, and himself in relation to her, in a different kind of
creation—the images of art.†

Neumann, was, however, writing before an event which
changed accepted ideas about the age of the earliest cultures.
Recent archeological excavations in the Near East, at such sites
as Jericho in Israel and Anatolia in Turkey, revealed cultures

* Unfortunately, this triad depends on a too-familiar dualism, between man/
culture/consciousness, and woman/nature/unconsciousness. As a woman
thinking, I experience no such division in my own being between nature
and culture, between my female body and my conscious thought. In bringing the light of critical thinking to bear on her subject, in the very act
of *becoming more conscious* of her situation in the world, a woman may
feel herself coming deeper than ever into touch with her unconscious and
with her body. Woman-reading-Neumann, woman-reading-Freud, woman-
reading-Engels or Lévi-Strauss, has to draw on her own deep experience for
strength and clarity in discrimination, analysis, criticism. She has to ask
herself, not merely, "What does my own prior intellectual training tell
me?" but "What do my own brain, my own body, tell me—my memories,
my sexuality, my dreams, my powers and energies?"
† Neumann, though a Jungian, has gone much further than Jung in trying to understand and bring into focus the role of the feminine in culture
and to acknowledge the force of misogyny. However, like Jung, he is primarily concerned with integrating the feminine into the masculine psyche
(again, as in Marcuse's coinage, "the femalization of the male") and his
bias is clearly masculine. Nevertheless, I find Neumann's interleaving of
several aspects of experience useful as a way of keeping in mind that we
are talking at one and the same time about the physical realm of human
biological reproduction and nurture, the cultural/historical realm of what
human beings have invented, prescribed, designed in their efforts to live
together, and the realm that exists within the individual psyche. Like
Briffault, Neumann has brought together an enormous mass of material relating to woman, specifically as mother, and many of their materials reinforce each other in suggesting certain aspects of prepatriarchal life.

existing in Asia Minor two thousand or more years before the presumed Neolithic cultures of Iraq, Iran, Syria, and Palestine, and producing evidence of a "proto-Neolithic" cult of worship, including figurines and "symbolically ornamented chapels—revealing, in superb display, practically all the basic motifs of the great mother-goddess mythologies of later ages."[13] James Mellaart, an archeologist active in the unearthing of the town of Çatal Hüyük in Anatolia, believes that the goddess-figurines, as well as the other art discovered there, were the work of women:

> What is particularly noteworthy . . . is the complete absence of sex [he means sexuality] in any of the figurines, statuettes, plaster reliefs or wall-paintings. The reproductive organs are never shown, representations of phallus and vulva are unknown, and this is the more remarkable as they were frequently portrayed both in the Upper Paleolithic and in the Neolithic and post-Neolithic cultures outside Anatolia. It seems that there is a very simple answer to this seemingly puzzling question, for emphasis on sex in art is invariably connected with male impulse and desire. If Neolithic woman was the creator of Neolithic religion, its absence is easily explained and a different symbolism was created in which breast, navel and pregnancy stand for the female principle, horns and horned animal heads for the male.[14]*

We can find some support for this hypothesis indirectly in both Briffault and Neumann, who cite numerous examples to show that the deeply reverenced art of pottery-making was invented by women, was taboo to men, was regarded as a sacred process and that "the making of the pot is just as much a part of the creative activity of the Feminine as is the making of the child. . . . In pottery making the woman experiences . . . primordial creative force . . . we know how great a role the sacred vessel played in the primordial era, particularly as a vehicle of magical action. In this magical implication the essential features of the feminine transformation character are

---

* It is tempting to ask why sexuality in art—Neolithic or otherwise—should "invariably (be) connected with male impulse and desire." But this is not the place in which to follow up that query. I quote from Mellaart to suggest that there is some documentation for the idea that the early images of women were created by women.

bound up with the vessel as a symbol of transformation."[15] Briffault describes the actual molding of pots by Zuñi women in the shape of a breast; he further states that "the manufacture of pots, like most operations in primitive society . . . partakes of a ritual or religious character" and that "the pot's identity with the Great Mother is deeply rooted in ancient belief through the greater part of the world."[16]

It does not seem unlikely that the woman potter molded, not simply vessels, but images of herself, the vessel of life, the transformer of blood into life and milk—that in so doing she was expressing, celebrating, and giving concrete form to her experience as a creative being possessed of indispensable powers. Without her biological endowment the child—the future and sustainer of the tribe—could not be born; without her invention and skill the pot or vessel—the most sacred of handmade objects —would not exist.

And the pot, vessel, urn, pitcher, was not an ornament or a casual container; it made possible the long-term storage of oils and grains, the transforming of raw food into cooked; it was also sometimes used to store the bones or ashes of the dead. The potential improvement and stabilization of life inherent in the development and elaboration of pottery-making could be likened to the most complex innovations of a technological age —the refining of crude petroleum, the adaptation of nuclear energy—which invest their controllers with immense power. And yet this analogy, even, fails us, because the relationship of the potter to the pot, invested with both an intimate and a communal spirit, is unknown in present-day technology.

Because of speculations like Erik Erikson's (wittily dissected by Kate Millett) as to the meaning and value of woman's "inner space," it is difficult to talk about women in connection with "containers" without evoking a negative if not derisive response.[17] The old associations start pouring in: woman is "receptive," a "receptacle"; little girls "instinctively" want to play with dollhouses while boys do not; woman's place is the "inner space" of the home; woman's anatomy lays on her an ethical imperative to be maternal in the sense of masochistic, patient, pacific; women without children are "unfulfilled," "barren," and "empty" women. My own negative associations with male derivations from female anatomy were so strong that for a long time I felt distaste, or profound ambivalence, when I looked at some of the early mother-goddess figures emphasizing breasts and belly. It took me a long time to get beyond patriarchally acquired responses and to connect with the power and integrity, the absolute nonfemininity, of posture and expression in those images. Bearing in mind, then, that we are talking not about "inner space" as some determinant of woman's proper social function, but about primordial clusters of association, we can see the extension of the woman/vessel association. (It must be also borne in mind that in primordial terms the vessel is anything but a "passive" receptacle: it is *transformative*—active, powerful.)

A diagram may be useful here:

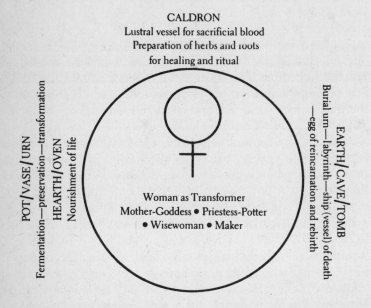

CALDRON
Lustral vessel for sacrificial blood
Preparation of herbs and roots
for healing and ritual

POT/VASE/URN
Fermentation—preservation—transformation

HEARTH/OVEN
Nourishment of life

Woman as Transformer
Mother-Goddess • Priestess-Potter
• Wisewoman • Maker

EARTH/CAVE/TOMB
Burial urn—labyrinth—ship (vessel) of death
—egg of reincarnation and rebirth

The transformations necessary for the continuation of life are thus, in terms of this early imagery, exercises of female power. According to Neumann, "the magical caldron or pot is always in the hands of the female mana figures, the priestess, or later, the witch."[18] The earliest religious activity had as its impulse not the contemplation of eternity but the struggle for survival; it was "practical, not speculative," as Briffault says, having to do with daily needs. And women were the people who filled those needs. He suggests further that sex inequality in our terms was unknown in prepatriarchal society; the kinds of administrative and bureaucratic power-relationships which developed in patriarchy simply did not exist.[19] Thus, not power *over others*, but *transforming* power, was the truly significant and essential power, and this, in prepatriarchal society, women knew for their own.

5

For a long time, the relationship between the sexual act and pregnancy went unrecognized. Sigmund Freud, in *Totem and Taboo*, Otto Rank, in *Beyond Psychology*, and Bronislaw Malinowski, in *The Sexual Life of Savages*, all noted this fact and suggested that here was not mere ignorance but active denial of the paternal role. This denial permitted men to believe that women were impregnated by spirits of the dead, symbolized in the totem animal of the clan. Rank suggested that two impulses could be at work here: the desire for personal immortality (i.e., in the form of rebirth in a later generation) and the desire for a system which would place responsibility for the survival of the tribe on someone other than the individual male—that is, on the totem animal.[20] Malinowski found that the Trobriand Islanders were aware that a virgin could not conceive and that a woman's vagina must be opened before she could become pregnant. They insisted, however, that pregnancy occurred when the spirit of a fully formed child was introduced into the woman's body by being placed on her head by another spirit of the clan.[21] Finally, of course, the visible, physical relationship of mother to child cannot help but seem more authentic than the indistinct paternal relationship, which depends so tangibly on the mother for its realization.

In prepatriarchal life the phallus (*herm*) had a quite different significance from the one it has acquired in androcentric (or phallocentric) culture. It was not worshiped on its own account or regarded as autonomously powerful; it existed as an adjunct to the Goddess, along with other figures such as the bull, the cow, the pig, the crescent moon, the serpent, the lunar axe or *labrys*, the small child in her lap. The tree in leaf is not phallic; it is a female symbol; "it bears, transforms, nourishes; its leaves, branches, twigs are 'contained' in it and dependent on it"; it is inhabited by its own spirit, which it also contains. The sacred grove is sacred to the Goddess. Neumann sees the distortion of the tree into a phallic-patriarchal symbol—as post or pillar, without leaves or natural roots—or into the world-tree whose roots are in the sky, an "unnatural symbol" (a patriarchal reversal of natural fact).[22] Prepatriarchal phallus-cults were the celebration by women of the fertilizing instrument, not the celebration by men of their "manhood" or of individual paternity. The Great Mother acknowledged no individual husband, only sons who become consorts.

Prepatriarchal, gynocentric motherhood preceded wifehood; the mother relation and status were far more important than the wife-status. The act of birth, as Barbara Seaman suggests, must have been perceived as profoundly awesome by primitives —even more so than today, when it is still accompanied, for many onlookers and participants, by intense feelings of transcendence.[23] Out of her body the woman created man, created woman, created continuing existence. Spiritualized into a divine being, she was the source of vegetation, fruition, fertility of every kind. Whether she bore children or not, as potter and weaver she created the first objects which were more than objects, were works of art, thus of magic, and which were also the products of the earliest scientific activity, including the lore of herbs and roots, the art of healing and that of nurturing the young.*

* "It was in neolithic times that man's [*sic*] mastery of the great arts of civilization—of pottery, weaving, agriculture, and the domestication of animals—became firmly established. No one today would any longer think of attributing these enormous advances to the fortuitous accumulation of a series of chance discoveries or believe them to have been revealed by the passive perception of certain natural phenomena. Each of these techniques assumes centuries of active and methodical observation, of bold hypotheses tested by means of endlessly repeated experiments" (Claude Lévi-Strauss, "The Science of the Concrete," in Vernon Gras, ed., *European Literary Theory and Practice: From Existential Phenomenology to Structuralism* [New York: Delta Books, 1973], pp. 138–39).

In biological motherhood, as in these other activities, woman was not merely a producer and stabilizer of life: there, too, she was a *transformer*. Menstrual blood was believed to be transformed into the infant (an idea which still persists—I recall my own mother, an intellectually curious and well-read woman, the wife of a physician, telling me that menstrual blood was "wasted baby") and into the milk which flowed from the mother's breasts. What to many women today may be experienced as a passive function, occurring beyond volition, once was felt to be *transformative power* and was associated, as we have seen, with other kinds of transformation, including reincarnation. If the pot, or vessel, was associated with the woman's body, the conversion of raw fibers into thread was connected with power over life and death; the spider who spins thread out of her own body, Ariadne providing the clue to the labyrinth, the figures of the Fates or Norns or old spinning-women who cut the thread of life or spin it further, are all associated with this process.

Woman did not simply give birth; she made it possible for the child to go on living. Her breasts furnished the first food, but her concern for the child led her beyond that one-to-one relationship. Briffault sees the primitive division of labor as created by the development of hunting. He cites many examples of women in preliterate societies who show great proficiency in hunting, and concludes that the more prevalent pattern of the all-male hunt arose, not from "the respective powers or aptitudes of the sexes or . . . any physical inferiority in woman, but by the functional necessity which bound her to the care of the off-spring and prevented her from undertaking pursuits entailing absence."[24] The human species is dependent on maternal (or adult) care in infancy much longer than any other animal species, and in creating a situation in which they could nurture and rear infants safely and effectively, women became the civilizers, the inventors of agriculture, of community, some maintain of language itself.*

* A recent study uses "implicational analysis" to show that the sexual division of labor in a standard cross-cultural sample derives from the basic fact that "because men cannot nurse infants, the women of any preindustrial society, taken as a group, have primary responsibility for the care of small

6

The woman's body, with its potential for gestating, bringing
forth and nourishing new life, has been through the ages a field
of contradictions: a space invested with power, and an acute
vulnerability; a numinous figure and the incarnation of evil; a
hoard of ambivalences, most of which have worked to dis-
qualify women from the collective act of defining culture. This
matrix of life has been fundamental to the earliest division of
labor; but also, as Bruno Bettelheim has shown, males have
everywhere tried to imitate, annex, and magically share in the
physical powers of the female.[25] The highly developed (and
highly dubious) technology of modern obstetrics is merely a
late stage in what Suzanne Arms has called "the gradual attempt by man to extricate the process of birth from women and
call it his own." "Overpopulation" is today regarded as a
global problem; yet there is far more concern with sterilizing
(chiefly black and Third-World) women, and limiting births,
than with finding new ways to produce and distribute food
throughout the globe. Not simply Western capitalism, but a
male need to feel in control of female reproductive power, is
at issue here.

In his study of primitive mythology Joseph Campbell compares the energy-releasing response to myth (and poetry) with
the innate biological response to certain signs that have been
identified by students of animal behavior. (The wooden model

---

children" and that "women will not undertake activities which would require large numbers of women to work simultaneously in situations which
are dangerous to children," whether this means activities such as hunting
or plowing, or activities near the home involving heavy materials or im-
plements. The authors suggest that these constraints on women's roles
proliferate throughout role behavior through the sequences of production
(clearing land, tilling, sowing, harvesting) and that they derive from a
need for "efficient utilization of human resources" (D. White, M. Burton,
L. Brudner, J. Gunn, "Implicational Structures in the Sexual Division of
Labor," unpublished, 1974). The avoidance of dangerous or physically
taxing work by women *for the protection of unweaned children* has, of
course, no implications whatsoever for the innate capacity of women to
engage in such activities. It tells us nothing whatsoever about *necessary*
constraints in the role of a nonnursing, or childless female; the only "innate
constraint" would seem to be upon men who are incapable of breast-feeding.

or the actual shadow of a hawk, drawn over a cage of newly
hatched chicks, will cause them to dart for shelter; the model or
shadow of a gull or other bird will not. The human infant will
respond to masks resembling a human face, but the mask must
embody certain specific features or it will evoke no response.)
He identifies certain early imprintings of the human mind—the
paradisical bliss of the infant still floating weightlessly in
amniotic waters, the struggle and fear of suffocation on drawing
the first breath, the suckling at the mother's breast and the
sense of abandonment at her absence—which are endlessly re-
lived, sought, or evaded, and which myth, poetry, and art cause
us to experience again as powerful reverberations. He goes on
to acknowledge that "The fear of menstrual blood and isolation
of women during their periods, the rites of birth, and all the
lore of magic associated with human fecundity make it evident
that we are here in the field of one of the major centers of
interest of the human imagination. . . . The fear of woman
and the mystery of her motherhood have been for the male no
less impressive imprinting forces than the fears and mysteries of
the world of nature itself."[26]

Obviously there was a very ancient and powerful tangle of
relationships between a cycle in woman associated with fertility,
the cycle of the moon to which it so mysteriously corresponds,
the need for women to protect themselves at times from men's
unwanted sexual aggression, and the reaction of men to that
curb on their sexuality. Into these play still other relationships—
between the remission of menstruation during pregnancy, the
end of menstruation which marks the end of fertility, the kinds
of knowledge about herself that even primitive woman has
through her menses—whether she is pregnant, whether she can
become so.

Generally it seems to be assumed that the menstrual taboo
(withdrawal of the woman from her usual activities, including
sex) is the original taboo; where authorities differ is on whether
it was first imposed by women or men. Briffault sees it as "the
veto originally laid by women on the exercise of the sexual
instincts of the male. . . . These prohibitions represent the
repulse of the men by the women . . ." According to his
studies, both of menstrual taboos and those of childbirth, the

woman is author of the prohibition, and her self-segregation is felt by men to suggest that at such times she is emitting "dangerous influences."[27] C. G. Hartley claims that the egoistic, nonsocial tyranny of the early male group forced the female group to establish laws of social conduct.[28] Neumann says that woman "domesticated the male through the taboos that she imposed on him, and so created the first human culture."[29] According to his view, sexual initiation originates, not with male puberty rites but with the ritual surrounding the first menstrual period; taboo with the menstrual taboos imposed on men by women; and exogamy (marriage outside the kinship group) as an incest taboo aimed at preventing the sexual exploitation of women by the men living closest to them. What a contemporary woman experiences as her "uncleanness," prepatriarchal women may well have understood as one of their sacred mysteries.

According to the Jungian psychologist Esther Harding:

> In primitive communities a woman's whole life is focused around the regular changes of her physiological cycle. Periods of work at home and in the community of social life with her neighbors and of marital relationship with her husband, alternate with periods of seclusion. At regular intervals she is obliged to go away alone; she may not cook, nor tend the cultivated patch, nor walk abroad; she is precluded from performing any of her customary tasks; she is compelled to be alone, to go down into herself, to introvert. Anthropologists, who, as a rule, are more interested in the customs of a tribe than in the psychology of individuals, have not asked what effects these customs have on the women themselves. Yet, this periodic seclusion must inevitably have had a profound effect on the woman's relation to life.[30]

Both Harding and Bettelheim suggest that the puberty initiation rites practiced by men—which include seclusion, purification, fasting, and the "seeking of a vision"—are attempts to achieve the power inherent in the kind of inwardness which women have come by organically in their periodic menstrual and puerperal withdrawals. Harding suggests that the contemporary woman may still need to use her period as a time for reaching into her subjectivity, living closer to the rhythms of her deepest being—not because the menses are a time of neurotic illness or demonic possession, but because they can be, if used, a source of insight.

Mary Douglas, in her study of pollution and taboo, *Purity and Danger*, points out that where male dominance is unquestioned, and women are totally and violently subjugated (as among the Walbiri, a desert people of central Australia) no menstrual taboo exists; it is, in her opinion, a male-imposed taboo calculated to protect men from the dangers felt to emanate from women.[31] Various other writers, including Margaret Mead, have assumed that the menstrual taboo was created by men out of a primitive fear of blood. But, as Paula Weideger notes in *Menstruation and Menopause*, "if all blood is a source of mana, why is it that men and *only* men consider menstrual blood identical in spiritual substance with other blood? What makes women's attitude toward blood so very different? . . . Primitive peoples are not victims of arrested development who are incapable of learning about the existence of natural events with repeated exposure. . . . Every woman learns the lesson of menstrual blood quite early in life and so might every man."[32]

Whether or not woman was actually the originator of taboo, the mere existence of a menstrual taboo signifies, for better or for worse, *powers only half-understood; the fear of woman and the mystery of her motherhood.* I would suggest that if women first created a menstrual taboo, whether from a sense of their own sacred mysteries or out of a need to control and socialize the male, this taboo itself must have added to their apparent powers, investing them with the charisma of ritual. The deliberate withdrawal of women from men has almost always been seen as a potentially dangerous or hostile act, a conspiracy, a subversion, a needless and grotesque thing, while the exclusion of women from men's groups is rationalized by arguments familiar to us all, whether the group is a priesthood, a dining club, a fishing expedition, an academic committee, or a Mafioso rendezvous. The *self*-segregation of women (most of all in lesbian relationships, but also as in the group which formed around Anne Hutchinson, or as in the women's political clubs in the French revolution of 1848, or in present-day women's

classes or consciousness-raising groups) is to this day seen as
threatening to men; presumably in a culture attuned to magic
it would have terrifying overtones.

Certainly, the menstrual cycle is yet another aspect of female
experience which patriarchal thinking has turned inside out,
rendering it sinister or disadvantageous. Internalizing this attitude, we actually perceive ourselves as polluted. Our tendency
to flesh-loathing (the aversion to the female body passed on to
us by men) is underscored; religious taboos are laid on us even
in "advanced" societies.* A man whose unconscious is saturated
with the fear of menstrual blood will make a woman feel that
her period is a time of pollution, the visitation of an evil spirit,
physically repulsive. Men often exalt and romanticize the
spermal fluid (one man I knew compared its smell to the scent
of chestnut-blossom) while degrading menstrual blood as unnatural and distasteful (another man assured me that intercourse with a menstruating woman did not appall *him*, but that
it resulted in irritation of "the" penis).

It is recognized today that the menstrual and premenstrual
periods can be characterized by depression, anxiety, flashes of
anger. Water retention and hormonal fluctuation may contribute their share, but there are also deep psychic and cultural
factors. An ambivalence of pride and shame (and fear) have
marked, under patriarchy, the onset of the menses; sometimes a
young woman will experience outright denial and revulsion. A
similar ambivalence of fear and relief often marks the beginning
of menopause. For woman-defined-as-mother, the event may
mean, at last, an end to unwanted pregnancies, but also her
death as a woman (thus defined), as a sexual being, and as
someone with a function.

* In order to be legally married in contemporary Israel, a woman must
present herself at the Chief Rabbinate and declare the date of her last
period; her wedding-date will be set thereby so that she does not go "unclean" to her husband. It is still believed that a Jewish woman having intercourse with her husband during her period may cause him to be killed in
war. There is, of course, an ancient background. The *Mishnah* compares a
menstruating woman's "uncleanliness" to that of males with gonorrhea, of
lepers, of human corpses, animal carrion, dead reptiles, and incestuous
sexual relations (Personal communication, Dr. Myra Schotz, Ben-Gurion
University, Israel; Emily Culpeper, "Niddah: Unclean or Sacred Sign?"
unpublished paper, Harvard Divinity School, 1973).

Male attitudes toward menstrual blood aside, the years of menstruation are the years when a woman is potentially, if not actually, a mother. Under patriarchy, until very recently (and still only with immense difficulty) a childbearing woman *could not* be unto-herself, a *virgin* in the ancient, authoritative, sense of the word. The unmarried mother has borne the most savage excoriations of church and society, and still carries a heavy burden of economic and social pressures which penalize her for her choice. Somewhere in the feelings, latent and overt, that women carry through menstruation, there is an association of the menstrual period with a profound ambivalence toward our pregnability, and toward institutionalized motherhood.

8

Prepatriarchal religion acknowledged the female presence in every part of the cosmos. The moon is generally held to have been the first object of nature-worship, and the moon, to whose phases the menstrual cycle corresponds, is anciently associated with women. The Moon Mothers, according to Harding, were virgins, in the great primal sense of the word—not the undeflorated girl, but the woman who belongs to herself, or, in the Eskimo phrase, "She-who-will-not-have-a-husband." She has many lovers, and many sons, and the son often grows up to be a lover. Sometimes the moon is herself female, represented by a goddess like Selene, Artemis, Luna; sometimes the moon is the impregnator, the male source of the Great Mother's fertility (and that of all women); but even so, still associated primarily with what Harding terms "Woman's Mysteries." In other words, whether female or male, the lunar deity has been first and foremost related to the Virgin-Mother-Goddess, who is "for-herself" and whose power radiates out from her maternal aspect to the fertilization of the whole earth, the planting and harvesting of crops, the cycle of seasons, the dialogue of humankind and nature.[33]

But the moon is merely one aspect of the female presence once felt to dominate the universe. Prepatriarchal thought gynomorphized everything. Out of the earth-womb vegetation and nourishment emerged, as the human child out of the woman's body. The words for mother and mud (earth, slime, the *matter* of which the planet is composed, the dust or clay of which "man" is built) are extremely close in many languages: *mutter, madre, mater, materia, moeder, modder.* The name "Mother Earth" still has currency, although, significantly, in our time, it has acquired a quaint, archaic, sentimental ring.

In winter, vegetation retreats back into the earth-womb; and in death the human body, too, returns into that womb, to await rebirth. Ancient Mid-Eastern tombs were deliberately designed to resemble the body of the mother—with labyrinths and spirals intended to represent her internal anatomy—so that the spirit could be reborn there. G. Rachel Levy suggests that this design originated in the caves of Neolithic culture, which were natural symbols of the Mother. Here we see one of many connections between the idea of the Mother and the idea of death—an association which remains powerful in patriarchal thought.[34]

The ocean whose tides respond, like woman's menses, to the pull of the moon, the ocean which corresponds to the amniotic fluid in which human life begins, the ocean on whose surface vessels (personified as female) can ride but in whose depth sailors meet their death and monsters conceal themselves—this ocean lies somewhere between the earth and moon in the gynomorphizing of nature. From human eye-level the ocean is approachable as the moon is not; it is unstable and threatening as the earth is not; it spawns new life daily, yet swallows up lives; it is changeable like the moon, unregulated, yet indestructible and eternal. The ocean cannot be planted or plowed; it is a sterile, salty field, yet it produces, spontaneously, its own life, rich, nourishing, yet very different from the life of vegetation and animals onshore. The Great Goddess is found in all water: "the sea of heaven on which sail the barks of the gods of light, the circular, life-generating ocean above and below the earth. To her belong all waters, streams, fountains, ponds and springs, as well as the rain."[35]

The moon was sometimes perceived as a male deity which impregnated both women and the earth. But gynocentric pantheism imagined the sky itself to be female, with the sun and moon as her sons. "The female sky is the fixed and enduring element," in a number of cultures and myths cited by Neumann: Egyptian, Aztec, Vedic, Babylonian. The Great Mother, the female principle, was originally personified both in darkness and in light, in the depths of the water and the heights of the sky. Only with the development of a patriarchal cosmogony do we find her restricted to a purely "chthonic" or tellurian presence, represented by darkness, unconsciousness, and sleep.

V THE DOMESTICATION OF MOTHERHOOD

===

. . . there is a Persian myth of the creation of the World which precedes the biblical one. In that myth a woman creates the world, and she creates it by the act of natural creativity which is hers and which cannot be duplicated by men. She gives birth to a great number of sons. The sons, greatly puzzled by this act which they cannot duplicate, become frightened. They think, "Who can tell us, that if she can *give* life, she cannot also *take life*." And so, because of their fear of this mysterious ability of woman, and of its reversible possibility, they kill her.

—Frieda Fromm-Reichmann,
"On the Denial of Woman's Sexual Pleasure."

Frederick Engels identified father-right and the end of the matrilineal clan with the beginnings of private ownership and slavery. He saw women as forced into marriage and prostitution through economic dependency, and predicted that sexual emancipation would come with the abolition of private property and the end of male economic supremacy. For Engels (as for succeeding generations of Marxists) the oppression of women has, simply, an economic cause, and an economic solution. He actually discourages our trying to speculate on *how* the transition to sexual equality would come about:

What we can now conjecture about the way in which sexual relations will be ordered after the impending overthrow of capitalist production is mainly of a negative character, limited for the most part to what will disappear. But what will there be new? That will be answered when a new generation has grown up: a generation of men who never in their lives have known what it is to buy a woman's surrender with money or any other social instrument of power, a generation of women who have never known what it is to give themselves to a man from any other considerations than real love, or to refuse to give themselves to their lover from fear of the economic consequences. When these people are in the world, they will care precious little what anybody today thinks they ought to do; they will make their own practice and their corresponding public opinion about the practice of each individual—and there will be the end of it.[1]

This is an excellent illustration of what Karen Horney means when she says that "it is in the interest of men to obscure [the fact that there is a struggle between the sexes]; and the emphasis they place on their ideologies has caused women, also, to adopt these theories." In her delicately worded essay, "The Distrust Between the Sexes," Horney speaks of the resentment and anxiety harbored by all men toward women—even, she says, by "men who consciously have a very positive relationship with women and hold them in high esteem as human beings."[2]* Materialist analysis and masculine bias allow Engels to assume that an economic solution will cleanse false consciousness, create a new concept of gender, purge the future of the pathologies of

* Erich Neumann goes much further. In an essay called "Psychological Stages of Feminine Development" (translated by Rebecca Jacobson and revised for *Spring* by Hildegarde Nagel and Jane Pratt), he discusses the myth of feminine evil and the use of woman as scapegoat "which . . . means that the feminine is 'recognized' as evil by the patriarchally stamped cultures, the Judeo-Christian, Mohammedan and Hindu. Therefore, it is suppressed, enslaved, and outwardly eliminated from life, or else—which is what happens in witch trials—persecuted and done to death as the carrier of evil. *Only the fact that man cannot exist without woman has prevented the extirpation . . . of this group of 'evil' humans upon whom the dangerousness of the unconscious has been projected.*" (Emphasis mine.) This raises the question of how extrauterine reproduction and cloning techniques could be applied toward a gynocidal future, if they remain under male control.

the past. But he fails to understand that it is the mother-son and mother-daughter relationship, as much as, perhaps more than, that between man the buyer and woman the bought, which creates the sexual politics of male supremacism. Even under the pressures of a growing, worldwide, women's consciousness, the overwhelming bias of socialist and revolutionary movements is male, and reflects a wish to have a social revolution which would leave male leadership and control essentially untouched.* Eli Zaretsky has at least attempted to respond to the challenge directed by radical feminism at socialism, acknowledging that in the Bolshevik Revolution,

> Revolution through economic development left intact a major part of women's oppression. The psychosocial heritage of male supremacy was scarcely challenged by the entry of women into industry; while the strengthening of the family encouraged a resurgence of traditional patriarchal ideals, such as the exaltation of motherhood . . .

and that Marxism has assumed the traditional division of labor within the family along with heterosexuality as a "natural" condition.[3] But the effort to marry psychoanalysis and Marxism —two creations of the nineteenth-century masculine intellect— seems unavailing, since we find that it is "the family" which is seen as the problem, rather than the attitudes—acknowledged and hidden—held toward women by men. A woman is for a man both more and less than a person: she is something terribly necessary and necessarily terrible. She is not simply "more than an exploited worker";[4] she is not simply the "other"; she is first of all the Mother who has to be possessed, reduced, controlled, lest she swallow him back into her dark caves, or stare him into stone.

Rationalizations of patriarchy which deny this fact exist, of course, outside the Left. In a little book on kinship systems,

---

* Horney notes that to confess dread of women is far more threatening to masculine self-regard than to acknowledge dread of a man. Since the notion of class assumes that women are merely subsumed under either the dominant males of the ruling class, or the oppressed males of the working class, it has perhaps been only natural that class analysis, male-created, has taken precedence over a sexual analysis.

the anthropologist Robin Fox describes, in several bland sentences, the "basic female function." After acknowledging that the essential human bond, the foundation of all social bonds, is that between mother and child, he goes on to explain how the longer extrauterine gestation required by the upright, bipedal human has resulted in woman's necessary preoccupation with bearing and nurturing for long periods, "probably getting pregnant again while doing so." This necessitated, according to Fox, a system whereby the mothers, thus incapacitated, had to be "protected." Where Engels sees male dominance as evolving from the possession of private property, Fox sees it as naturally evolving from this "protective" role: "it was the men who hunted the game, fought the enemies, and *made the decisions.*" (Emphasis mine.)[5] Apart from the question of how far decisions must be made by a protective group, we have already seen that, in fact, decision-making—in whatever sense that concept would have had meaning in elementary society—was probably originally inseparable from the maternal role. Fox creates a somewhat Victorian image of the early male (and, incidentally of himself), implying that "protection" rather than power and force, is at issue—a familiar rhetoric. If, however, we are to assume that from woman's original child-nurturing function flowed a "natural" division of all labor, generally accepted as natural by women and men, how do we account for the fact that laws, legends, and prohibitions relating to women have, from the early patriarchal myths (e.g., Eve) through the medieval witch-massacres and the gynocide of female infants down to the modern rape laws, mother-in-law jokes, and sadistic pornography of our time, been hostile and defensive, rather than "protective"?

One of the themes of post-Freudian psychology is that man's contributions to culture are his way of compensating for the lack of the one, elemental, creative power of motherhood. Bruno Bettelheim has analyzed male initiation rituals as outgrowths of deep male envy of this female power.[6] Horney suggests that, despite male dominance in every other sphere, a residual envy and resentment has remained which has expressed itself in phallocentric thinking (including such concepts as "penis envy"), in the devaluation (I would call it *reduction*) of motherhood, and in a generally misogynist civilization.*

She finds that besides the very ancient resentment of woman's power to create new life, there is fear of her apparent power to affect the male genitals. Woman as elemental force, and as sexual temptress and consumer of his sexual energies, thus becomes, for man, a figure generating anxiety: "Woman is a mysterious being who communicates with spirits and thus has magic powers that she can use to hurt the male. He must therefore protect himself against her powers by keeping her subjugated." (It is possible that the more "rational" and antisubjective the male, the greater his unconscious servitude to these magical ideas.) "Motherliness" is split off from both sexual attractiveness (the temptress) and "motherhood" (the power-

* Misogyny is not a projection of women who resent men. That it exists, and has been validated by patriarchal culture at all times, is clearly documented. There are a number of recent works—all by men—on this subject, most of them quite interestingly misogynist in their leanings and conclusions. R. E. L. Masters and Eduard Lea, in an anthology called *The Anti-Sex* (1964), assert at regular intervals that "true misogyny is an unwarranted generalization" and suggest that despite the evidence to the contrary they have accumulated, misogyny is really an aberrant strain in human culture. At the same time they admit that misogyny is "cultural and ideological" rather than individual. Both Masters and Lea, and Wolfgang Lederer (*The Fear of Women* [1968]) deny in the dedications of their books that they are misogynists. Lederer accumulates vast research on male fear of the female, but his conclusion is that it is justified because women's drive to reproduce ("Some women are excessively—one is tempted to say, pathologically—fertile") is a genuine threat to civilization. What man really fears is not woman, but an overcrowded planet on which *she* is determined to go on breeding. A similar case of denial is found in the classical scholar H. F. Kitto, who, after amassing evidence of the repression of Athenian women, writes: "What is wrong is the picture it gives of the Athenian man. The Athenian had his faults, but pre-eminent among his qualities were lively intelligence, humanity and curiosity. To say that he habitually treated one-half of his own race with indifference, even contempt, does not, to my mind, make sense" (*The Greeks* [Baltimore: Penguin, 1960], p. 222).

H. R. Hays, who nowhere in his book presents credentials of gynophilia, has written the least misogynist treatment of the subject. His *The Dangerous Sex* (New York: Putnam, 1964) is an attempt "to make men aware of the shameful burden of fantasy and rationalization which they have been trailing down the ages . . . By using this symbolic magic he has either imprisoned [woman], made her an outcast or treated her as a scapegoat" (p. 295). Hays's book is unhysterical and straightforward and should be basic reading for men who want to think seriously about sexual politics.

ful Goddess) and is acceptable in its "nurturing, selfless, self-sacrificing" form: thus, in the fourteenth century, the Virgin Mary could be worshiped while living women were brutalized and burnt as witches.

2

Joseph Campbell, tracing the universality of the Great Goddess or Great Mother image from prehistory onward, asserts that "there can be no doubt that in the very earliest ages of human history the magical force and wonder of the female was no less a marvel than the universe itself; and this gave to woman a prodigious power, which it has been one of the chief concerns of the masculine part of the population to break, control and employ to its own ends."[7] He associates the glorification of hunting over agriculture, and the disappearance of female figurines at the end of the Aurignacian period (c. 30,000 B.C.), with the rise of this male self-assertion against the elemental power of woman. Female figurines were, he finds, "the first objects of worship by the species Homo sapiens. But there is a shift in the magic, ritual and imagery of Homo sapiens from the vagina to the phallus, and from an essentially plant-oriented to a purely animal-oriented mythology."

G. Rachel Levy offers a convincing and beautifully concrete recreation of Neolithic consciousness. She bases her conclusions, which are never dogmatic, on her actual explorations of Aurignacian caves, on a great variety of artifacts and wall-tracings, on the architecture of post-Neolithic cultures, and on studies of the prehistoric movements of wild herds and the distribution of wild grasses throughout Eastern and Western Europe. She suggests that a unified life-giving principle—the female principle embodied in the caves themselves and the goddess-cult figurines found within them—informed the existence of the hunting peoples. The beginnings of animal domestication and grazing, the development of agriculture, led, she feels, to the first consciousness of "movement in time"—i.e., the seasons' cycles, the rotation of the stars, the gestation, birth, and death of animals and crops. This earliest sense of "movement in time" generated a sense of numerical relation, balance, cyclic symmetry which in turn made possible such advances as the development of pottery.[8] But one essential by-product of this "mental revolution" was a growing consciousness of *duality*—a way of perceiving which, carried to its extreme and bifurcated, was later to become fundamental to patriarchal consciousness.

To acknowledge a cyclic change of aspects (that birth is followed by death, death by reincarnation; that tides ebb and flow, winter alternates with summer, the full moon with the dark of the moon) is to acknowledge that process and continuity embrace both positive and negative events—although, as parts of a process, events are less likely to become stamped as purely "positive" or "negative." Prepatriarchal consciousness, according to Levy, begins with an elemental unity which is sensed as female; and proceeds to an awareness of dynamics still presided over by a female presence: "In the growing consciousness of duality, the Mother retained her former abiding and fundamental status as the earth into which men return and out of which all birth emanates . . . no cult of a male divinity is discoverable in Neolithic archaeology. . . . Female potency [was] the great subject of Aurignacian sculpture."[9]

Even death was part of a movement in time, part of the cycle leading to reincarnation and rebirth. A "dark" or "negative" aspect of the Great Mother was thus already present from the beginning, inseparable from her benign, life-giving aspect. And, like death, violence, bloodshed, destructive power, were always there, the potentially "evil" half of the Mother's profile, which, once completely split off, would become separately personified as the fanged blood-goddess Kali, the killer-mother Medea, the lewd and malign witch, the "castrating" wife or mother. (As I was writing this, one of my sons showed me the cover of the current *National Geographic*—the photograph of a Peruvian Indian rowing a pure white llama to the annual ceremony on Titicaca Island where it would be sacrificed to the Earth Mother in exchange for a good harvest. This ceremony is performed by sorceresses and the llama's blood sprinkled onto "Pacha Mama" [Mother Earth].[10] Thus the bringing of life— i.e., food—is associated, as in ancient times, with bloodshed and killing, and both are associated with the Great Mother. Such customs, if rare today, were once legion.)

Women's blood is different from the blood of men or animals. It is associated not only with the "curse" and mysteries of the menstrual taboo, but with the *mana* of defloration, the transformation mystery of birth, and with fertility itself. There is thus a complex fusion of associations derived from the several aspects of the female, which might be visualized as a cluster like the one below:

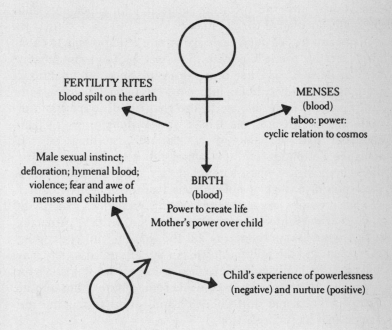

FERTILITY RITES
blood spilt on the earth

MENSES
(blood)
taboo: power:
cyclic relation to cosmos

Male sexual instinct;
defloration; hymenal blood;
violence; fear and awe of
menses and childbirth

BIRTH
(blood)
Power to create life
Mother's power over child

Child's experience of powerlessness
(negative) and nurture (positive)

As Joseph Campbell acknowledges: "the natural mysteries of childbirth and menstruation are as directly convincing as death itself, and remain to this day what they must also have been in the beginning, primary sources of a religious awe."[11]

In the recurrent hero myth, the male infant grows up into the son/lover, who later undergoes *violence* (murder or castration) at his mother's hands. The myth of killing the dragon (another violence/blood myth) recounts the test by which the

young man tries to surmount his dread of the Terrible Mother—
his elemental fear of women. According to Mycenean myth,
Apollo had to battle a female dragon before he could enter
Delphi, which became his shrine.[12]

The Neolithic triangle or the *yoni*—female genital symbols
anciently inscribed at the entrance to a sacred area—become,
in this struggle against female power, fanged Kali, or Medusa's
face with its snarl of snaky hair. The beneficient "Cow Goddess
beyond the grave" who "suckled the souls of the newly dead" is
transformed into the pregnant monster, "hippopotamus and
crocodile, lioness and woman in one."[13]

Neumann sees an *adult* male ego as one which is able to enter
into a creative connection with the Great Mother—presumably
both in her dark and her benign aspects, since full adulthood
requires eventually entering into some creative relationship with
death itself. It is the adolescent ego that is still so uncertain of
itself that it perceives the female as threatening; as "the unconscious and the non-ego . . . darkness, nothingness, the
void, the bottomless pit." Of course the issue here is not one
of a chronological phase ending at, say, twenty, or even of a
more primitive stage of human consciousness, but of an aspect
of male sexuality, which in a great many, probably a majority of
men, continues into middle life and beyond. In fact, patriarchy
is by nature always trying to "kill the dragon," in its negation
of women; and the fully adult woman in patriarchal society may
still often find only an adolescent son/lover, who wants her for
his emotional sustenance even while somewhere within him he
fears castration and death at her hands. This fear is the real
dragon that has to be destroyed.

3

Woman has always known herself both as daughter and as potential mother, while in his dissociation from the process of
conception man first experiences himself as son, and only much
later as father. When he began to assert his paternity and to
make certain claims to power over women and children on that
basis, we begin to see emerging the process through which he

compensated for—one could say, took revenge for—his previous condition as son-of-the-mother.

Patriarchal monotheism did not simply change the sex of the divine presence; it stripped the universe of female divinity, and permitted woman to be sanctified, as if by an unholy irony, only and exclusively as mother (without the extended *mana* that she possessed prepatriarchally)—or as the daughter of a divine father. She becomes the property of the husband-father, and must come to him *virgo intacta*, not as "second-hand goods"; or she must be ritually deflorated. If he is to know "his" children, he must have control over their reproduction, which means he must possess their mother exclusively. The question of "legitimacy" probably goes deeper than even the desire to hand on one's possessions to one's own blood-line; it cuts back to the male need to say: "I, too, have the power of procreation—these are *my* seed, *my* own begotten children, *my* proof of elemental power." In addition, of course, the children are the future receivers of the patrimony; by their prayers and sacrifices, they will ensure the father's spirit a safe passage after death; but they are also present assets, able bodies to work fields, fish, hunt, fight against hostile tribes. A wife's "barrenness" (until very recently it was the woman who was declared "barren" rather than the husband infertile) was a curse because she was, finally, the means of reproduction. A man needed children to enhance his position in the world, and especially, a man needed sons. The command of Yahweh: "Be fruitful and multiply,"* is an entirely partiarchal one; he is not invoking the Great Mother but bidding his sons beget still more sons. Thus, Engels is correct in his famous statement that in the patriarchal family the husband is the bourgeois and the wife and children the proletariat. But each is something more to each, something which both cements and can outlast economic bondage.

In the Middle East to this day, God is believed to strike a woman barren as punishment for some impiety (the woman is

---

* That imperative in Genesis is of course preceded by the myth of Adam, in which woman's procreative power is denied and *she* is taken out of the man's body. When Adam and Eve are cursed, Eve is told that "in sorrow [she] will bring forth children."

assumed to be the sinner, not her husband) and the production of daughters is a disaster, not simply for the mother, but for the daughters. The Hebrew scholar Raphael Patai says that "we know from historical documents relating to the Arab world from pre-historic times down to the 19th century that often a father decided to put to death a daughter either immediately upon her birth or at a later date. The usual method of putting a newborn daughter to death was to bury her in the sands of the desert." He quotes from the Koran the words of a father who asks himself, of his newborn daughter: "Shall he keep it in contempt, or bury it in the dust?"[14] The earlier background of female primacy I have described needs to be held in mind against the violence of this question—along with the fact that the Yahwists savagely repressed the cults of Astarte (originally Tanit, Asherah, or Ishtar) and denounced all worship of the Goddess as "an abomination." [15]

The Mother Goddess is gradually devalued and rejected; the human woman finds her scope and dignity increasingly reduced. Patriarchal man impregnates "his" wife and expects her to deliver "his" child; her elemental power is perceived more and more as a service she renders, a function she performs. In the *Eumenides* of Aeschylus, the Erinyes, representing mother-right, claim vengeance on Orestes for the crime of matricide. But Apollo declares that Orestes's murder of his mother was a just act because it avenged the death of his father Agamemnon; and he continues:

> The mother is no parent of that which is called her child, but only nurse of the newplanted seed that grows. The parent is he who mounts.

Athena, also a representative of father-right, denies having had any mother; she sprang from her father Zeus's brain and she acts like a true token woman, loyal only to "the man" as she does not hesitate to announce.[16] And the medieval church held that a minuscule, fully formed *homunculus*, complete with soul, was deposited by the male in the female body, which simply acted as incubator.[17]*

* Margaret Mead notes that it has always been more difficult to obscure the woman's role in procreation than the man's—yet she gives contemporary examples—the Rossel Islanders, the Montenegrins—of cultures in which

The image of the divine family also changes. The Goddess, whether in Sumer, Minos, Mycenae, Phrygia, Knossos, or Syria, had often been represented with a young god, her son, servant, or consort, but always subsidiary to her. E. O. James perceives these young male images as the first sign of recognition of the male's part in fertilization. But for a long time the young god remained more son than husband, more consort than equal. Mellaart finds the role of the son of the goddess "strictly subordinate to hers"; of a male figure found in one of the Çatal Hüyük shrines, he says: "Presumably he represents an aspect of hunting, which alone was responsible for the presence of an independent male deity in the neolithic of Çatal Hüyük."[18] But in his earliest appearance he is a vegetation god, who must die and be reborn for the vegetative cycle to continue. In a sense, he is thus still annexed to the Mother of grains, fruits, and growing things. Later, the virgin-mother with her youthful childmate is replaced by a father, his wife, and his children. In contrast to the "Divine Triad" of Mycenae cited by Leonard Palmer, which consists of two queens and a king, we find such images as the Egyptian Amarnan family, consisting of a father, his son, and his small grandson.[19] The mother is no longer virgin, "she-unto-herself"; she is "unto-the-husband," his unequal consort or his possession and subordinate, to be reckoned up with his cattle.*

Devaluations of the Goddess are legion. Patai describes the struggle of Jewish patriarchal monotheism with the goddess-cults, of which the golden calf was one remnant (the horned bull or cow having been sacred to the Goddess throughout the world.)† He tells of women weaving "houses"—possibly gar-

the mother's role is held to be purely passive or is denied outright (*Male and Female* [New York: Morrow, 1975], pp. 59–60).

* In Judaism there is no divine family. Christianity's Holy Family—really the human family of Jesus—is distinct from the Trinity, or three-part Godhead of Father, Son, and Holy Spirit. Daly notes the ambiguity surrounding the Holy Spirit, which is invested with stereotypically "feminine" qualities but referred to by a masculine pronoun and supposed to have impregnated the Virgin Mary. As for the human family of Jesus, his words spoken to the Virgin Mary in the Gospels are suggestive: "Woman, what have I to do with thee?" The Virgin is, of course, *virgo intacta*, not *virgo* in the sense associated with the cult of Artemis.

† In his *Ancient Judaism*, Max Weber hints at the rejection of "chthonic and vegetative" cults by the Hebrews; he is, of course, talking about cults

ments—for Asherah in the temple at Jerusalem, and the baking
of cakes for Astarte or Anath. Some remnant of female presence
—heavily laden with what Jung would call anima-projection—
survived in the concept of the Shekhina, "the loving, rejoicing,
motherly, suffering, mourning and in general emotion-charged
aspect of deity" (with what implications for centuries of Jewish
mothers?). A female deity also reemerged in the Kabbalistic
renascence of the thirteenth century, under the name Matronit,
who, acording to Patai is a distinct and often independent presence, but who seems to have left few ripples in the mainstream
of Judaism.[20] The pig, declared an unclean animal in the Koran
and the Old Testament, was a reiterative figure in goddess-
religion; the sow was sacred in Crete, sometimes appeared as
an embodiment of Isis, was sacrificed at the feast of Aphrodite,
and was a symbol of the Eleusinian cult of Demeter. "Wherever
the eating of pork is forbidden and the pig is held to be unclean, we can be sure of its originally sacred character."[21]

Jane Harrison describes the descent (in every sense) of the
Hellenic figure of Pandora from the Cretan Earth-Mother, her
conversion from the All-Giver to merely a beautiful girl dowered
with gifts by all the Olympians and then sent as a temptress to
man. Pandora's famous "box" which when opened released
every kind of grief and trouble among men, was originally a
pithos or *jar* in which the Earth-Mother stored all the goods of
wine, grain, and fruits. Jane Harrison was struck by the "ugly
and malicious theological animus" in Hesiod's telling of this
tale: "he is all for the *Father* and the Father will have no great
Earth-Goddess in his man-made Olympus."[22]

Slater sees the entire Olympian mythology as saturated with
fear of the mature, maternal woman; the much-admired goddess, Athena, is born from her father Zeus's brain, is virginal,
childless, and, as has been seen, affirms her loyalty to the male.
Hera is a jealous, competitive consort, and destructive mothers
like Gaea, Rhea, Medea, and Clytemnestra abound. He the-
orizes that this fear of the maternal woman derived from the
sexual politics of fifth-century Greece, where women were ill-
educated, were sold into marriage, and had no role except as

of the Mother-Goddess. Another example of the method Daly has named
"The Great Silence."

producers of children, the sexual interest of men was homo-
erotic, and for intellectual friendships a man sought out hetaeras
(usually foreign-born women) or other men. He assumes the
mother to have been filled with resentment and envy of her
sons, and, in her own frustration, excessively controlling of her
male children in their earliest years. Her feelings would have
been experienced by her sons as a potentially destructive hostility which is later embodied in mythology and classical drama.[23]*

4

Sun-worship, which always postdates worship of a lunar deity
(whether feminine or masculine) is another feature of patriarchal thought. The ancients saw the moon not as a reflector
of solar light, but as independently glowing in the darkness of
night; the sun was the inhabitant, rather than the source of
daylight.

It is extraordinary to see concretely, as in Egyptian art of the
Amarna period, the coming-into-dominance of the sun. Although a solar deity had long been central in Egyptian religion,
there was still a strong goddess-cult embodied in the figures of
Isis, Hathor, Nut, Nepthys. The fourteenth-century B.C. pharaoh
Akhenaton revolutionized Egyptian cosmology in setting up the
Aten, or sun-disk, as the sole embodiment of a new religion. In
his capital, the seat of the Aten at Tell-el-Amarna, he encouraged an art which over and over, in the sun-disk with its spreading rays, asserts the message of a monotheistic, heliocentric, and
patriarchal universe.

When we think of Amarnan art we tend to think of the fa-

* Slater is another writer who comes close to a denunciation of patriarchy
yet gets deflected. His thesis is that maternal overinvolvement with the
son, deriving from the inferior and reduced status of women, results—in
America as in fifth-century Greece—in a narcissistic male consciousness,
given to "proving" itself through war, often through meaningless achievement and acquisitiveness, and through competition. He does not, like some
writers, leave the problem at the mother's door; he is refreshingly aware
that her relationship to her son occurs in a social context, the *reductio-ad-
matrem* which gives no other opportunity for action, makes motherhood
the definition of womanhood, and child-care (in the middle classes) a full-
time, exclusively female occupation. Though many of Slater's observations
are useful, his failure to connect the psychic pattern with the patriarchal
context leaves his insights regrettably incomplete.

mous portrait bust of Nefertite. But her popularity in our times should not make us exaggerate her importance in her own. Amarnan art, in fact, reiterates images of woman and of the family which do not seem very different from contemporary stereotypes. In these incised or carven images, Akhenaton is already both patriarch and deity (Incarnation of the Aten). With him is his queen, Nefertite, of extraordinary bearing and elegance, who comes far closer to contemporary ideals of feminine, aristocratic beauty than do most prepatriarchal female images. But she is unmistakenly second; a consort, even a royal deity, depicted with dignity and pride, but essentially a token woman. In one *stele*, the royal family (Akhenaton, Nefertite, and three of their daughters) are represented in an informal, even intimate family scene showing a good deal of physical affection. But above them the Aten holds forth its rays, and *it* is the real center and keystone of the composition.

In establishing the worship of the Aten, Akhenaton not only ordered the destruction of many images of the earlier gods, and removed their names from monuments, but prohibited the plural form of the word "god." A reference in Cyril Aldred to the fact that "the words for 'mother' and 'truth' were cleansed of their old associations" is tantalizing, since the hieroglyph for "house" or "town" also symbolizes "mother," emphasizing the principle of collective as well as individual nurture.[24]

In the *Eumenides* of Aeschylus, Apollo, the Hellenic sun-god, becomes the spokesman for father-right, upheld by Athena, the goddess who denies her mother. Apollo is god of poetry and the lyre, twin brother of an independent sister, associated with light, with trees, with the art of healing. Jane Harrison notes that Apollo is derived from the god Paean, of the land where the styptic peony grows, and that this herb, which could stanch blood, was held in reverence throughout the East. But Artemis, his sister, is likewise associated with healing herbs, in her diminished state as goddess. Apollo's relationship to trees is interesting: The nymph Daphne, to escape rape by him, had herself turned into a laurel tree. This tree Apollo made his personal symbol; and it was with a laurel branch in his hand that he came to take over the oracular shrine of the earth-goddess,

Themis, at Delphi[25]—killing, as we have seen, a female dragon on the way.

Thus Apollo assimilated a number of attractive aspects of the Great Mother—even to being paired with the moon. The Mother of Trees, of healing herbs and the preservation of life, becomes a male god; the lunar goddess becomes his sister. Slater calls him "the personification of anti-matriarchy, the epitome of the sky-god, a crusader against Earth-deities. He is all sunlight, Olympian, manifest, rational."[26] Now this of course is an extreme case of patriarchal "splitting"—in Jane Harrison's words, Greek orthodoxy would allow "no deed or dream of darkness" about Apollo. All was to be lucidity, radiant masculinity. Harding suggests that the worship of the moon embodies respect for the wisdom of instinct and natural law, and that sun-worship has to do with the idea of control of natural forces.[27] Indeed, Apollo is personified as driving the steeds of the sun. The "Apollonian" rational control of nature, as opposed to the instinctual excesses of the cult of Dionysus, the power of consciousness as opposed to the unconscious, the celebration of father-right over mother-right, come together in this mythology.

Why the sun should have come to embody a split consciousness, while the worship of the moon allowed for coexistent opposites, a holistic process, is an interesting question. The fact that the moon is itself continually changing, and is visible in so many forms, while the sun presents itself in one, single, unvarying form, may account for the kinds of human perceptions which would be powerfully drawn to one or the other. At all events, with the advent of solar religion, the Great Mother, in her manifold persons and expressions, begins to suffer reduction; parts of her are split off, some undergo a gender change, and henceforth woman herself will be living on patriarchal terms, under the laws of male divinities and in the light of male judgments.

5

There are really two modes in which man has related to woman-as-mother: the practical and the magical. He has, at one time, been utterly dependent on her. Predominantly, in all cultures, it is from women that both women and men have learned about caresses, about affectionate play, about the comfort of a need satisfied—and also about the anxiety and wretchedness of a need deferred.

Briffault was convinced that maternal sentiment far predated the mating instinct; the first love being the love of mother and child. He perceived tender feelings as a secondary female sexual characteristic, derived in the course of female evolution from the biological nature of the female organism. It was the desire for that tenderness, which the male experienced from his mother, that originally induced him to modify his own sexual instinct in accordance with the mating, or stabilizing, impulse of woman.[28] According to Margaret Mead,

> The relationship in the male between his innate sexual impulses and reproduction seems to be a learned response. . . . Male sexuality seems originally focussed to no goal beyond immediate discharge; it is society that provides the male with a desire for children, for patterned interpersonal relationships that order, control, and elaborate his original impulses.[29]

Thus in prepatriarchal life the male child early perceived that the female power of procreation was charged with *mana*. The sacred, the potent, the creative were symbolized as female. When not absorbed in fending for existence, or ritually acknowledging the (female) powers ruling life and death, prepatriarchal man must have felt something of an outsider. As Mead remarks: "His equipment for love [sex] is manifest to the very small boy—but what is it to be a father? This is something that goes on outside one's own body, in the body of another."[30] The anthropologist Leo Frobenius gives us the words of an Abyssinian woman commenting on the richness and complexity of a woman's biological endowment as contrasted with a man's: "His life and body are always the same. . . . He knows nothing."[31]

Patriarchal man created—out of a mixture of sexual and affective frustration, blind need, physical force, ignorance, and intelligence split from its emotional grounding, a system which turned against woman her own organic nature, the source of her awe and her original powers. In a sense, female evolution was mutilated, and we have no way now of imagining what its development hitherto might have been; we can only try, at last, to take it into female hands.

The mother-child relationship is the essential human relationship. In the creation of the patriarchal family, violence is done to this fundamental human unit. It is not simply that woman in her full meaning and capacity is domesticated and confined within strictly defined limits. Even safely caged in a single aspect of her being—the maternal—she remains an object of mistrust, suspicion, misogyny in both overt and insidious forms. And the female generative organs, the matrix of human life, have become a prime target of patriarchal technology.

VI HANDS OF FLESH, HANDS OF IRON

How have women given birth, who has helped them, and how, and why? These are not simply questions of the history of midwifery and obstetrics: they are political questions. The woman awaiting her period, or the onset of labor, the woman lying on a table undergoing abortion or pushing her baby out, the woman inserting a diaphragm or swallowing her daily pill, is doing these things under the influence of centuries of imprinting. Her choices—when she has any—are made, or outlawed, within the context of laws and professional codes, religious sanctions and ethnic traditions, from whose creation women have been historically excluded.

In Judeo-Christian theology, woman's pain in childbirth is punishment from God. (The notion of birth-pain as punitive is found, as well, in other cultures.) Since the curse laid on Eve in Genesis was taken literally well into the nineteenth century, the mother in labor had to expect to suffer; but what was even more significant, it was assumed until the last three decades that she must suffer *passively*. In 1591 a midwife, Agnes Simpson, was burned at the stake for having attempted to relieve birth pangs with opium or laudanum.[1] In the nineteenth century, chloroform was finally allowed to blot the laboring woman from consciousness, rendering her so totally passive that she awoke unaware that she had delivered. Others would *do to* her what had to be done. "Nature" is often referred to in manuals of early midwifery as wiser than the "art" of the surgeon with his hooks and forceps; but that a woman might learn to understand the process herself, and bring to it her own character and intelligence, her own instinctive and physical equipment, is never hinted. The "courage" of passive suffering is the highest praise accorded the lying-in mother.

I began thinking about childbirth with the hypothesis that men had gradually annexed the role of birth-attendant and thus assumed authority over the very sphere which had originally been one source of female power and charisma. But for many reasons—the advent of the male midwife and obstetrician being one—passive suffering and the archetypal female experience of childbirth have been seen as identical. Passive suffering has thus been seen as a universal, "natural," female destiny, carried into every sphere of our experience; and until we understand this fully, we will not have the self-knowledge to move from a centuries-old "endurance" of suffering to a new active being.

A surprising number of women—not simply poor and illiterate but educated and middle-class—approach labor insisting that they want to know as little about it as possible: "Just put me out and let the doctor handle it." I was one of these women myself, in the fifties: literate, intellectual, an artist curious about the psyche, yet convinced that the knowledge of my body was a matter for "experts" and that birth was the specialty of the obstetrician. A part of me, even then, could not tolerate passivity, but I identified that part with the "unwomanly" and in becoming a mother I was trying to affirm myself as a "womanly woman." If passivity was required, I would conform myself to the expectation. I was also, of course, mistrustful of and alienated from my body. Later, in the mid-sixties, I underwent a series of operations for arthritis which demanded my active engagement in painful physiotherapy if I was to walk freely again. "Womanliness" was not in question then; but also, I brought with me into that experience certain political ideas about resistance, about the conversion of suffering into activism, and about the need to analyze what was happening to me. I kept a notebook in which I tried to explore the efforts of the hospital system to reduce the patient to a child or an object and to induce passive reactions, even though immense will and determination were needed to go through the postoperative exercises. I understood then, as I had not in bearing my three children, that I could not afford to become an object; and I knew, later, that I could probably have given birth with the same active engagement in whatever pain there was.

In reading the history of childbirth, we have to "read between the lines" of histories of obstetrics by contemporary medical men; we can also examine the passionate debate-by-pamphlet that went on between those who opposed and those who argued for the female midwife. But it is important to remember that the writers were by no means disinterested, that they were engaged in both a rhetorical and a political battle—and that the one group whose opinions and documentation we long to have —the mothers—are, as usual, almost entirely unheard-from.

2

Benjamin Rush, the eighteenth-century physician, reported of Native-American mothers that

> Nature is their only midwife. Their labors are short, accompanied with little pain. Each woman is delivered in a private cabin, without so much as one of her own sex to attend her. After washing herself in cold water, she returns in a few days to her usual employment.[2]

Of course, a great deal of glib romanticizing surrounds the notion of the "primitive" woman giving birth without pain or fuss and then getting on with the day's work. However, certain physical facts do suggest that women in a homogeneous elementary culture might have shorter and easier *normal* labors than women of a heterogeneous and urbanized culture.

First, in the earliest human groups, all human beings were smaller; and a small fetus is easier to deliver. Moreover, the fetus and the mother were of the same body-type. A small-boned woman from the Mediterranean did not meet or mate with a tall, heavy-boned man from the north; consequently she did not have to deliver a large-boned, large-skulled child through a narrow pelvis. She began bearing her children in the second decade of life, soon after first menstruation; she did not wait till some age of consent to mate, and youth gave her a muscular tone and flexibility already diminished in a woman of thirty.[3] She was not likely to have a pelvis misshapen by rickets —this, too, came later, along with urbanization and a more indoor life. She was not likely to contract infection, since she gave birth alone and no one touched her internally. Moreover, she gave birth in an instinctively natural, squatting position, which allowed the force of gravity to aid her in expelling the child. All this was true for normal labors; however, complications—a breech presentation, twins, prematurity—would be almost necessarily fatal to mother or child, since a woman laboring alone cannot manipulate her own body and the body of the child to facilitate a difficult birth.

Throughout the literature of childbirth runs the theme that the majority of births, even today, *are* "normal," and that the chief work of the birth-attendant is to be with the mother prenatally and during labor, to help expel the placenta, cut the umbilical cord, and attend to the newborn. So we can assume that the majority of births before recorded history were also normal ones.

When the father recognized his fatherhood, some men probably attended at births. There are accounts of women in elementary societies giving birth on the father's knees, as on an obstetrical stool, assisted by a woman relative. Before paternity was acknowledged or understood, it seems improbable that the father assisted at births, as one contemporary obstetrician asserts.[4] In fact, in many cultures a pregnant or laboring woman is still today taboo to all but her female relatives, and men are excluded from the birth-chamber.[5] Most commonly, a woman would give birth with the help and moral support of the grandmother, a woman friend or relative, or a group of women who had been through the experience. Finally certain of these would become known as "experienced" or "wise" women.[6]

No one disputes that within recorded history, until the eighteenth century, childbirth was overwhelmingly the province of women. This seems utterly natural, if only because women were experienced firsthand in the process; but even in early times there were male rationalizations as to why it should be so. For instance: we are told on the one hand that the Athenian midwife knew far more about the female reproductive organs than the Hippocratic physician (which seems highly likely); on the other, that the practice of midwifery was "beneath the dignity" of the male physician. The latter view of course corresponds with the low opinion held of women—in particular mothers, as Slater has shown—by the Athenian male.

Athenian midwives were more than birth-assistants; they prescribed aphrodisiacs and contraceptives, gave advice on sexual problems, and induced abortions. They were often accompanied by priestesses who chanted and recited spells to ease labor. The physician was forbidden to perform abortions; but only he was permitted to perform podalic version;[7] and this type of specialization was to give the male practitioner a kind of power which, though it hovers for many centuries in the background, can be traced throughout the history of midwifery.

The technique of podalic version, or the turning of the child in its descent through the birth-canal from an upside-down head position to a breech presentation, for better traction, was practiced as early as 1500 B.C. in Egypt—not by midwives or physicians, but by priests.* Greek physicians were called in only when labor became acutely difficult; we are told that podalic version was practiced by them with skill.[8] Throughout the historical literature on midwifery runs the assertion that midwives took care of normal births but that in emergency a male physician (or priest) had to be summoned.† (Women, of course, could not be physicians in fifth-century Greece.) But podalic version is not a surgical operation, nor part of the treatment of disease. It is a technique relevant *only* to obstetrics, and it necessitates a good deal of knowledge about the normal birth-process and the inner organs of women. It is hard to see how podalic version could have been mysteriously at the command of Hippocrates, unless he had learnt it originally from the midwives.

* The oldest existing medical treatise, the Ebers Papyrus of Egypt, mentions childbirth only once, according to R. P. Finney (*The Story of Motherhood* [New York: Liveright, 1937], p. 23).
† One exception is that of high-caste Hindu women of the early centuries A.D., who were apparently delivered by a priest-physician even in normal labors, while lower-caste women had midwives. (See Harvey Graham, *Eternal Eve* [London: Hutchinson, 1960], p. 23; Finney, *op. cit.*, pp. 26–38.)

Caesarean section—removal of the child from the mother's abdomen through an incision—was apparently performed by the Hindus and by Hippocrates, but usually at the expense of the mother's life. (It was reinvented in Western Europe in 1500, having been a lost art for centuries, not by a physician but by a sow-gelder.) But before version and Caesarean section, the efforts to deliver a child in a difficult labor were probably more excruciating than the labor itself. There are accounts, from many cultures, of birth-attendants "stripping" the abdomen (squeezing it downward like a cow's udder to force the child's descent), trampling on the abdomen directly above the fetus, or tying tight clothes around the mother's body to force expulsion. If her contractions were weak she might be "shaken" in a sheet or hung from a tree.* Repeatedly and for centuries, hooks were used to extract the fetus in pieces—a practice appropriately known as "destructive obstetrics," with subdivisions including craniotomy, embryotomy, hook extraction, and amputation of limbs. This was the specialty of the male physician as taught by Hippocrates and Galen; Galen specifically declared it a male domain.[9]

Whatever the frequency of such labors, they can only have left their mark on the consciousness of any woman who witnessed them, underwent them, or heard them described. Very early, the process of labor—the most natural process in the world—becomes tinged with cultural reverberations of terror, and a peculiar resonance of punishment. In some cultures an infant who did not get born easily was assumed to be evil, or possessed of demons; it was condemned to death, and the mother sometimes shared in the penalty, since to be pregnant with such a child was surely a judgment on her.

Three types of midwives practiced in Rome: the obstetrical midwife, her assistant, and the female priest who chanted pray-

---

* "Sometimes it worked. . . . And each time it did seem to work, those who had conceived the idea became convinced of their power to influence and control nature. That the midwife would have waited for the natural process to move at its own pace, and that her quiet assistance would have been enough to see the process through to a safe conclusion, were often forgotten in the face of such dramatic evidence that man's power to reason could shape and control nature" (Suzanne Arms, *Immaculate Deception* [Boston, Houghton Mifflin, 1975], p. 10).

ers for a successful delivery. Soranus of Ephesus, a physician of the second century A.D., produced an obstetrical treatise giving instructions for midwives;[10] again, it is difficult to know where he could have obtained his knowledge unless from the midwives themselves, since the male birth-attendant did not attend at normal births. But women did not write books; and the real history of the development of birthing as an art, the expertise accumulated and passed on by the actual practitioners, is blotted out in the history of male obstetrics. Only after the Middle Ages, when male influence and the struggle for male control of midwifery were well underway, do we begin to hear of the "heroes" of this branch of medicine. And indeed, there were some heroes, men who fought to save the lives of women in labor; but the names of the great midwives are mostly lost.

3

The establishment of Christianity in the West had its own effect on childbirth. Of the two great classical sources of medical learning, Hippocrates and Galen, the Church preferred Galen, not on the basis of his science but for his monotheism. Galen taught that surgery was unrelated to medicine, so that surgery remained for centuries a technique rather than a science, requiring at best a strong stomach and a certain brutal self-confidence. Where obstetrical surgery was called for, it was performed "by barbers and sow-gelders."[11] During the Middle Ages and beyond, midwifery was in any case seen as an unclean profession. The misogyny of the Church Fathers, which saw woman—especially her reproductive organs—as evil incarnate, attached itself to the birth-process, so that males were forbidden to attend at births, and the midwife was exhorted to make her primary concern not the comfort and welfare of the mother, but the baptism of the infant—*in utero*, with a syringe of holy water if necessary.[12] With convenient double think, the midwife was classified with the sow-gelder as performing a necessary but degraded function; however, she, and she alone, except for the priest, could baptize—because an infant might die in damnation if it failed to survive until a priest could be called.

The male physician, in any case, would have a fairly limited

notion of the female organs, since the Church also forbade the
dissection of corpses, thus arresting and retarding the study of
anatomy in general. So for several centuries, the knowledge of
pregnancy, of the birth-process, of female anatomy, and of
methods for facilitating labor, was being accumulated entirely
by women. As late as the fifteenth century, only women birth-
attendants are depicted in paintings and engravings.[13] Only by
the seventeenth century do we find the man-midwife appearing
on the scene, and he appears at the moment when the male
medical profession is beginning to control the practice of healing, refusing "professional" status to women and to those who
had for centuries worked among the poor. He appears first in
the Court, attending upper-class women; rapidly he begins to
assert the inferiority of the midwife and to make her name
synonymous with dirt, ignorance, and superstition.

In their classic pamphlet, *Witches, Midwives and Nurses: A
History of Women Healers*, Barbara Ehrenreich and Deirdre
English trace the rise of this élitist male medical profession,
which emerged out of the suppression of women healers during
the centuries of witch-hunting, persecution, and murder. Eighty-
five percent of the many millions executed as witches were
women. They were charged with an imaginative variety of
crimes, from causing a man's genitals to disappear to bringing
about the death of a neighbor's cow; but wisewomen, healers,
and midwives were especially singled out by the witch-hunters.
I have already cited one English midwife who was executed for
prescribing a pain-reliever during labor; and many more were
charged with using "heathen" charms and spells, under the direction of the devil. In the Massachusetts Bay Colony in America, midwives were often viewed with suspicion and charged
with witchcraft.

The case of Anne Hutchinson is instructive because it illuminates the many levels on which the American Puritan midwife
was seen as threatening and subversive. The doctrine of "the
priesthood of all believers" and the Puritan emphasis on the
individual conscience as the primary mediator with God, had
seemed to encourage freedom of thought for women and men
alike. But in practice, a male theology and a male magistracy
stood between the individual woman's conscience and intellect,

and God. To men was assigned the task of interpreting God's "unknowable omnipotence"—specifically, his power of damnation or salvation; and in order for men to be free to wrestle with the problems of covenant theology, women must devote themselves to the management of "Secular Cares"; in short, stay in the home and keep off the masculine turf of theology. God was to be revealed to women by men. Ben Barker-Benfield suggests that the anxiety, frustration, and impotence experienced by the seventeenth-century New England woman, living under the double pressure of God's unknowable will and man's exclusion of her from active participation in interpreting that will, drove some women to infanticide, attempted murder, suicide, and "utter desperation." Others, more vocally aggressive, were whipped for challenging the male hierarchy.

Anne Hutchinson was a midwife and a thinking woman, "of haughty and fierce carriage, of a nimble wit and very active spirit, and a very voluble tongue, more bold than a man," as Governor Winthrop, no admirer, described her. She held classes in Boston of sixty to eighty women, meeting weekly, to discuss issues of doctrine and interpret scripture. As Barker-Benfield sees,

> It was through this virtually exclusive female province—obstetrical care—that Hutchinson reached out to address the need which the size and composition of her classes demonstrated was there, and intensely enough to drive some women to murder their children. Women's turning to a midwife, an assistant at the springing forth of life, starkly contrasts with their dumb stifling of self and child where the spiritual assistants were exclusively male . . . [Governor] Winthrop saw an intimate connection between Hutchinson's claim to invade male mysteries and her role in childbearing.

Childbearing was, of course, intimately associated with sexuality; and the Puritan midwife was believed to administer aphrodisiacs, to empower women to get control of their men's sexuality (another variant of the witch's supposed power to take away the penis). John Cotton saw that "filthie Sinne of the Communitie of Women"—i.e., the coming-together of Hutchinson with other women to discuss doctrine—as leading to total sexual promiscuity. If the male-dominated hierarchy of

Puritan society were to change, that is, if women were to become thinkers and formulators of the relationship between human beings and God, pure anarchy and bestiality would result. Thus, the midwife, with her already formidable expertise and power in the matter of life itself, became completely threatening when she challenged religious doctrine. She became a witch. Anne Hutchinson was not alone. The first person executed in the Massachusetts Bay Colony was Margaret Jones, a midwife convicted of witchcraft. And a Mistress Hawkins, a colleague of Hutchinson's in midwifery, was charged with "familiarity with the devill."[14]

It seems obvious that throughout history, as one of the few professions open to women, midwifery must have attracted women of unusual intelligence, competence, and self-respect.* While acknowledging that many remedies used by the witches were "purely magical" and worked, if at all, by suggestion, Ehrenreich and English point out an important distinction between the witch-healer and the medical man of the late Middle Ages:

> . . . the witch was an empiricist; She relied on her senses rather than on faith or doctrine, she believed in trial and error, cause and effect. Her attitude was not religiously passive, but actively inquiring. She trusted her ability to find ways to deal with disease, pregnancy and childbirth—whether through medication or charms. In short, her magic was the science of her time.

---

* The term "midwife" has been so downgraded and so associated with ignorance and dirt, that we can easily lose sight of that fact. Kathleen Barry suggests a connection between the idea of the "filthy" midwife and the male physician's view of women's bodies, and the doctoring of women, as "dirty." If woman's flesh is intrinsically foul and evil, these qualities become attributed to those who have to do with her, particularly at a time as charged with fear and mystery for men as the moment of giving birth. (See "The Cutting Edge: A Look at Male Motivation in Obstetrics and Gynecology," unpublished, copyright, 1972, by Kathleen Barry.) This is not simply a Western male cultural bias. "Since God, who made disease, had conveniently decreed that women were inferior, unclean and blood-producing creatures, and Chinese physicians had diagnosed pregnancy as a disease of the blood, religious tenets held that the gravid female was unclean. If menstruating or pregnant, a woman could not walk through the torii, or arches, of shrines" (M. W. Standlee, *The Great Pulse: Japanese Midwifery and Obstetrics Through the Ages* [Rutland, Vt.: Chas. E. Tuttle, 1959], p. 26).

By contrast:

> There was nothing in late mediaeval medical training that con-
> flicted with church doctrine, and little that we would recognize
> as "science". Medical students . . . spent years studying Plato,
> Aristotle and Christian theology. . . . While a student, a doc-
> tor rarely saw any patients at all, and no experimentation of any
> kind was taught. . . . Confronted with a sick person, the
> university-trained physician had little to go on but supersti-
> tion. . . . Such was the state of medical "science" at the time
> when witch-healers were persecuted for being practitioners of
> "magic".[15]

Since asepsis and the transmission of disease through bacteria
and unwashed hands was utterly unknown until the latter part
of the nineteenth century, dirt was a presence in any medical
situation—real dirt, not the misogynistic dirt associated by
males with the female body. The midwife, who attended only
women in labor, carried fewer disease bacteria with her than the
physician.

But the climate of misogyny surrounding the woman in child-
birth took many forms. There was much opposition to *The
Byrthe of Mankynde,* a translation into English in 1540 of a
Latin text on midwifery, *De Partu Hominis*—possibly because
it would then be available to the common people who knew no
Latin. But this was the argument against it:

> it is not meete ne fitting that such matters to be intreated of so
> plainly in our mother and vulgar language to the dishonour
> . . . of womanhood . . . whereof men it reading or hearing
> shall be moved thereby the more *to abhor and loathe the com-
> pany of women,* every boy and knave reading them as openly
> as the tales of Robin Hood. (Emphasis mine.)[16]

In short, the facts of woman's physicality could only be repulsive; and flesh-loathing toward woman—especially in her role
as mother—was taken for granted as a fact of the male character.

The ancient physician held midwifery beneath his dignity;
the male practitioner of the Christian Era was forbidden to
degrade his manhood in the birth-chamber. Over and over, the
historians of medicine declare that obstetrics could only move

forward once the male midwife or physician took the place of the female midwife. Rongy states that "the backward state of obstetrical knowledge was the direct result of this complete monopoly by women."[17] Another obstetric historian makes the unconsciously revealing observation that "perhaps even today the medical practice of midwifery seems less distinguished than some of the other specialities because it was originally *wrested from the hands of women*, and for centuries was considered an inappropriate occupation for men." (Emphasis mine.)[18] Yet, as Ehrenreich and English point out, the women were in many ways, relative to their time, more scientific than the men; they knew female anatomy as men did not, and they were more often than not dealing with a physical process which they themselves had experienced. The unacknowledged assumption in the quotations above is, of course, that only men could be physicians.

4

The beginning of the transformation of obstetrics into a male province is usually dated from the attendance of a court physician named Boucher on Louise de la Vallière, the favorite mistress of Louis XIV, in 1663. The fad of employing a man-midwife, or *accoucheur*, soon spread within the French upper classes. As one historian bluntly expresses it: "The few physicians who were known to be qualified in this art soon found themselves besieged by royalty and the well-to-do, and amazed at this sudden turn in their fortunes, they promptly limited their practice to obstetrics."[19] They also, of course, limited it to those who could pay well.

The male physicians had for at least fifty years been using their privileged situation to discover skills unknown to their profession since classical times or known only to witches and wisewomen. In 1551 the physician Ambroise Paré wrote an obstetrical treatise in which he revived the technique of podalic version. We will probably never know whether podalic version had actually been practiced all along by midwives while it remained a lost art to physicians; at all events, Paré made it again available to anyone who could read vernacular French.[20] In the last decade of the sixteenth century the medical faculty at Marburg stumbled on the effects of ergot, a fungus found in blighted grain, which had been used for centuries by witches and midwives to induce labor and strengthen weak contractions.* The female healers had long observed the effects of mild ergot poisoning in pregnant women in their care, and deduced that, in minute quantities, the substance could be effective in childbirth. Now the physicians of Marburg recognized the value of this "witches'" remedy.

The books written by male *accoucheurs* generally seem to conform to what Rongy says of Eucharius Rösslin: "His book consists in the main of a collection of standard authorities and scraps of information conveyed to the author by midwives with whom he was in contact. So limited was his own knowledge that the woodcuts he used as illustration of the foetus within the uterus convey a fantastic, altogether false picture."[21]† It was not until the seventeenth century that William Harvey, celebrated for his discovery of the circulation of the blood, was able to describe the female reproductive organs from his own dissections and observations.

The first great woman practitioner of obstetrics—"great" in the sense that she both practiced and trained other women (and men) and wrote three books on midwifery—was Louise Bourgeois, herself a mother and married to a barber-surgeon. Her husband had been trained by Ambroise Paré, and when, after her first child was born, Bourgeois became interested in midwifery, she took instruction both from her husband and from his famous teacher. She was licensed as a midwife and practiced both at Court and at the Hôtel Dieu, the public hospital of Paris, where she directed the training of midwives and taught obstetrics to surgeons. Her midwifery text, *Observations*

---

* The mild form of ergot poisoning caused abortion in pregnant women; the severe form was a disease called "St. Anthony's Fire" which caused the limbs of the afflicted to become blackened and gangrenous and to fall off— one of those peculiarly horrible and mysterious diseases of the Middle Ages which must have lent credence to the idea of Hell.

† In 1522, a Dr. Wortt of Hamburg had the temerity to dress in women's clothes in order to be present at a delivery. For this indecency and degradation of his profession he was burned at the stake. Yet the majority of books on midwifery were written by men—Rösslin, Damian Carbon in Spain, Paré in France, among many others.

Diverses, first published in 1609, was widely translated.[22] She also published an account of the lyings-in of Marie de Médicis, whom she had attended. In the latter book, written as a series of letters to "ma fille"—a daughter or younger midwife—she urges that the midwife attending in poor households accept as little as possible in the way of fee ("for little may seem much to them") and give her services to those who can afford nothing. Her sense of the ethics and dignity of her profession is high:

> Undertake, till the last day of your life, to learn; which to do readily requires a great humbleness, for the proud do not win the hearts of those who know secrets. Never in your life venture to employ any medicine in which you have been instructed, neither on the poor nor on the rich, unless you are certain of its virtue and that it can do no harm, whether taken within the body or applied upon it. Nor hide the medicines you know of from physicians or midwives, lest these be as little regarded as the charlatans who employ their medicines alike on every occasion, and yet claim to know wonders and, in all they do, hide their practice.[23]

The waste of female lives through these centuries was partly unavoidable; mortality of both sexes, and from all causes, was high before the discovery of asepsis and the refinement of anatomical knowledge with dissection. But much of it *was* avoidable, if we remember that a pregnant woman, a woman in labor, is not usually suffering from disease. The midwives' ignorance of progress in medicine and surgery, on the one hand, and the physician's ignorance of female anatomy and techniques relating to childbirth, on the other, were not inevitable; they were the consequences of institutionalized misogyny. The midwives' work was either stolen and reproduced in the form of treatises by "learned" scientists, or treated as "heathen charms," "old wives' tales," and derogated as the pretensions of "high and lofty conceited midwives, that will leave nothing unattempted to save their credits and cloak their ignorances," as Percival Willughby (1596–1685), a friend of Harvey, wrote in his *Observations on Midwifery*.[24]

The effectiveness of the midwife who for centuries practiced her "degraded" craft among her sisters, was reduced and diminished with the growth of an élite medical profession from which women were barred. The female hands of flesh that had delivered millions of children and soothed the labor of millions of mothers were denied the possibility of working with the tools later developed to facilitate the practice of obstetrics in difficult labor. The masculine "hands of iron"—the forceps—were, and still are, often used with mechanistic brutality and unconcern to hasten a normal labor, causing brain damage to the infant and perforation of delicate tissues in the mother, both totally unnecessary. The wasteful and disastrous split in the profession must be laid at the door of male prejudice and the power of a male-dominated establishment to discredit and drive out even the most talented women practitioners.*

5

"The obstetric forceps, more than any other instrument, symbolizes the art of the obstetrician."[25] The history of the forceps is a peculiar one, involving three male generations of a family, the commercial exploitation of a scientific invention, and the effective displacement of the midwife through a male monopoly of that invention.

It begins in the late sixteenth century with William Chamberlen, a Huguenot who emigrated to England to avoid religious persecution under the Catholic Church in France. This Chamberlen had numerous children and two of them, both male midwives, bore the same name, Peter. (Like royalty, they have become known as Peter I and Peter II.) These two Peters became known for their pushiness, "impudence," and antiestablishment ideas; they were known to all the midwives, and Peter II

* One of the less covert misogynists, Augustus K. Gardner, M.D., used to deliver an introductory lecture to his course in midwifery at the Philadelphia College of Physicians and Surgeons "showing the Past Inefficiency and Present Natural Incapacity of Females in the Practise of Obstetrics." He inveighs against "a proposition mooted—springing from the same high source which advocates women's rights, the Bloomer costume, and other similar nonsensical theories—to give again the portion of the healing art of which I am treating, if not the whole domain of medicine, to the females." Gardner was also opposed to birth control and to higher education for women (*A History of the Art of Midwifery* [New York: 1852], pp. 26–27, 30–31).

was formally rebuked by the College of Physicians for trying to organize the midwives into a society with credentials and corporate status. It is difficult to know whether the midwives thus organized could have become an independent body or whether, as is more likely, they were intended to become part of Peter II's entourage. But clearly the two Peters and the son of Peter II (also, to further confuse matters, a Peter) were in running conflict with the College of Physicians, and were much sought after, practicing at Court. Peter III actually acquired his M.D. after studying at Heidelberg, Padua, and Oxford, thus bringing unimpeachable status to the family name.

The Chamberlens were not simply flashy and fashionable; they had their Secret. A mystique grew up around them: two of them attended at each difficult birth, arriving in a carriage and carrying between them a massive carved chest whose contents were revealed to no one. Even the women they delivered were blindfolded. And they were dramatically successful at delivering in difficult labors.

This family Secret, kept for nearly a century, consisted of a kit of three instruments: a pair of obstetric forceps, a vectis or lever to be used in grasping the back of the head of the fetus, and a fillet or cord used to help in drawing the fetus, once disengaged from an abnormal position, out through the birthcanal. Ironically, although these instruments ensured the success of the Chamberlens for many years, they failed in the test when Hugh Chamberlen, son of Peter III, and also a manmidwife in the family tradition, tried to sell the Secret to the celebrated French obstetrician, François Mariceau. Mariceau challenged him to deliver successfully a case which appeared to be beyond hope. The patient was a dwarfed woman with inflammation of the spine and a deformed pelvis, in labor with her first child.* Chamberlen failed, and Mariceau declined to purchase the Secret at the exotic price demanded.

* In all accounts of this case I have read, the woman is referred to as a "rachitic dwarf primapara." It took me some time to understand that the creature thus described was a woman, presumably terrified, probably a victim of rape, whose entire existence must have been psychically and physically painful, and who died in torture. (Hugh Chamberlen "worked over" her for three hours with his forceps in the unsuccessful attempt to prove his method; she had been similarly "worked over" earlier by other

Arrogant to the core, Chamberlen did not fail, in writing his introduction to the English translation of Mariceau's midwifery text, to remind readers that the famous Frenchman did not possess "the Secret":

> My Father, Brothers, and myself (tho none other else in Europe as I know) have, by God's Blessing and our Industry, attained to, and long practised a way to deliver women in this case, without any prejudice to them or their infants; tho all others . . . do and must endanger, if not destroy, one or both with hooks.[26]

In Chamberlen's words we hear the readiness to sacrifice thousands of women's and children's lives, smugly and complacently, knowing how easily they could be saved, and to justify the withholding of that information in terms of "God's Blessing and our Industry." The men who developed the forceps, symbol of the art of the obstetrician, were profiteers.
True to their principled tradition, the Chamberlens finally sold their Secret to a Dutch practitioner. When they had received their money and the Secret was handed over, they proved to have tricked him and to have supplied him with—one-half of a forceps. A Belgian barber-surgeon, Jean Palfyne, guessed at the whole instrument, either from seeing the part sold to the Dutchman, or from putting together rumors of the Chamberlen apparatus, and presented his recreation entire to the Paris Academy of Science in 1721. In the words of Harvey Graham, it consisted of:

> . . . two large spoons set in round wooden handles. These were known as the *mains de fer* [hands of iron], and were of course crude artificial hands designed to grasp the infant's head. They derived from the large spoon-shaped *cuillers* which had been used for many years to remove parts of the foetus piecemeal after operations intended to destroy the child. The most important difference was in the curve of the blades and their shanks. The long axis of all earlier instruments was straight. Since the birth passage from the womb to the vulva is deeply

---

methods.) Possibly before the advent of asepsis, analgesia, and safe Caesarean section, she could not have been saved. But beneath the medical jargon we can easily forget that here, too, lived a victim of obstetrical indifference, nameless and deprived even of her humanity.

curved, a correspondingly curved instrument will obviously penetrate much farther and more effectively than any straight instrument.[27]

The actual design of the Chamberlen forceps—perfected over three generations of secretive monopolization—was finally revealed by the surgeon and man-midwife Edward Chapman, in his *Essay for the Improvement of Midwifery* in 1773. From then on, the forceps was available to all male—and to almost no female—practitioners of the obstetric art.[28]

6

With the public knowledge of the Chamberlen device, a public struggle broke out between the midwives and the surgeons. In scanning the rhetorical and theoretical arguments on both sides, it is important to bear several facts in mind. The practice of surgery was considered a lower craft than that of medicine and the barber-surgeon was not a fully trained physician. Moreover, we have to rid ourselves of the opposite stereotypes of the highly trained, spotlessly aseptic male obstetrician, clad in sterile gown, masked and gloved, and the filthy peasant crone muttering over her bag of charms. Contagion and asepsis were unknown to physician, surgeon, and midwife alike. John Leake, M.D., in his late–eighteenth-century treatise on midwifery, argues for the examination and certification of obstetrical attendants "as is usual in other branches of physic and surgery. We should not then find the town and country overrun with ignorant and half-instructed practitioners *of both sexes*." (Emphasis mine.)[29] The male physician's standards of cleanliness were not, by contemporary standards, high; there is no evidence that the average doctor was more scrupulous than the average midwife. The midwife was far more experienced in the pragmatic conduct of normal births than the surgeon or physician; and, perhaps as important, she felt by tradition and gender-sympathy at home in the birth-chamber, while the male practitioner was still emotionally, if not practically, under the cloud of a tradition of misogyny which made it a sin and a crime for him to be there except in extreme emergencies. Finally, it was the male practitioners, such as Julien Clement in France and John Leake in England, who established the lithotomy (lying down, therefore passive) position as the preferred one for women in labor. The midwife used the obstetrical chair or the upright position, which is still universal outside Western culture and cultures in which Western medical influence prevails,[30] and which is now just beginning to be revived, against the resistance of the profession, in North and South America.*

The forceps was the masculine weapon in this struggle; but it was not maneuvered with equal enthusiasm by all men. Leake warned that "the safety of the patient more immediately depends on the operator's skill in this, than in any other brand of physic or surgery." In his instructions on the use of forceps he points out that a too forceful application of this lever can cause dangerous bruising to vagina and bladder, and even tear apart the two bones forming the pubis.[31] The midwives were even more outspokenly opposed to the forceps, and soon many were writing pamphlets and handbooks in defense of their own methods. Justine Siegmundin in Germany, Sarah Stone in England, among others, warned against the overuse and abuse of instruments. Stone also demanded regulation of the profession of midwifery, with requirements of several years apprenticeship and training.[32] Meanwhile, the Chamberlen forceps were being modified and developed by others, in particular André Levret in France and William Smellie in England, both surgeons. Smellie became the target for one of the most detailed and passionate attacks on male midwifery, published in 1760 by Elizabeth Nihell, a graduate of the Hôtel Dieu midwife school.

Nihell's *Treatise on the Art of Midwifery* deserves a place in the history of feminist polemics. It is an exhaustive argument against the use of instruments, and on behalf of the patience,

---

* "Use of the lithotomy (supine) position has two purposes: It makes maintenance of asepsis easier and it contributes greatly to *the convenience of the obstetrician*. These advantages more than compensate for the somewhat unphysiologic posture and *the discomfort of the position itself*" (emphasis mine) (Bryand, Danforth, Davis, "The Conduct of Normal Labor" in D. N. Danforth, ed., *Textbook of Obstetrics and Gynecology* [New York: Harper and Row, 1966] pp. 532–33. This text was written by forty-two men and one woman.)

expertise, and natural capability of women for assisting at births. She accuses the surgeons of using forceps to force labor prematurely and to shorten the time of normal deliveries, for their own convenience or for experimental purposes. She acknowledges her own lack of experience with instruments, but has read Levret and others who describe their use. She maintains that during her apprenticeship at the Hôtel Dieu she never saw a birth where instruments were necessary, although five to six hundred women were delivered there monthly. She sees the hand as the proper "instrument" for facilitating labor, guided by a knowledge of female anatomy, and the forceps, reserved to male surgeons, as a means of preempting the practice of women.

> I own however there are but too few midwives who are sufficiently mistresses in their professions. In this they are . . . but too near a level with the men-midwives, with this difference . . . that they are incapable of doing so much actual mischief as the male ones, . . . who with less tenderness and more rashness go to work with their instruments, where the skill and management of a good midwife would . . . prove more efficacious toward saving both mother and child; *always with due preference however to the mother.* (Emphasis mine.)[33]

Her three major arguments run as follows:

1. There is no "plea of superior safety" in the entrance of men into midwifery; consequently it is not worth the "sacrifice . . . of decency and modesty." Here she is probably playing on the puritan sentiments of her public.

2. Men have justified their intrusion into the profession by "forging the phantom of incapacity in women" and by "the necessity of murderous instruments." (It is likely that all instruments bore a certain taint by association with the hooks and blades used for destructive obstetrics in the past. But we also know that the forceps itself was often used unnecessarily and could become destructive in awkward or unpracticed hands.*)

---

* "The forceps was to afford men-midwives with the means by which they could expedite a laborious labor, without any serious consequences either to mother or child. At first far too many of them used this new weapon blindly and roughly . . . Smellie only used his forceps on rare occasions. . . . Some of Smellie's pupils were even more cautious in their use for the forceps, and in particular William Hunter . . . who is reputed to

3. The surgeons themselves disagree as to which instruments are preferable, in spite of having used "the lives and limbs of so many women and children" as subjects for experimentation.

Nihell is not above shifting her ground in order to create an argument which bristles in all directions. She asserts that some occupations are "naturally" more proper for women than for men: spinning, bed-making, pickling, and preserving—at the end of which list she casually slips in midwifery. Women, she maintains, would of course not be encouraged to set up fencing academies. On the other hand, she takes considerable pride in the professionalism of the Hôtel Dieu school for midwives, which had a woman at its head, and where women taught surgeons—not the other way around. She is thoroughly cynical about the sudden enthusiasm of men for midwifery:

> . . . the nobility of this art is only begun to be sounded so high by the men, till they discovered the possibility of making it a lucrative one to themselves. . . . The art with all its nobility was for so many ages thought beneath the exercise of the noble sex; it was held unmanly, indecent, and they might safely have added impracticable for them.

She is most eloquent and convincing when she describes the surgeon's style of birthing, as contrasted with the midwife's:

> In the men, with all their boasted erudition, you may observe a certain clumsy untoward stiffness, an *unaffectionate perfunctory air*, an ungainly management, that plainly prove it to be an acquisition of art, or rather the rickety production of interest begot upon art . . . (Emphasis mine; the portrait certainly rings true.)

> In women, with all their supposed ignorance, you may observe a certain shrewd vivacity, a grace of ease, a hardiness of performance, and especially a kind of unction of the heart . . . there is something that would be prodigious, if anything natural could properly be termed prodigious, in that supremely tender

have told his class that it was 'a thousand pities that it was ever invented'. There is no doubt that instruments were resorted to far too readily by brash and enthusiastic man-midwives, and it was necessary for the leading men in the profession to teach some measure of restraint, especially with the forceps" (Walter Radcliffe, *Milestones in Midwifery* [Bristol: Wright, 1967], pp. 48–49).

sensibility with which women in general are so strongly impressed toward one another in the case of lying-in.[34]

She also reiterates the midwife's constant and intimate experience with the female body and with normal birth, which left male students of midwifery at a severe disadvantage. According to her, Smellie instructed his students of midwifery on a machine, invented by himself, which consisted of

> . . . a wooden statue, representing a woman with child, whose belly was of leather, in which a bladder full, perhaps, of small beer, represented the uterus. This bladder was stopped with a cork . . . in the middle of the bladder was a wax doll, to which were given various positions.

On the other hand, she says that a physician should absolutely be called in the event of complications. She sees women as less prideful than men, readier to admit their ignorance and ask for help. But "lying-in women principally require an early assistance" and *patience*. She makes a convincing argument that the forceps became a quick-delivery trick, rather than a device to be used with great care and caution in manifestly difficult cases. She constantly reiterates that labor must not be rushed, that nature must be allowed to take its course, though the midwife can alleviate pain manually and through "a thousand little tender attentions suggested by nature and improved by experience." Her trust in process, and her sense that women are more capable of understanding and moving with process, makes us trust her, finally; her sarcasm and anger at the sudden descent of men upon a field formerly left to women as degraded, we can well understand.

Why did not more of the midwives make an effort to learn the use of the forceps and retain control of the profession? After all, the leading professional midwives must have been exceptionally strong, self-confident women. But strong, self-confident women of the twentieth century are still battling uphill against prejudice and institutional obstacles, particularly in the field of health and science. And the centuries of witchcraft trials, during which midwives were a particular target, were not far behind in the eighteenth-century memory. Presumably a midwife still would have been cautious about "going too far" and arousing the hostility of an entire society. Moreover, the midwives had seen the horrors of "destructive surgery" in obstetrics—the child dragged from the mother's body piecemeal, the mother's pubic bone and vagina used as a fulcrum and often permanently mutilated. Many of them must sincerely have felt that the forceps could only be a refinement of these tools of force. Nihell herself notes:

> A few, and very few indeed of the midwives, dazzled with that vogue into which the instruments brought the men . . . attempted to employ them, and though certainly they could handle them at least as dexterously as the men, they soon discovered that they were at once insignificant and dangerous substitutes to their own hands, with which they were sure of conducting their operations both more safely, more effectually, and with less pain to the patient.[35]

Had the forceps been freely permitted to women, would Nihell have condemned their use so sweepingly? Perhaps not; like Sarah Stone, she would probably have taught that they should be used as a last resort, and with great judiciousness and care.* Her pride in the midwife's multiplicity of skills, "small hands" with their feminine dexterity, and "tenderness" of heart toward the women in her care, suggests that for Nihell and others like her, the forceps would never have become the major symbol of the obstetrical profession.†

Finally, one major difference distinguished the midwife and the male obstetrician. The midwife not only gave prenatal care and advice, but came to the woman at the beginning of her labor and stayed with her till after delivery. She gave not only physical assistance but psychological support. The male birth-attendant was historically called in only to perform the functions (podalic version, Caesarean, forceps delivery) which were forbidden to the midwife. He was a technician rather than a counselor, guide, and source of morale; he worked "on" rather than "with" the mother. And this difference has persisted into

---

* Stone, in her *Complete Practice of Midwifery* (1737) asserts that out of three hundred cases she delivered in one year, she used instruments in only four.

† The pride of contemporary midwives, from California to Denmark, in the use of their hands, bears this out, as documented by Suzanne Arms, *op. cit.*

the present, where the obstetrician, though he may see the mother during her pregnancy, often does not appear until the late stage of labor and sometimes arrives too late for the delivery; while the midwife (literally, "with-woman") stays with the mother throughout her labor, as a friend and teacher in the birth-chamber.[36]

7

In the seventeenth century began a two centuries' plague of puerperal fever which was directly related to the increase in obstetric practice by men. (Again, we must remember that antisepsis, asepsis, contagion, and bacterial infection were still unheard-of; the hands of the physician or surgeon and those of the midwife were both potential carriers of bacteria. But the hands of the physician or of the surgeon, unlike those of the midwife, often came directly from cases of disease to cases of childbirth, and the chance for communication of infection was much higher. Moreover, the man-midwife attended many cases of labor, arriving in time to perform a forceps delivery and then going his way; the midwife stayed with one woman in labor from the beginning of her pains till after delivery, often for several days in difficult birth.) With the growth of lying-in hospitals in the cities of Europe, the disease—rarely known in earlier times—reached epidemic proportions. In the French province of Lombardy in one year no single woman survived childbirth; in the month of February 1866 a quarter of the women who gave birth in the Maternité Hospital in Paris died.[37]

Puerperal fever was thought to be an epidemic, and "epidemic influences" were "hitherto inexplicable, atmospheric, cosmic, telluric changes, which sometimes disseminate themselves over whole countrysides."[38] The conditions of all hospitals were unsanitary enough—hospitals were for the poor, who could not pay a doctor to attend them at home. Even the dubious standards of sanitation in an average middle-class home were superior to those of the hospitals, with their overcrowding, unwashed linens, open barrels of organic waste and used bandages, lack of ventilation, and the visible presence of death.

Between the seventeenth and nineteenth centuries the lying-in
clinics were as bad or worse than other wards, and often
adjoined them. One observer of a new hospital in Budapest in
1860 reported that

> . . . there poor lying-in women are to be found, some of them
> partly on straw, spread on the floor, some of them on wooden
> benches, others crouching in any corner of the room, weary
> and worn-out . . . everywhere you find dirty bed linen, with
> bedclothes old and worn and almost in rags.[39]

Oliver Wendell Holmes says that in the 1840s, in the Vienna
Lying-In Hospital, the mortality from "childbed fever" was so
high that women were buried two in a coffin to disguise the
actual rate of death.[40]

Childbed or puerperal fever was a misnomer for a deadly kind
of blood-poisoning. In the seventeenth century, William
Harvey, the first physician to dissect a female body and observe
the reproductive organs at firsthand, had described the post-
partum uterus as resembling "an open wound"—highly absorp-
tive and extremely vulnerable to contamination. Any decom-
posing organic substances carried on the hands of a birth-
attendant became fatal when introduced into the vagina of a
woman in labor or one who had just given birth. But for
centuries the disease was regarded as a mysterious epidemic,
part of the curse of Eve. Women knew that delivery in the
hospitals meant a far greater likelihood of death than deliveries
at home. However, the majority of poor women seeking
obstetric help were required to have their babies in public
hospitals, probably in part because they were material for teaching and experimentation, just as today. Many ran from the
hospitals, others committed suicide rather than enter.

Meanwhile, the potential sources of the disease went unexplored, and women continued to die—not from giving birth
but from acute streptococcal infection of the uterus, in no way
inevitably linked with the birth-process. It killed one Mary
Wollstonecraft, of whom we know, and thousands of women
of whom we know nothing, whose potential genius and influence we can only try to imagine. And the specter of death,
larger than ever before in the history of maternity, darkened the

spirit in which any woman came to term. Anxiety, depression, the sense of being a sacrificial victim, all familiar components of female experience, became more than ever the invisible attendants at pregnancy and labor.

A certain indifference and fatalism toward the diseases of women, which persists to this day in the male gynecological and surgical professions, was reflected in the indifference and outright hostility encountered by the three men who, over two hundred years, did choose to look further. As early as 1795, Alexander Gordon, a Scottish physician, published his observations that childbed fever "seized such women only as were visited or delivered by a practitioner, or taken care of by a nurse, who had previously attended patients affected with the disease." In other words, the disease was not a mysterious epidemic, but was contagious—that is, communicated on contact from one body to another. Others corroborated Gordon's experience, yet the possible contagiousness of puerperal fever continued to go unmentioned in the texts and handbooks of gynecology and midwifery.

Nearly fifty years later, the young American doctor Oliver Wendell Holmes followed up Gordon's observations with his own detailed studies of contagion in cases he had seen or which were reported to him. He demonstrated even more solidly that the disease was carried by the physician from patient to patient.[41] The response of his profession was outrage at the implication that the hands of the physician could be unclean; uncleanliness was the very charge the doctors had long been leveling at the midwives. Holmes was abused and attacked as an irresponsible and sensation-seeking young upstart. His essay on "The Contagiousness of Puerperal Fever" was to become a medical classic, but not until many years later.

In 1861 Ignaz Philipp Semmelweis, a Viennese physician, published a passionate and obsessive book: *The Etiology, the Concept and the Prophylaxis of Childbed Fever*. Semmelweis had observed births and deaths over five years in two sections of the Vienna Lying-In Hospital. (The First Clinic was staffed entirely by physicians and medical students, the Second Clinic entirely by midwives.) He found that poor women who literally gave birth in the streets of Vienna had a lower mortality rate than those giving birth in the First Clinic. He became convinced that puerperal fever was not an epidemic raging in the community at large; it was somehow connected with the hospital, and in particular with the clinic staffed by physicians. Even the poor women of Vienna knew that they were likelier to survive in the midwives' than in the physicians' section. "That they really dread the First Division can readily be demonstrated, because one must endure heart-rending scenes, when women, wringing their hands, beg on bended knee for their release, in order to seek admission to the Second Division after having hit upon the First Division because of the unfamiliarity of the place, which the presence of many men made clear to them."[42]

Semmelweis was possessed by the spectacle of this suffering and these deaths. Yet he was unable to grasp the source of them, until a crevice broke open in his personal life. He had gone on holiday to Venice to look at the paintings there, and while he was away a close friend and colleague died of a wound in his finger acquired during a post-mortem dissection. Semmelweis returned to the news of this fresh death. By his own account,

> Professor Kolletschka . . . became ill with lymphangitis and phlebitis . . . and died, during my absence in Venice, of a bilateral pleuritis, pericarditis, peritonitis, and meningitis, and some days before his death a metastasis formed in one eye. Still animated by my visit to the Venetian treasure houses, still much agitated by the report of Kolletschka's death, there was forced on my mind with irresistible clarity in this excited state the identity of this disease, of which Kolletschka died, with that from which I had seen so many hundred puerpera die.[43]

What Semmelweis recognized was that cadaveric particles, which could not be removed by ordinary washing, were being carried from the dissecting rooms to the women in childbirth. Just as the cut in Kolletschka's hand had absorbed these particles from the cadaver into his bloodstream as deadly poisons, so a hand retaining these particles could introduce them into the uterus, with fatal results. Semmelweis mounted a campaign to compel all physicians and medical students to wash their hands in chlorinated lime on entering a labor room. The death rate in the First Clinic soon fell to that of the Second Clinic.[44]

Semmelweis's findings, and his polemics against other doctors and clinics, met with such antagonism that he was professionally discredited by politically powerful physicians, who saw to it that he was not promoted at Vienna. Yet he arraigned no one more harshly than himself.

> Because of my convictions, I must here confess that God only knows the number of patients that have gone prematurely to their graves by my fault. I have handled cadavers extensively, more than most accoucheurs. If I say the same of another physician, it is only to bring to light a truth, which was unknown for many centuries, with direful results for the human race.[45]

He was forced to leave Vienna for Budapest, taking a post in a lying-in clinic where "directly under the windows of the obstetrical department is found the open sewer, into which all the liquid refuse of the . . . pathological anatomy is thrown."[46] To work under these destructive conditions, and to see his laboriously amassed findings rejected in one country after another, affected the mind of this emotionally vulnerable man, and in 1865 he was committed to the Vienna Insane Asylum. A few days before his commitment he had wounded his hand while operating, and he died soon after—the same death as Kolletschka, and the thousands of women whose fate had obsessed him. Twenty years later, following Lister's presentation of the principle of asepsis in surgery, and Pasteur's demonstration of the reality of bacterial infection, Semmelweis's plea for doctors to wash their hands finally became accepted practice, and a statue was erected to him in Budapest.[47] The two hundred years of puerperal fever were coming to an end. The age of anesthetized, technologized childbirth was simultaneously beginning.

VII ALIENATED LABOR

Metaphors of midwifery and childbirth recur in the literature of the contemporary women's movement: a feminist poster bears the inscription, *I am a woman giving birth to myself.** Such an image implies a process which is painful, chosen, purposive: the creation of the new. But for most women actual childbirth has involved no choice whatever, and very little consciousness. Since prehistoric times, the anticipation of labor has been associated with fear, physical anguish or death, a stream of superstitions, misinformation, theological and medical theories—in short, all we have been taught we should feel, from willing victimization to ecstatic fulfillment.

The Hebrews saw in women's travail the working of Eve's curse for tempting Adam to the Fall. The Romans called it *poena magna*—the "great pain." But *poena* also means punishment, penalty. We are told over and over by ancient writers that childbirth is the most terrible pain endured in human life. In a 1950 study of the myth of "painless childbirth" in primitive societies, Lawrence Freedman and Vera Ferguson conclude that the expectation of agony in childbirth is as common in elementary as in postindustrial societies. Margaret Mead suggests that "whether they are allowed to see births or not, men contribute their share to the way in which child-birth is viewed, and I have seen male informants writhe on the floor, in magnificent pantomine of a painful delivery, who have never themselves seen or heard a woman in labour."[1] Nancy Fuller and Brigitte Jordan report that in their field work with Mayan

* Published by Times Change Press, 62 West Fourteenth St., New York.

Indian women, they have observed both difficult and easy births, but that pain is expected and is taken for granted by the midwife and birth-attendants, and the husband is expected to be present, not only to help but "to see how women suffer."[2]

A woman preparing to swim the English Channel, or to climb in high altitudes, is aware that her system will undergo stress, her courage will be tested, and her life may even be in danger; but despite the demands to be expected on her heart, her lungs, her muscular coordination, her nerves, during such an effort, she thinks of it primarily in terms not of pain but of *challenge*. The majority of women, literate or illiterate, come to childbirth as a charged, discrete happening: mysterious, sometimes polluted, often magical, as torture rack or as "peak experience." Rarely has it been viewed as one way of knowing and coming to terms with our bodies, of discovering our physical and psychic resources.

It is as difficult to think about pain as about love; both are charged with associations going back to early life, and with cultural attitudes wrought into language itself. Yet pain, like love, is embedded in the ideology of motherhood, and it has so much depth of allusion for all women, mothers or not, that we need to examine its meaning more closely. The attempt is sometimes made to divide pain into the categories of sensory perception—a response to a measurable stimulus—and psychological experience.[3] To separate sense from emotion, body from mind, is hardly useful when we are trying to understand the whole of female experience, and in particular a function—childbirth—so charged with unconscious and subjective power, and so dramatic in its physical sensations.

The experience of pain is historical—framed by memory and anticipation—and it is relative. Thresholds of what we call pain vary greatly among individuals, and the conditions under which pain is experienced can alter the sufferer's definition of pain. Pain is also expressed differently in different cultures. Briffault cites examples of Maori and African women in labor for whom it was traditional not to utter a groan.[4] Emotional display is more acceptable in some cultures than in others, and behavior during childbirth may reflect an overall style of expressiveness.

But the pains of labor have a peculiar centrality for women, and for women's relationship—both as mothers and simply as female beings—to other kinds of painful experience. What, anyway, is this primal idea which seems to take women—not only in childbirth—in its grasp and press the self out of us, or, even worse, to *become* our selfhood? Can we distinguish physical pain from alienation and fear? Is there creative pain and destructive pain? And who or what determines the causes and nature and duration of our suffering? In different cultures there are different answers; but women live, bear children, and suffer in all cultures.

The remarkable philosopher-mystic Simone Weil makes the distinction between suffering—characterized by pain yet leading to growth and enlightenment—and affliction—the condition of the oppressed, the slave, the concentration-camp victim forced to haul heavy stones back and forth across a yard, endlessly and to no purpose. She reiterates that pain is not to be sought, and she objects to putting oneself in the way of unnecessary affliction. But where it is unavoidable, pain can be transformed into something usable, something which takes us beyond the limits of the experience itself into a further grasp of the essentials of life and the possibilities within us. However, over and over she equates pure affliction with powerlessness, with waiting, disconnectedness, inertia, the "fragmented time" of one who is at others' disposal.[5] This insight illuminates much of the female condition, but in particular the experience of giving birth.

Weil's image of the prison camp is also an image of forced labor—labor as contrasted with work, which has a real goal and a meaning. The labor of childbirth has been a form of forced labor. For centuries, most women had no means of preventing conception, and they carried the scriptural penalty of Eve's curse with them into the birth-chamber. Then, in the nineteenth century, the possibility of eliminating "pain and travail" created a new kind of prison for women—the prison of unconsciousness, of numbed sensations, of amnesia, and complete passivity. Women could choose anesthesia, and for many of the women who first did so it was a conscious, even a daring choice. But the avoidance of pain—psychic or physical—is a dangerous mechanism, which can cause us to lose touch not just with our painful sensations but with ourselves. And, in the case of childbirth, pain has been a label indiscriminately applied to the range of sensations during labor, a label which appropriates and denies the complexity of the individual woman's physical experience.

2

Patriarchy has told the woman in labor that her suffering was purposive—was *the* purpose of her existence; that the new life she was bringing forth (especially if male) was of value and that her own value depended on bringing it forth. As the means of reproduction without which cities and colonies could not expand, without which a family would die out and its prosperity pass into the hands of strangers, she has found herself at the center of purposes, not hers, which she has often incorporated and made into her own. The woman in labor might perceive herself as bringing forth a new soldier to fight for the tribe or nation-state, a new head of the rising yeoman or bourgeois family, a new priest or rabbi for her fathers' faith, or a new mother to take up the renewal of life. Given this patriarchal purpose she could obliterate herself in fertility as her body swelled year after year, and pain and suffering might well become associated, for her, with her ultimate value in the world. She might equally know that her pregnancy and labor would result in a life without a future, a child who could not be fed, or who would be strangled at birth; a wasted human life.

In the twelfth century, with the beginnings of the romantic love-cult in the West, still another element enters the tangle of feelings and attitudes surrounding childbirth. The courtly love tradition perceived marriage quite correctly for what it was— a property settlement—and located the real springs of feeling, intensity, vital energy as dwelling in passion-love, a secret and usually doomed relationship. To bear the child of a man with whom one was entangled in passion-love became an assertion of the seeming uniqueness of that love; to bear *this man's child* was to bring this love to a tangible consummation. Bastards were believed to be exceptionally vital and dynamic beings, begotten

in the intensity of passion rather than between the dull, oblig-
atory sheets of marriage. The child thus becomes not only the
expression of a forbidden love, but an incorporation of the lover
into the woman's body. He may desert her, they may be parted
by fate, but she continues to possess him in "his" child—
especially if a son. To bear an "illegitimate" child proudly and
by choice in the face of societal judgment has, paradoxically,
been one way in which women have defied patriarchy. Hester
Prynne's needlework in which she splendidly dresses her daughter Pearl and decorates her own label of "adulteress" in *The
Scarlet Letter* is a gesture of such defiance. Childbirth, then,
may be painful, dangerous, and unchosen; but it has also
been converted into a purpose, an act of self-assertion by a
woman forced to assert herself primarily through her biology.

From the sense of producing a necessary person, or persons,
and of carrying out one's destiny as a woman, to the ambivalence toward, or rejection of motherhood by many twentieth-
century women, there is a continuing thread of unexamined
emotions. The twentieth-century, educated young woman, looking perhaps at her mother's life, or trying to create an autonomous self in a society which insists that she is destined primarily
for reproduction, has with good reason felt that the choice was
an inescapable either/or: motherhood or individuation, motherhood or creativity, motherhood or freedom. Doris Lessing's
heroine, Martha Quest,

> . . . saw it all so very clearly. That phrase, "having a baby,"
> which was every girl's way of thinking of a first child, was
> nothing but a mask to conceal the truth. One saw a fluttering
> image of a madonna-like woman with a helpless infant in her
> arms; nothing could be more attractive. What one did not see,
> what everyone conspired to prevent one seeing, was the middle-
> aged woman who had done nothing but produce two or three
> commonplace and tedious citizens in a world that was already
> too full of them.[6]

Not only is the world already "too full," but Martha resists the
notion of the child as an end-in-itself; she sees, with bitter
clarity, beyond the sentimental image of "motherhood" to the
life-span of the woman defined as mother; instead of a "peak

experience" she perceives a continuing condition. For a creative woman, as for a woman living in poverty, the child can be perceived as a disaster, as an "enemy within." In Cora Sandel's *Alberta and Freedom*, Alberta, an impoverished young woman writer, has become pregnant by her lover; she confesses to her friend Liesel, also an artist:

> "Only today I thought I could see some way in my work," she said half to herself. "I had such a desire to write, but in quite a different form from before."
> "Oh—." Liesel gestured away from herself with her hand. "That's precisely when it happens, when we think we're beginning to achieve something. Then it comes and interrupts it all . . ."

But there is a need—whether instinctual or psychogenic or acculturated, to come to terms with the disaster. Alberta begins to notice the mothers with their children in the streets.

> They had nobody to look after them, they were tied by them from morning to night, forced to forget everything else for sake of the white bundle, sacrifice everything for it. And Alberta felt mutinous. She thought: I'm not ready with myself yet, I haven't achieved anything, must I start thinking only about someone else, unable even to look in any other direction? At the same time she surprised herself noticing how such bundles were carried and dressed, and attempted instinctively to catch glimpses of the tiny, well-wrapped faces . . .

Finally, she sees an African woman with her child in the tent of a traveling exhibition; the mother, noticing that Alberta is pregnant, smiles and nods wordlessly to her.

> For the first time she felt without defiance and coldness that she was to become a mother. The approaching enemy was a little naked child, with only herself to turn to and trust. Boundless sympathy for it streamed towards her heart and eyes . . .[7]

The depths of this conflict, between self-preservation and maternal feelings, can be experienced—I have experienced it— as a primal agony. And this is not the least of the pains of childbirth.

Finally, a woman who has experienced her own mother as a

destructive force—however justified or unjustified the charge—
may dread the possibility that in becoming a mother she too
will become somehow destructive. The mother of the laboring
woman is, in any case, for better or worse, living or dead, a
powerful ghost in the birth-chamber.

3

Throughout the world, certain powerful attitudes surround
pregnancy and childbirth.[8] Nowhere is the pregnant woman
taken for granted; she may be viewed as proof of her husband's
sexual adequacy; as dangerous to crops or to men; as especially
vulnerable to the evil eye or other maleficent influences; as an
embarrassment; as possessed of curative powers.* These attitudes culminate in the birth itself. The lack of material on the
conduct of normal births and on the actual behavior of mothers
in normal labors in different cultures is due to the scarcity, until
recently, of women observing women's behavior, and the fact
that male anthropologists have usually been excluded from
births unless the delivery was abnormal, when males (as medicine man, witch doctor, or priest) would be admitted.[9] However, there are emotional responses shared by laboring women of
all cultures.

Grantly Dick-Read, the early crusader for "natural" childbirth, identified a dynamic, in labor, between fear, tension, and
pain. Fear stands high on the list. In the woman bearing her
first child there is first of all fear of the unknown. She has heard
all her life tales of "how women suffer"; she may have attended
births and witnessed for herself; above all, there is the sense of
her body going into powerful, involuntary contractions, almost
a sense of becoming possessed. In most of our history, women
have not been told to identify these as "contractions"; they have
been described by midwives, surgeons, priests, mothers alike as
"pains," and even as punishment. Instead of visualizing a functional physical process the woman may perceive herself simply

* During my own first pregnancy, I was invited to give a poetry reading at
an old and famous boys' preparatory school in New England. When the
master responsible for inviting me realized that I was seven months pregnant he canceled the invitation, saying that the fact of my pregnancy would
make it impossible for the boys to listen to my poetry. This was in 1955.

as invaded by pain.* Not only has she been socialized to expect suffering, but the mysteriousness of the process generates fear. Freedman and Ferguson's study of childbirth, cited above, concludes that the fear of suffering derives from "empirically derived knowledge of mutilations and deaths" or of the births of monstrosities. The fear of death is inextricable from fear of the unknown.

In many cultures the woman in labor is believed to be particularly vulnerable to malign occult influences, just as during pregnancy. Closely related to this is the notion of childbirth as illness. Niles Newton cites the Cuna Indians of Panama, who "regard childbirth as so abnormal that the mother goes to the medicine man daily throughout pregnancy for medicine to help her and is under constant medication during labor." In the American hospital delivery, similarly, birth is frequently treated as an operation, and always as a medical event.

The idea of birth as defilement is widespread. Indian village midwives are usually of the "untouchable" caste, and in some parts of India the mother is supposedly "untouchable" during birth and for ten days after. Similarly, Vietnamese women were reported (in 1951) to be secluded for a lengthy time after giving birth in order not to bring bad luck upon others. Arapesh women give birth in an area "reserved for excretion, menstrual huts, and foraging pigs." The ritual purification of women after childbirth is found among Jews, Christians, and Arabs, and from the Caucasus to South Africa. Newton observes that (as with menstrual taboos) post-partum "defilement" may at least procure for the mother some relief from her daily tasks and an opportunity for uninterrupted and peaceful concentration on the new relationship with her baby. But even where this is so, the cost exacted is still female flesh-loathing; and physical self-hatred and suspicion of one's own body is scarcely a favorable emotion with which to enter an intense physical experience.[10]

Finally, there is the pain of sexual guilt. In some cultures,

* K. D. Keele points out that "in primitive thought, pain is closely associated with the intrusion of an object or of a spirit into the body; painful disease is often thought to be caused by the spirit of another person, dead or living, which seeks a new body. Pregnancy has widely been thought to result from the entrance of a spirit seeking rebirth into the woman's body" (*Anatomies of Pain* [Oxford: Blackwell, 1957], p. 2).

confessions of adultery are extorted from women in labor.[11]
The sexual connotations of pregnancy and birth can give rise,
not only to shame and embarrassment during pregnancy, but
feelings of guilt in the intimate exposure of the birth-chamber.
The dread of giving birth to monsters, as Sheila Kitzinger observes, has to do with "the crystallization of deep-seated feelings
of guilt. The girl wants to punish herself, to wipe away her
guilt by atonement—by producing this monstrosity from within
her own body, the living embodiment of her own evil."[12] Again,
sexual guilt and physical defilement in women are inextricably
associated, and throughout the world are sources of enormous
tension.

Such negative attitudes, found in nonliterate as well as literate cultures, make childbirth an ordeal both psychically and
physically. There is a deep and prevalent sense of the woman's
body as magical, as either vulnerable to or emanating evil—as
unclean, and as the embodiment of guilt. These beliefs, internalized in her, affect her relationship to the birth-process as
much as do ignorance, or the actual, verifiable reality of risk
and danger. But contemporary Western culture shares many
of these attitudes, and has made its own special contributions
to the alienation of women from the birth-process.

4

The fear of pain of childbirth in literate as in nonliterate societies may come (and often does) from verbal tales, phrases,
anecdotes; it is further reinforced by literature. As a girl of
twelve or thirteen, I read and reread passages in novels which
recounted births, trying to imagine what actually happened.
I had no films, no photographs of childbirth to enlighten me;
but in my favorite novel, *Anna Karenina,* I found the account
of Kitty Levin's labor, as perceived by her husband.

> Kitty's flushed, agonized face, a lock of hair clinging to her
> clammy forehead, was turned to him, seeking his eyes. . . .
> She spoke fast, and tried to smile, but suddenly her face dis-
> torted with pain and she pushed him away.
> "Oh, this is terrible! I am dying . . . I shall die! Go away,

go away!" she cried, and the same unearthly shriek echoed through the house. . . .

Leaning his head against the doorpost, he stood in the next room and heard someone shrieking and moaning in a way he had never heard before, and knew that these sounds came from what had once been Kitty. . . .

Beside himself, he rushed into the bedroom again. The first thing he saw was the midwife's face looking more frowning and stern than ever. Kitty's face was not there. In its place was something fearful—fearful in its strained distortion and the sounds that issued from it. . . . The terrible screams followed each other quickly until they seemed to reach the utmost limit of horror, when they suddenly ceased . . . and he heard a soft stir, a bustle, and the sound of hurried breathing, and her voice, faltering, vibrant, tender and blissful as she whispered, "It's over!"[13]

The outcome for Princess Lise, in *War and Peace*, was less blissful:

The screaming ceased, and a few more seconds went by. Then suddenly a terrible shriek—it could not be hers, she could not scream like that—came from the bedroom. Prince Andrew ran to the door; the scream ceased and he heard the wail of an infant.

. . . A woman rushed out and seeing Prince Andrew stopped, hesitating on the threshold. He went into his wife's room. She was lying dead, in the same position he had seen her in five minutes before . . .[14]

Both these passages, of course, were composed by a man, and written through the consciousness of the father.

I considered myself a young woman enlightened in "the facts of life"; my mother, unlike the mothers of many of my friends, had described sexual intercourse and conception in general terms, quite unhysterically. But the process of labor was mysterious to me. I imagined that the pains could only be caused by the squeezing of an infant's head through the tiny opening of the vagina—how could that be anything but painful? I had heard of "forceps" deliveries and imagined a huge instrument which would lacerate the mother while grasping the child's body. But how was it possible that the pain could end immedi-

ately after the child was born? And how could Lise simply have
died there, "in the same position he had seen her in five minutes before?" *What killed her?* How could it all happen so
suddenly? And there was something terrifying in the metamor-
phosis which Tolstoy implied women underwent in the sufferings of labor: "these sounds came from what had once been
Kitty" . . . "a terrible shriek—it could not be hers, she could
not scream like that—." One became, then, possessed or dehu-
manized, with pain.

Beyond the accounts of childbirth—few and far between—
in novels (Pearl Buck's *The Good Earth* was another source),
I knew that my own birth had been long and slow, that my
mother had been accounted "a heroine" for enduring my coming. In my father's library I stole glances at a thick, dark red
volume, Williams's *Obstetrics*, a textbook written by the obstetrician who had delivered me. Nowhere was the *face* of a
laboring mother visible in its photographs; all was perineum,
episiotomy, the nether parts I recognized as like and unlike my
own, stretched beyond belief by the crowning infant head. Like
many a young girl, I simply could not imagine that my body
was built to withstand the cataclysm.

Dick-Read says that he was told by many women that they
cried out, not from pain but the fear of pain, and demanded to
be put to sleep in order to escape from the terrors of the unknown. For centuries, notably the centuries of puerperal fever,
death-fantasies had a literal, unassailable basis in statistical fact.
Yet, even in a place and time where maternal mortality is low,
a woman's fantasies of her own death in childbirth have the
accuracy of metaphor. Typically, under patriarchy, the mother's
life is exchanged for the child; her autonomy as a separate being
seems fated to conflict with the infant she will bear. The self-
denying, self-annihilative role of the Good Mother (linked im-
plicitly with suffering and with the repression of anger) will
spell the "death" of the woman or girl who once had hopes, expectations, fantasies *for herself*—especially when those hopes
and fantasies have never been acted-on. For a poor woman, or
one who has only herself to depend on economically, the birth
of an infant can imply another kind of death—a new liability in
the struggle merely to survive.

There is another kind of fear which does seem elemental; the fear of change, of transformation, of the unfamiliar. Pregnancy may be experienced as the extinguishing of an earlier self, as the diary notes of a European woman suggest:

> My face in the mirror looked alien to me. My character blurred. Childish violent desires, unknown to me, came over me, and childish violent dislikes. I am a coldly logical thinker, but at that time, my reasoning blurred and dissolved, impotent, into tears, another helpless, childish creature's tears, not mine. I was one and the other at once. It stirred inside of me. Could I control its movements with my will? Sometimes I thought I could, at other times I realized it was beyond my control. I couldn't control anything. I was not myself. And not for a brief, passing moment of rapture, which men, too, experience, but for nine watchful quiet months. . . . Then it was born. I heard it scream with a voice that was no longer mine.[15]

Not every woman, of course, feels pregnancy as "imposing" "alien traits" on her, as did this woman with her "coldly logical" self-image. It could be said of her that what appeared most alien and unfamiliar were really buried, denied aspects of her own nature. But pregnancy and birth do herald enormous changes in the life of any mother. Even a woman who gives up her child for adoption at birth has undergone irreversible physiological and psychic changes in the process of carrying it to term and bearing it. And the woman who continues to mother will find the rhythms and priorities of her life changed in the most profound and also the most trivial ways. The woman who has long wanted and awaited a child can anticipate becoming a mother with imaginative eagerness; but she too must move from the familiar to the strange, and this is never a simple process.

5

The forceps and its monopoly by male practitioners were decisive in annexing childbirth to the new male medical establishment. In 1842 a Georgia physician discovered that pain could be annulled by ether-inhalation; both ether and nitrous oxide were rapidly introduced in dentistry; and the term *anesthesia*, suggested by Oliver Wendell Holmes, soon became current. In

1847, using ether in a case of childbirth, James Simpson in
Scotland showed that contractions of the uterus would continue even if the woman was unconscious, and proceeded to
experiment with and to use chloroform to relieve the pains of
labor. A fierce theological opposition arose; the clergy attacked
anesthesia as "a decay of Satan, apparently offering itself to
bless women; but in the end it will harden society and rob God
of the deep earnest cries which arise in time of trouble for
help."[16] The lifting of Eve's curse seemed to threaten the foundations of patriarchal religion; the cries of women in childbirth
were for the glory of God the Father. An alleviation of female
suffering was seen as "hardening" society, as if the sole alternative to the *mater dolorosa*—the eternally suffering and suppliant
mother as epitomized by the Virgin—must be the Medusa
whose look turns men to stone.

This view still finds expression in antiabortion rhetoric, and
extends beyond any single issue to feminism in general. After
the horrible and lingering death of Mary Wollstonecraft from
septicemia, the Rev. Richard Polwhele complacently observed
that "she had died a death that strongly marked the distinction
of the sexes, by pointing out the destiny of women, and the
diseases to which they were peculiarly liable."[17]

The identification of womanhood with suffering—by women*
as well as men—has been tied to the concept of woman-as-
mother. The idea that woman's passive suffering is inevitable has
worn many guises in history; not only those of Eve or the Virgin
Mary but also later ones such as Helene Deutsch's association
of passivity and masochism with "normal" femininity. If the
medieval woman saw herself as paying by each childbirth for
Eve's transgression, the nineteenth-century middle-class woman
could play the Angel in the House, the martyr, her womanhood

---

* Olive Schreiner wrote in 1888 to Havelock Ellis: "Once God Almighty
said: 'I will produce a self-working, automatic machine for enduring suffering, which shall be capable of the largest amount of suffering in a given
space,' and he made woman. But he wasn't satisfied that he had reached
the highest point of perfection; so he made a man of genius. He was not
satisfied yet. So he combined the two and made a woman of genius—and
he was satisfied. That's the real theory—but in the end he defeated himself
because the machine he'd constructed to endure suffering could enjoy bliss
too . . ." (*Letters of Olive Schreiner, 1826–1920*, S. C. Cronwright-
Schreiner, ed. [London: T. Fisher Unwin, 1924]).

affirmed by her agonies suffered in travail. Oliver Wendell Holmes supplies us with one version of the rhetoric:

> The woman about to become a mother, or with her newborn infant upon her bosom, should be the object of trembling care and sympathy wherever she bears her tender burden or stretches her aching limbs. The very outcast of the streets has pity upon her sister in degradation when the seal of promised maternity is impressed upon her. The remorseless vengeance of the law . . . is arrested in its fall at a word which reveals her transient claim for mercy. The solemn prayer of the liturgy singles out her sorrows from the multiplied trials of life, to plead for her in her hour of peril.[18]*

The value of a woman's life would appear to be contingent on her being pregnant or newly delivered. Women who refuse to become mothers are not merely emotionally suspect, but are dangerous. Not only do they refuse to continue the species; they also deprive society of its emotional leaven—the suffering of the mother. As late as the 1920s, it was assumed that "the suffering which a woman undergoes in labor is one of the strongest elements in the love she bears her offspring."[19]

It was therefore a radical act—*the* truly radical act of her entire reign—when Queen Victoria accepted anesthesia by chloroform for the birth of her seventh child in 1853. In so doing she opposed clerical and patriarchal tradition and its entire view of women; but her influence and prestige were strong enough that her decision opened the way for anesthesia as an accepted obstetrical practice.

It was also in the Victorian period that the female body became more taboo, more mysterious, more suspected of "complaints and disorders," and the focus of more ignorant speculation, than ever before. The male gynecological establishment viewed female sexual responsiveness of any kind as pathological, and the "myth of female frailty" haunted the existence of middle- and upper-class women. If education was supposed to

---

* This of course was purely sentimental. In the nineteenth century, as before and since, women gave birth in prisons and workhouses. See, for example, Emmeline Pankhurst's account of listening to the cries of a woman in childbirth in the prison cell next to hers (Midge MacKenzie, ed., *Shoulder to Shoulder* [New York: Knopf, 1975], pp. 72, 91).

atrophy the female reproductive organs, women's suffrage was
seen as creating "insane asylums in every county, and . . . a divorce court in every town." Clitoridectomies and ovariotomies
were performed on women as a form of behavior modification
for "troublesomeness," "attempted suicide," and "erotic ten-
dencies." The much professed "reverence" for women (of the
upper classes) in Victorian England and America consisted
largely in an exaggerated prudery.[20] At the onset of labor, the
woman was placed in the lithotomy (supine) position, chloro-
formed, and turned into the completely passive body on which
the obstetrician could perform as on a mannequin. The labor
room became an operating theatre, and childbirth a medical
drama with the physician as its hero.

In the early twentieth century various forms of anesthesia
were developed specifically for labor: "Twilight Sleep," a compound of morphine and scopolamine, was widely used until it
was discovered to have a highly toxic effect on the infant.
Sodium amytal and nembutal were found to produce after-
amnesia (while only partly blunting pain); of nembutal Sylvia
Plath's heroine in *The Bell Jar* bitterly remarks, "I thought it
sounded just like the sort of drug a man would invent."[21] The
development of caudal or saddle-block anesthesia meant that a
woman could remain conscious and see her baby born, though
she was paralyzed from the waist down. Speert and Guttmacher,
in their textbook *Obstetric Practice*, admit that the use of
caudal or saddle-block anesthesia can prolong the second stage
of labor, by producing "uterine inertia . . . [and] the absence
of voluntary expulsive efforts by the mother," thus rendering a
forceps delivery "necessary" where the child might otherwise
have been born more swiftly and without instruments. (Not
to mention the fact that in inexperienced hands the possibility
of permanent damage has to be considered.)

There are certain valid indications for the prevention of exer-
tion by the mother—such as heart disease, tuberculosis, or a
previous Caesarean,[22] but women are now asking what psychic
effect a state of semihelplessness has on a healthy mother, awake
during the birth, yet prevented from participating actively in
delivery. No more devastating image could be invented for the
bondage of woman: sheeted, supine, drugged, her wrists strapped

down and her legs in stirrups, at the very moment when she is bringing new life into the world. This "freedom from pain," like "sexual liberation," places a woman physically at men's disposal, though still estranged from the potentialities of her own body. While in no way altering her subjection, it can be advertised as a progressive development.*

6

In the 1940s, Dick-Read observed that pain sensations arose out of fear and tension and began to train prospective mothers to relax, to breathe correctly, to understand the stages of the labor process, and to develop muscular control through exercises. Dick-Read also placed great emphasis on the presence of calm, supportive birth-attendants throughout labor, especially the obstetrician, who was to act as a source of confidence and security rather than as a surgeon needlessly interfering with or accelerating the birth process. He held that anesthesia should always be available but never involuntarily imposed on the woman or administered routinely. Dick-Read's work was path-breaking, and many of his observations are still valuable. However, his attitude to women is essentially patriarchal: While in genuine awe of

---

* A physician of the 1930s offers us this description of the perfections of American obstetrical technology:

> Arriving (at the hospital) . . . she is immediately given the benefit of one of the modern analgesics or pain-killers. Soon she is in a dreamy, half-conscious state at the height of a pain, sound asleep between spasms. Though hours must elapse before the infant appears, her conscious self is through; the rest is up to the doctor and her own reflexes.

> She knows nothing about being taken to a spotlessly clean delivery room, placed on a sterile table, draped with sterile sheets; neither does she see . . . the doctor and nurses, garbed for her protection in sterile white gowns and gloves; nor the shiny boiled instruments and antiseptic solutions. She does not hear the cry of her baby when first he feels the chill of this cold world, nor see the care with which the doctor repairs such lacerations as may have occurred. She is, as most of us want to be when severe pain has us in its grasp—asleep—Finally she awakes in smiles, a mother with no recollection of having become one.

(R. P. Finney, *The Story of Motherhood* [New York: Liveright, 1937], pp. 6–7.)

the female capacity to produce new life, he writes of "the in-
born dependence of woman" which finds its natural outlet in
her dependence on the doctor. He perceives the birth process as
naturally "ecstatic": "Biologically, motherhood is her desire,"
he remarks; and at one point: "*Varium et mutabile semper
femina,* but never more so than in childbirth." For him, childbirth is a woman's glory, her purpose in life, her peak experience. Remove fear, reinforce ecstasy, and childbirth can be
"natural"—that is, virtually without pain. But the male obstetrician is still in control of the situation.[23]

During the thirties and forties, several Soviet obstetricians
began applying Pavlov's theories of the conditioned reflex to
childbirth. Successful deliveries in Russia under hypnosis and
in posthypnotic states led to increased emphasis on "suggestion," which was the basis for the first prenatal training: the
creation, during pregnancy, of "complex chains of conditioned
reflexes which will be applicable at the confinement. The pregnant woman learns to give birth as the child learns to read or
swim." The conditioning towards pain was to be altered and
new reflexes set up; the method is described as "verbal analgesia."[24] Pavlov had observed that

> . . . for man speech provides conditioned stimuli which are
> just as real as any other stimuli. . . . Speech, an account of
> the whole preceding life of the adult, is connected up with the
> internal and external stimuli which can reach the cortex, sig-
> nalling all of them, and replacing all of them, and therefore it
> can call forth all those reactions of the organism which are
> normally determined by the actual stimuli themselves.[25]

In 1951, Fernand Lamaze, a French physician, visited maternity
clinics in the U.S.S.R. which used the "psychoprophylactic
method," and introduced the method in the West, at the maternity hospital under his direction, serving the members of the
Metallurgists' Union. Lamaze, far more than Dick-Read, emphasized the active participation of the mother in every stage
of labor, and developed a precise and controlled breathing drill
to be used during each stage. Where Dick-Read encourages a
level of "dulled consciousness" in the second stage, Lamaze
would have the mother aware and conscious, responding to a

series of verbal cues from the birth-attendant by panting, pushing, and blowing. Suzanne Arms suggests, however, that the Lamaze method "has the unfortunate side-effect of greatly altering a woman's natural experience of birth from one of deep involvement inside her body to a controlled distraction." In her "militant control over her body," she is "separate and detached from the sensations, smells and sights of her body giving birth. She is too involved in . . . control . . ."[26]

The "psychosexual" method of Sheila Kitzinger, in England, involves a much broader concept of childbearing as part of the context of a woman's entire existence. She stresses that a woman must learn to "trust her body and her instincts" and to understand the complex emotional network in which she comes to parturition. Kitzinger insists on both physical and psychic education for childbirth if the mother is to retain "the power of self-direction, of self-control, of choice, of voluntary decision and active cooperation with doctor and nurse" and she strongly favors giving birth at home, usually with a midwife.

The mother of five children herself, she unequivocally states that "pain in labour is real enough." But she also describes the sensuous experience of the opening of the vagina during expulsion—not as painless, but as powerful and often exhilarating. Her grasp of female reality is much broader than that of Dick-Read or Lamaze, but she, like other writers on prepared childbirth, assumes that babies are born only to married couples, and that the husband—present and emotionally dependable—will be a primary figure in the birth-chamber; and she unhesitatingly states that "the experience of bearing a child is central to a woman's life."[27]

More recently, in the United States, there has been widespread interest in various combinations of the Dick-Read, Lamaze, and Kitzinger approaches. The move toward midwife deliveries and away from the male obstetrician and the depersonalization of the hospital has been a crucial aspect of "taking our bodies back" and of the women's health-care movement. In the late sixties there began to appear a sprinkling of volumes celebrating home births, glamorized with photographs of very young and lovely pregnant women, naked or in flowered dresses, in rural communes, romanticized as hippie earth-mothers. The conditions which affect the majority of women in labor—poverty, malnutrition, desertion by the father of the child, inadequate prenatal care—are ignored in these books (where, again, an eager young father is usually present at the birth). "Prepared" or "natural" childbirth in the United States has been a middle-class phenomenon; but even its crusaders acknowledge that the context of a woman's life may have something to do with her experience of labor. A French obstetrician Pierre Vellay says that in "normal" cases (normal pelvis, good presentation, *good physical and psychological conditions*) "the woman can expect childbirth without any pain, provided that no family, money or social worries upset her just before the birth. . . . A light, pleasant house with plenty of room, enough money and no fear for the future are the best conditions in which a woman can bear a baby."[28] Lamaze admits that "the addition of a child to a family may be a real source of anxiety when the house is too small or the father's income inadequate . . . it is natural for a mother to feel depressed about her child's future when her own is overcast." Shulamith Firestone, as an early theorist of the contemporary women's movement, was understandably skeptical of "natural" childbirth as part of a reactionary counterculture having little to do with the liberation of women as a whole.

Firestone sees childbearing, however, as purely and simply the victimizing experience it has often been under patriarchy. "Pregnancy is barbaric," she declares; "Childbirth *hurts*." She discards biological motherhood from this shallow and unexamined point of view, without taking full account of what the experience of biological pregnancy and birth might be in a wholly different political and emotional context. Her attitudes toward pregnancy ("the husband's guilty waning of sexual desire; the woman's tears in front of the mirror at eight months") are male-derived.[29] Finally, Firestone is so eager to move on to technology that she fails to explore the relationship between maternity and sensuality, pain and female alienation.

Ideally, of course, women would choose not only whether, when, and where to bear children, and the circumstances of labor, but also between biological and artificial reproduction. Ideally, the process of creating another life would be freely and intelligently undertaken, much as a woman might prepare herself physically and mentally for a trip across country by jeep, or an archeological "dig"; or might choose to do something else altogether. But I do not think we can project any such idea onto the future—and hope to realize it—without examining the shadow-images we carry out of the magical thinking of Eve's curse and the social victimization of women-as-mothers. To do so is to deny aspects of ourselves which will rise up sooner or later to claim recognition.

7

In 1955, 1957, and 1959, I gave birth to my three children—all essentially normal births—under general anesthesia. In my first labor, an allergic reaction to pregnancy, which was assumed to be measles, may have justified medical intervention. But in each subsequent pregnancy I used the same obstetrician, and was "put out" as completely as I had been for the first. During my first pregnancy I and many of the women I knew were reading Grantly Dick-Read's *Natural Childbirth*. I found myself suspicious of his claims that giving birth was *the* ecstatic and exhilarating experience for women. I was only beginning a long process of reunion with the body I had been split from at puberty; my mind lived on one plane, my body on another, and physical pleasure, even in sex, was problematic to me. I had known exhilaration in language, in music, in ideas, in landscape, in talk, in painting; even in Dick-Read's book I could identify more with the obstetrician's exhilaration at a "natural" labor than with what he believed his patients experienced. I was vaguely interested in his theories, but did not consider trying them for myself. Labor seemed to me something to be gotten through, the child—and the state of motherhood—being the mysterious and desired goal.

During and after those years, I often felt apologetic in talking with women who had delivered by some variant of the Dick-Read method, or had attempted it. I was told: "It hurt like hell, but it was worth it"; or, "It was the most painful, ecstatic experience of my entire life." Some women asserted that the promised ecstasy had been, in fact, agony, and that they had ended crying for anesthesia. Others had been, on the delivery table, anesthetized against their will. At that time, even more than now, the "choice" a woman made as to the mode of delivery was likely to be her obstetrician's choice. However, among those who were awake at delivery, a premium seemed to be placed on the *pain endured* rather than on an active physical experience. Sometimes I felt that my three unconscious deliveries were yet another sign of my half-suspected inadequacy as a woman; the "real" mothers were those who had been "awake through it all." I think now that my refusal of consciousness (approved and implemented by my physician) and my friends' exhilaration at having experienced and surmounted pain (approved and implemented by their physicians) had a common source: we were trying in our several ways to contain the expected female fate of passive suffering. None of us, I think, had much sense of being in any real command of the experience. Ignorant of our bodies, we were essentially nineteenth-century women as far as childbirth (and much else) was concerned. (But, unlike our European sisters, none of us dreamed of having our babies at home, with a midwife. In the United States, that was a fate reserved for the rural poor.)

We were, above all, in the hands of male medical technology. The hierarchal atmosphere of the hospital, the definition of childbirth as a medical emergency, the fragmentation of body from mind, were the environment in which we gave birth, with or without analgesia. The only female presences were nurses, whose training and schedules precluded much female tenderness. (I remember the gratitude and amazement I felt waking in the "recovery room" after my third delivery to find a young student nurse holding my hand.) The experience of lying half-awake in a barred crib, in a labor room with other women moaning in a drugged condition, where "no one comes" except to do a pelvic examination or give an injection, is a classic experience of alienated childbirth. The loneliness, the sense of abandonment, of being imprisoned, powerless, and depersonalized is the chief collective memory of women who have given birth in American hospitals.

But not just American hospitals. Cora Sandel describes the

sensations of her heroine Alberta, giving birth to her illegitimate
child in a Paris hospital at the turn of the century:

> She was sitting up to her neck in water in a bath tub, for-
> saken by God and man. They had closed the door and gone
> away, as if she were quite capable of looking after herself. Sup-
> pose they forgot her? Suppose the pain came back before she
> was safe in bed? With sinking heart she stared at the door.
>
> There they were! She breathed again.
>
> But it was only a hand which snatched her clothes from the
> chair on which they were lying, placed some kind of white linen
> robe there instead, and closed the door again. She called. No-
> body answered. She was a prisoner, with no chance of flight.
>
> What was happening was inevitable. Outside night lay over
> the city. . . . Far, far away, in another world, lived people she
> knew who were close to her . . . shades, left behind in an
> earlier life, incapable of helping her. Nor had they any suspicion
> of how bitterly forsaken she was in this machine composed of
> curt, white-clad persons and shining tiled walls, which had her
> in its clutches and would not release her again until she was
> transformed, one became two, or until—[30]

Brigitte Jordan, an anthropologist studying childbirth cross-
culturally, describes routine hospital delivery in the United
States as

> . . . a complex of practices which are justified, on medical
> grounds, as being in the best interest of mother and child . . .
> induction and stimulation of labor with drugs, the routine ad-
> ministration of sedatives and of medication for pain relief, the
> separation of the laboring woman from any sources of psycho-
> logical support, surgical rupturing of the membranes, routine
> episiotomy, routine forceps delivery, and the lithotomy position
> for delivery, to name just a few.

Jordan is saying that childbirth is a "culturally produced event,"
and that in the United States the same relentless consistency of
method is pursued without regard to individual aspects of a
particular labor. Yes, episiotomies are done to avoid tearing of
the perineum, but tearing is much *more* likely when the lithotomy position is used than when a woman gives birth squatting,

on a birth-stool, or (as in the Yucatan) supported in a hammock. Forceps deliveries are also more often necessary in the lithotomy position, where the pull of gravity cannot aid in the expulsion of the child.[31]

Tucho Perussi, an Argentine doctor, urges a return to the obstetrical stool, pointing out that in the lithotomy position a contraction which has pushed the fetus downward can be compensated against by the sliding-back of the fetus, lengthening the labor unnecessarily. In the vertical position gravity naturally works with the contractions. Roberto Caldeyro-Barcia of Argentina puts it succinctly: "Except for being hanged by the feet . . . the supine position is the worst conceivable position for labor and delivery." Moreover, vertical delivery seems to minimize the loss of oxygen to the fetus which results when the uterus is lying on the largest vein in the body (the vena cava). The chief objection to the use of the obstetrical stool or chair seems to be the obstetricians' belief that it would inconvenience them.[32]*

The artificial induction and stimulation of labor, widely resorted to in the United States, produces longer, stronger contractions with less relaxation-span between them than the contractions of normal labor. This in turn leads to the use of pain-relieving drugs; as so often, medical technology creates its own artificial problem for which an artificial remedy must be found. These unnaturally strong and lengthy contractions can deprive the fetus of oxygen, while the analgesic drugs interfere with its respiration.† If labor in the United States were induced

---

* Brigitte Jordan reports, however, that contemporary European delivery tables allow for greater diversity of position, having "a moveable backrest (which can be cranked up to support the woman in a semi-sitting position, where that isn't possible either the husband or midwife will hold the pushing woman up); secondly, the middle part; thirdly, the footend which can be inclined, left flat, or wheeled away or pushed under the middle part in case it becomes desirable to put the woman in the lithotomy position (for repair of episiotomies, for example). Routinely, then, pushing is done with the woman in a semi-upright position, hooking her hands under her thighs. Some delivery tables have hand holds (nowhere are a woman's hands tied down), some have foot supports, but nowhere is the lithotomy position used for routine delivery" (Personal communication, October 1974).

† A study of over 50,000 infants from birth to one year of age, prepared by the National Institute of Neurological Diseases and Stroke, revealed the

only in cases of medical necessity, only about 3 percent of births would be induced. In fact, at least one in five births are drug-induced or drug-stimulated, for the physician's convenience and with no physiologic justification whatever.[33]

In cultures as different as Sweden and the Yucatan, women have a part in the decision-making process during their deliveries. The Yucatan midwife emphasizes that "every woman has to 'buscar la forma,' find her own way, and that it is the midwife's task to assist with whatever decision is made."[34] This does not mean that births are painless, but that needless pain is prevented, birth is not treated as a "medical event," and the woman's individual temperament and physique are trusted and respected.

Thirty years ago, in *Male and Female*, Margaret Mead wrote of the violence done by American hospital obstetrics to both infant and mother in the first hours of life.[35] In 1972 Doris Haire, of the International Childbirth Education Association, published a report on "The Cultural Warping of Childbirth." In it she pointed out that of sixteen developed countries in 1971 and 1972, the United States had the highest infant mortality rate (number of infant deaths per 1000 live births, in the first year of life). She surveyed the routine methods used in American hospital obstetrics, researched the literature on each, and compared them with practices found in countries where infant mortality is especially low. Among practices routinely followed in this country, which she found to be damaging both to mother and child, she lists the following:

Withholding information on the disadvantages of obstetrical medication
Requiring all normal women to give birth in the hospital
Elective induction of labor (without clear medical indication)

---

ironic fact that there was a greater incidence of neurologic damage among white than among black children of one year old, and that "in one New York hospital during 1970 there was twice the incidence of depressed babies among private patients as among clinic patients." ."Although the incidence of low birth weight, prematurity and undernutrition is decidedly greater among our black population, black patients, who are more often clinic patients, traditionally receive less medication during labor and birth" (Doris Haire, "The Cultural Warping of Childbirth," International Childbirth Education Association, 1972, 1974).

Separating the mother from familial support during labor and
  birth
Confining the normal laboring woman to bed
Shaving the birth area
Professional dependence on technology and pharmacological
  methods of pain relief
Chemical stimulation of labor
Delaying birth until the physician arrives
Requiring the mother to assume the lithotomy position for
  birth
Routine use of regional or general anesthesia for delivery
Routine episiotomy
Separating the mother from her newborn infant
Delaying the first breast-feeding[36]

Writers like Haire, Sheila Kitzinger, and Suzanne Arms have
stressed the process of childbirth as a continuum, interwoven
inextricably with the entire spectrum of a woman's life. It is
not a drama torn from its context, a sudden crisis to be handled
by others because the mother is out of control of her body. Of
course actual medical crises occur during childbirth; but birth
itself is neither a disease nor a surgical operation. Nor should
infant and mother, immediately after parturition, be treated as
two separate creatures, to be cared for in separate parts of a
building by separate nursing staffs. They are still a continuum,
and sensitive treatment of the one is incomplete without closeness to the other. The very nature of the mother-child bond may
depend on the degree of contact in the first hours and days of
the child's life.

> Placed directly upon the mother's belly, while still connected
> to her placenta (by the unsevered umbilical cord) the baby
> finds the nipple and begins its first suckling activity. The mere
> licking of the mother's nipple triggers the nerves in her breast
> to alert the uterus that the baby is out and safe. In immediate
> response, the uterus clamps down to begin to expel the pla-
> centa. Meanwhile, the suckling action of the baby stimulates
> its breathing and heat productivity. Most important, the new-
> born finds peace and calm in direct contact with its mother's
> warm body. This moment of security is the first it has known
> since the onset of labor.[37]*

* Suzanne Arms reports that even as women in the United States are be-

Suzanne Arms both demystifies and pleads for a rehumaniza-
tion, a rewomanization, of the entire pregnancy, birth, and
post-partum process. She does not, of course, claim that the
hospital alone is the creator of pain in childbirth, although
she does point out that hospitals are associated with "disease
and disorder," an atmosphere of medical emergency which can
only increase the tension of the laboring woman. All labor, however, has to pass through the "transition" between the first
stage in which the cervix becomes fully dilated, and the expulsion of the child. Arms's description of the psychic and physical
stress of this part of labor is astute and revealing:

> At this point the woman, nearly sapped of energy, must rally
> her reserves to begin pushing the baby out, yet she is now con-
> fronted with contractions even more violent than before,
> coming so hard and fast that they seem to meld together in
> successive waves, culminating in a shattering explosion that
> overwhelms her entire body. . . . Suddenly nauseous and
> chilled to the bone, the woman turns to the nearest figure of au-
> thority with beseeching eyes and a look on her face that no one
> who has ever attended a delivery will forget. It is a look of
> shock and disbelief, a statement all its own that woman is never
> so completely and totally alone than at this moment. A be-
> seechingly, pleading, imploring cry for help, which looks like
> terror to the uninitiated, it is often articulated as "Do some-
> thing!" "I can't go on!" "Help me!" or words of similar
> dramatic power. The response of early Christian man might
> have been to read his wife the passages from the Scriptures
> telling her it was her lot to suffer so; the response of modern
> doctors's to inject drugs to end the suffering. Yet neither reac-
> tion is responsible. When primitive woman turned to the mid-
> wife with that same look of desperation, the midwife rightfully
> interpreted the plea to mean *"Assist me,"* "Support me," "Tell

ginning to demand home births, American obstetrical superhardware is
selling itself in countries like England, Holland, and Denmark which have
a long tradition of midwifery, maternity clinics, and home births, with a
complete back-up system of emergency medical care. Despite the much
lower infant mortality rate in Western Europe, the promise of "quick and
easy" technologized obstetrics is making inroads Meanwhile, in the United
States, "doctors resist any move to take birth out of the hospital or make
it a woman's event" (Suzanne Arms, *Immaculate Deception* [Boston:
Houghton Mifflin, 1975], p. 160).

me this is supposed to happen." The obstetrician reads it as a
cry to "Stop it," "Intervene," "Do it for me."[38]

She rightly observes that "after centuries of ingrained fear,
expectations of pain, and obeisance to male domination, the
mother cannot easily come to childbirth a 'changed woman'
after a few classes in natural childbirth or a heavy dose of
Women's Liberation."[39] What we bring to childbirth is nothing
less than our entire socialization as women.

The question is one of power and powerlessness, of the exercise of choice, whether a woman can choose to give birth at
home, attended by a woman, or at least in a maternity clinic
which is not a hospital. It is a question of the mother's right to
decide what *she* wants, to "buscar la forma." At this time in
America it is extremely difficult and usually illegal for a woman
to give birth to her child at home with the aid of a professional
midwife. The medical establishment continues to claim pregnancy and parturition to be a form of disease. The real issue,
underlying the economic profit of the medical profession, is the
mother's relation to childbirth, an experience in which women
have historically felt out of control, at the mercy of biology,
fate, or chance. To change the experience of childbirth means
to change women's relationship to fear and powerlessness, to
our bodies, to our children; it has far-reaching psychic and
political implications.

8

Childbirth is (or may be) one aspect of the entire process of
a woman's life, beginning with her own expulsion from her
mother's body, her own sensual suckling or being held by a
woman, through her earliest sensations of clitoral eroticism and
of the vulva as a source of pleasure, her growing sense of her
own body and its strengths, her masturbation, her menses, her
physical relationship to nature and to other human beings, her
first and subsequent orgasmic experiences with another's body,
her conception, pregnancy, to the moment of first holding her
child. But that moment is still only a point in the process if
we conceive it not according to patriarchal ideas of childbirth
as a kind of production, but as part of female experience.

Beyond birth comes nursing and physical relationship with an infant, and these are enmeshed with sexuality, with the ebb and flow of ovulation and menses, of sexual desire. During pregnancy the entire pelvic area increases in its vascularity (the production of arteries and veins) thus increasing the capacity for sexual tension and greatly increasing the frequency and intensity of the orgasm.[40] During pregnancy, the system is flooded with hormones which not only induce the growth of new blood vessels but increase clitoral responsiveness and strengthen the muscles effective in orgasm. A woman who has given birth has a biologically increased capacity for genital pleasure, unless her pelvic organs have been damaged obstetrically, as frequently happens. Many women experience orgasm for the first time after childbirth, or become erotically aroused while nursing. Frieda Fromm-Reichmann, Niles Newton, Masters and Johnson, and others have documented the erotic sensations experienced by women in actually giving birth. Since there are strong cultural forces which desexualize women as mothers, the orgasmic sensations felt in childbirth or while suckling infants have probably until recently been denied even by the women feeling them, or have evoked feelings of guilt. Yet, as Newton reminds us, "Women . . . have a more varied heritage of sexual enjoyment than men";[41] and the sociologist Alice Rossi observes,

> I suspect that the more male dominance characterizes a Western society, the greater is the dissociation between sexuality and maternalism. It is to men's sexual advantage to restrict women's sexual gratification to heterosexual coitus, though the price for the woman and a child may be a less psychologically and physically rewarding relationship.[42]

The divisions of labor and allocations of power in patriarchy demand not merely a suffering Mother, but one divested of sexuality: the Virgin Mary, *virgo intacta*, perfectly chaste. Women are permitted to be sexual only at a certain time of life, and the sensuality of mature—and certainly of aging—women has been perceived as grotesque, threatening, and inappropriate.

If motherhood and sexuality were not wedged resolutely

apart by male culture, if we could *choose* both the forms of our sexuality and the terms of our motherhood or nonmotherhood freely, women might achieve genuine sexual autonomy (as opposed to "sexual liberation"). The mother should be able to choose the means of conception (biological, artificial, or parthenogenetic), the place of birth, her own style of giving birth, and her birth-attendants: midwife or doctor as she wishes, a man she loves and trusts, women and men friends or kin, her other children. There is no reason why it should not be an "Amazon expedition" if she so desires, in which she is supported by women only, the midwife with whom she has worked throughout pregnancy, and women who simply love her. (At present, the father is the only nonmedical person legally admitted to the labor and delivery room in American hospitals, and even the biological father can be legally excluded over the mother's decision to have him there.)[43]

But taking birth out of the hospital does not mean simply shifting it into the home or into maternity clinics. Birth is not an isolated event. If there were local centers to which all women could go for contraceptive and abortion counseling, pregnancy testing, prenatal care, labor classes, films about pregnancy and birth, routine gynecological examinations, therapeutic and counseling groups through and after pregnancy, including a well-baby clinic, women could begin to think, read about, and discuss the entire process of conceiving, gestating, bearing, nursing their children, about the alternatives to motherhood, and about the wholeness of their lives. Birth might then become one event in the unfolding of our diverse and polymorphous sexuality: not a necessary consequence of sex, but one experience of liberating ourselves from fear, passivity, and alienation from our bodies.

9

I am a woman giving birth to myself. In that psychic process, too, there is a "transition period" when energy flags, the effort seems endless, and we feel spiritually and even physically "nauseous and chilled to the bone." In such periods, turning to doctors for help and support, thousands of women have been made into consumers of pain-numbing medication, which may quell anxiety or desperation at the price of cutting the woman off from her own necessary process. Unfortunately, there are too few trained, experienced psychic midwives for this kind of parturition; and the psycho-obstetricians, the pill-pushers, those who would keep us in a psychological lithotomy position, still dominate the psychotherapeutic profession.

There is a difference between crying out for help and asking to be "put under"; and women—both in psychic and physical labor—need to understand the extremity and the meaning of the "transition stage," to learn to demand active care and support, not "Twilight Sleep" or numbing. As long as birth—metaphorically or literally—remains an experience of passively handing over our minds and our bodies to male authority and technology, other kinds of social change can only minimally change our relationship to ourselves, to power, and to the world outside our bodies.

VIII MOTHER AND SON, WOMAN AND MAN

As her sons have seen her: the Mother in patriarchy: controlling, erotic, castrating, heart-suffering, guilt-ridden, and guilt-provoking; a marble brow, a huge breast, an avid cave; between her legs snakes, swamp-grass, or teeth; on her lap a helpless infant or a martyred son. She exists for one purpose: to bear and nourish the son. "I could never really take it in that there had been a time, even in *der heym*, when she had been simply a woman alone, with a life in which I had no part."[1] She finds in him her reason for existence: "A mother is only brought unlimited satisfaction by . . . a son; this is altogether the most perfect, the most free from ambivalence of all human relationships." "The relationship between . . . mother and son . . . furnishes the purest examples of unchanging tenderness, undisturbed by any egoistic consideration."[2] The mother as seducer, with whom the son longs to sleep, against whom the incest taboo is strongest: Jocasta, Gertrude.* Despite the very high incidence of actual father-daughter and brother-sister rape, it is mother-son incest which has been most consistently tabooed in every culture[3] and which has received the most obsessive attention in the literature men have written.

The mother-in-law, also cross-culturally tabooed; the potentially deadly surrogate for both wife and mother. The Banks

---

* Louis Malle's film, *Murmur of the Heart,* suggests another attitude toward the story; far from being a "dark legend," the mutual seduction of son and mother is merely a lighthearted family incident.

Islander son-in-law waits till the tide has erased her footprints
before he can follow her down the beach; the Navaho calls
her "doyshini," meaning "She whom I may not see"; in the
Yucatan an encounter with her is enough to sterilize a man.[4]
The mother unmanning the son, holding him back from life:
"It always starts with Mama, mine loved me. As testimony of
her love, and her fear of the fate of the man-child all slave
mothers hold, she attempted to press, hide, push, capture me
in the womb. The conflicts and contradictions that will follow
me to the tomb started right there in the womb . . . I pushed
out against my mother's strength September 23, 1941—I felt
free."[5] She who ought to have helped the son defy the father's
tyranny, handing him over instead to the male realm of judgment and force. "Mother unconsciously played the part of a
beater during a hunt. Even if your [his father's] method of up-
bringing might in some unlikely case have set me on my own
feet by means of promoting defiance, dislike, or even hate in
me, Mother canceled that out again by kindness, by talking
sensibly . . . by pleading for me, and I was again driven back
into your orbit, which I might otherwise have broken out of,
to your advantage and to my own."[6] She tries to prevent the
child from being born; she *is* the birth trauma. "It is *she* who
is the enemy. She who stands between the child and life. Only
one of them can prevail; it is mortal combat. . . . The monster
bears down one more time . . ."[7] She lurks in the past of the
criminal:

> "Oh mother, mother," he did cry!
> "You're to blame because I die;
> I was trained when I was young,
> For which this day I'm to be hung."[*8]

* More recently, when the "Boston Strangler" was terrorizing that city
with the sexual mutilation and strangling of a series of women,

[a] Medical-Psychiatric Committee, upon invitation of the stymied
police, had put together an imaginative, detailed profile of the phantom Strangler. Or, to be more precise, they put together an imaginative profile of the Strangler's mother. Struck by the advanced age of
the first victims, one of whom was 75, the committee postulated . . .
that the elusive killer was a neat, punctual, conservatively dressed,
possibly middle-aged, probably impotent, probably homosexual fellow
who was consumed by raging hatred for his "sweet, orderly, neat,
compulsive, seductive, punitive, overwhelming" mother. . . . Con-

She remains powerful and vampiristic after death: "What is
the use of a mother's sacrificing herself for her children if after
death her unappeased soul shall perforce return upon the child
and exact from it all the fulfillment that should have been
attained in the living flesh, and was not?"[9] And, at the two
ends of a spectrum which is really a continuum, she is Kali, the
"black mother" of Hindu religion, fangs ecstatically bared, a
necklace of skulls round her neck, dancing on her dead husband's body; while in Michelangelo's white-satin-marble *Pietà*
she bends her virginal mannequin's face above the icy, dandia-
cal corpse of the son on her lap.

Somehow her relationship to him is connected with death. Is
it simply that in looking at his mother (or any mature woman)
he is reminded, somewhere beyond repression, of his existence
as a mere speck, a weak, blind, clot of flesh growing inside her
body? Remembering a time when he was nothing, is he forced
to acknowledge a time when he will no longer exist?* Certainly
we know that he has chosen, for burial, caves, and tombs and
labyrinths imitating caves which represent the female body; or
the hollowed-out ship of death, which in the hero myths is also
a cradle.[10] He may fear—and long for—being lost again in a
female body, reincorporated, pulled back into a preconscious
state; to penetrate a woman can be an act filled with anxiety, in
which he must ignore or deny the human breathing person,

---

sumed by mother hatred, the psychiatrists divined, the Strangler had
chosen to murder and mutilate old women in a manner "both sadistic
and loving. . . ."

Albert DeSalvo, as he revealed himself and as his juvenile records
bore out, was genuinely attached to his mother. Moreover, she was
still alive and not particularly sweet, neat or overwhelming. The con-
suming rage DeSalvo bore was uncompromisingly directed against his
drunken, brutalizing father, who had regularly beaten him, his mother
and the other children during a wretched youth . . . engaged in sex
acts with prostitutes in front of his children, had taught his sons to
shoplift, had broken every finger on his wife's hand and knocked out
her teeth, and had . . . abandoned the family when Albert was eight.

(Susan Brownmiller, *Against Our Will: Men, Women and Rape* [New
York: Simon and Schuster, 1975], pp. 203–4.)

* Daughters may also dread being "redevoured" by their mothers; but the
daughter also knows herself potentially her mother's inheritor: she, also,
may bring life out of her body.

must conquer or possess her body like a territory, and even so
that body remains threatening to him.[11] (Before leaving the
Earth, astronauts, like warriors of the past, abstain from intercourse with women.) He must make a separation between the
sexual woman and the "motherly" woman;[12] and even so,
romantic sexual love is prevailingly associated with death.[13]

Denial of this anxiety toward the mother can take many
forms: the need to view her as Angel of the Home, unambiva-
lently loving, is merely one. A recently divorced mother of a
young child told me that a man she was seeing had assured
her: "Mothers turn me on—they are more real than other
women. They have a foothold in the future. Childless women
are already dead." Here the objectification of the woman to
whom he was speaking is mingled with some, no doubt buried,
need to outface, to exploit, even, her maternality. (This man's
first act in entering her apartment was always to open the
refrigerator.) I think it would be simplistic to say that he
was "looking for a mother"; rather, he was attempting to assert
his sexuality in the face of the mother who was already there.

But the mother is there, it seems, for better or worse, in
childless women as well; the mother looms in each woman for
the grown-up boy. Perhaps nowhere in literature has this been
so clarifyingly revealed as in the "Third Duino Elegy" of Rilke.
Here he addresses the "Mädchen" or young woman, the "be-
loved," trying to describe to her all that preceded her in his
consciousness, all that she represents for him. In so doing he
creates a landscape of the male psyche in its "prehistoric" apprehension of the mother (with whom the young girl becomes
almost immediately confused):

But did he ever begin himself?
Mother, *you* created him small, it was you who started him;
he was new for you, you bent over his new eyes
the friendly world, and warded off the unfriendly.
O where are those years when with your delicate figure
you simply stood between him and surging chaos?
You hid much from him thus; you rendered harmless
the eerie room at night; from your full heart's sanctuary
you mixed a more humane space into his space of night.
You placed the night-light, not in the darkness, no,
but in your closer being, and it shone with friendship.

There was nowhere a creak you couldn't explain away, smiling,
as though you'd long known when the floor would act that way.
And he listened, and calmed down . . .

He, the new, retreating one, how he was entangled
in the ever-growing vines of inner events
already twisted in patterns, into choking growth,
into beastlike stalking forms. How he gave himself—loved.
Loved his inner self, the wilderness inside him,
that jungle on whose quiet deadfall
his heart stood up, lightgreen. Loved. Left it, went
with his own roots, into a vast new beginning
where his insignificant birth was already forgotten. Loving
he went down into the older blood, the canyons
where lay the monstrous, still gorged with the fathers . . .
                         . . . this, woman, came before you . . .

So the young woman is to mediate for him in his "monstrous"
inner life, just as the mother mediated in his childhood with the
strange world and his own night-fears:

                            . . . Oh, slowly, slowly
do something kind for him each day, a task he can rely on
                              —bring him
close to the garden, give him the extra weight
of nights........
                  Keep him with you........

The woman, yet again, as healer, helper, bringer of tenderness
and security. The roles (or rules) are clear: nowhere in the
Elegies is it suggested that a man might do this for a woman, or
that the woman has her own inner complexity. Rilke grappled
at least once with the possibility of a change in roles. In *The
Notebooks of Malte Laurids Brigge*, he asks whether, since
women have done the work of "loving" for centuries, it might
not be time for men to take on their share of this work. "We
have been spoiled by easy enjoyment like all dilettanti and
stand in the odor of mastery. But what if we were to despise our
successes, what if we were to start from the very outset to learn
the work of love, which has always been done for us? What if
we were to go ahead and become beginners, now that much is
changing?"[14]

But nowhere in his musings does Rilke acknowledge even faintly what the cost of doing this "work of love" for men—in a word, mothering—has been for women. Depending for encouragement and protectiveness on a series of women, soulmates and patronesses, he remained essentially a son. In 1902 he writes of his recent marriage to the sculptor Clara Westhoff:

> Since December we have a dear little daughter, Ruth, and life has become much richer with her.—For the woman—according to my conviction—a child is a completion and a liberation from all strangeness and insecurity: it is, spiritually too, the mark of maturity; and I am filled with the conviction that the woman artist, who has had and has and loves a child, is, no less than the mature man, capable of reaching all the artistic heights the man can reach under the same conditions, that is, if he is an artist . . .
>
> In the past year I have had a little household with my wife (in a little village near Worpswede); but the houschold consumed too much, and so we have promised each other to live for our work, each as a bachelor of limited means, as before.[15]

But of course for Clara Westhoff, as the mother of a child, it could never again be "as before." Eventually she was to entrust Ruth to her own mother in order to go on with her work. But the meaning of what it is to have a child, for the woman artist or for any woman—the unending details of care, of forethought, of having to learn all that women are assumed simply to know "by nature," the actual physical, emotional work in one day of mothering, the night-risings which he remembers from a child's point of view, oblivious of the inroads of broken sleep on a woman's life and work—all this Rilke, childlike, takes for granted, as men have usually taken it.

We read Rilke in part because he often seems on the verge of saying—or seeing—further than other male writers, in the sense of knowing, at least, that the relationship of man to woman is more dubious, more obscure, than literature has assumed. By far the majority of men have written of women out of the unexplored depths of their fears, guilt, centered on our relationship to them, that is, to women perceived as either mothers or antimothers.

It is these grown-up male children who have told us and each other: in Mesopotamia that we were "a pitfall, a hole, a ditch" (a grave?);[16] under Hindu law, that we were by nature seductive and impure and required to live under male control, whatever our caste;[17] in the Christian Era, that we were "the head of sin, a weapon of the devil, expulsion from Paradise, mother of guilt";[18] that as Eternal Woman we wore the word "mystery" inscribed on our brows and that self-sacrifice was our privilege;[19] that our wombs were "unbridled" breeding-places of "brackish, nitrous, voracious humours";[20] by the Victorian medical experts, both that we had no sensuality and that "voluptuous spasms" would make us barren, also that "the real woman regards all men . . . as a sort of stepson, towards whom her heart goes out in motherly tenderness";[21] in the aftermath of the Bolshevik Revolution, that we were victims of our own "biological tragedy" which no legal and social changes could undo;[22] by the neo-Freudians, that "the syndrome of decay, the evil tendency in man, is basically rooted in the mother-child relationship";[23] in the People's Republic of China that the love of women for women is a bourgeois aberration, a function of capitalism.

But before we were mothers, we have been, first of all, women, with actual bodies and actual minds.

2

The first thing I remember hearing about mothers and sons, at the age of about six, was the story of the "brave Spartan mothers" who sent their sons forth to battle with the adjuration: *With your shield or on it*, meaning that the young man was to return victorious, or dead. Over and over a picture played itself out in my mind: the young man, wounded, without his shield, finds his way back to his mother's door. Would she really refuse to open it?

Vous travaillez pour l'armée, madame?

I still have a children's book, much-read in my early years, which quotes the following letter:

Dear Madam:

I have been shown in the files of the War Department that you are the mother of five sons who have died gloriously on the field of battle. I feel how weak and fruitless must be any words of mine which should attempt to beguile you from the grief of a loss so overwhelming. But I cannot refrain from tendering to you the consolation that may be found in the thanks of the Republic they died to save. I pray that our heavenly Father may assuage the anguish of your bereavement, and leave you only the cherished memory of the loved and lost, and the solemn pride that must be yours to have laid so costly a sacrifice upon the altar of freedom.

> Yours very sincerely and respectfully,
> Abraham Lincoln[24]

Despite these early impressions, when I first became pregnant I set my heart on a son. (In our childish "acting-out" games I had always preferred the masculine roles and persuaded or forced my younger sister to act the feminine ones.) I still identified more with men than with women; the men I knew seemed less held back by self-doubt and ambivalence, more choices seemed open to them. I wanted to give birth, at twenty-five, to my unborn self, the self that our father-centered family had suppressed in me, someone independent, actively willing, original—those possibilities I had felt in myself in flashes as a young student and writer, and from which, during pregnancy, I was to close myself off. If I wanted to give birth to myself as a male, it was because males seemed to inherit those qualities by right of gender. And I wanted a son because my husband spoke hopefully of "a little boy." Probably he, too, wanted to give birth to himself, to start afresh. A man, he wanted a male child. A Jew, and a first-born, he wanted a first-born son. An adult male, he wanted "a little boy."

I wanted a son, also, in order to do what my mother had not done: bring forth a man-child. I wanted him as a defiance to my father, who had begotten "only" daughters. My eldest son was born, as it happened, on my father's birthday.

Vous travaillez pour l'armée, madame? For generations, we have entered our sons in some kind of combat: not always so direct and bloody as those of Sparta or the Civil War. Giving birth to sons has been one means through which a woman could leave "her" mark on the world. After my youngest son was born, six years later, a woman friend, intelligent and talented herself, wrote to me: "This one . . . will be the genius. That's so obviously why it had to be born with a penis instead of a vagina."

But, having borne three sons, I found myself living, at the deepest levels of passion and confusion, with three small bodies, soon three persons, whose care I often felt was eating away at my life, but whose beauty, humor, and physical affection were amazing to me. I saw them, not as "sons" and potential inheritors of patriarchy, but as the sweet flesh of infants, the delicate insistency of exploring bodies, the purity of concentration, grief, or joy which exists undiluted in young children, dipping into which connected me with long-forgotten zones in myself. I was a restless, impatient, tired, inconsistent mother, the shock of motherhood had left me reeling; but I knew I passionately loved those three young beings.

I remember one summer, living in a friend's house in Vermont. My husband was working abroad for several weeks, and my three sons—nine, seven, and five years old—and I dwelt for most of that time by ourselves. Without a male adult in the house, without any reason for schedules, naps, regular mealtimes, or early bedtimes so the two parents could talk, we fell into what I felt to be a delicious and sinful rhythm. It was a spell of unusually hot, clear weather, and we ate nearly all our meals outdoors, hand-to-mouth; we lived half-naked, stayed up to watch bats and stars and fireflies, read and told stories, slept late. I watched their slender little-boys' bodies grow brown, we washed in water warm from the garden hose lying in the sun, we lived like castaways on some island of mothers and children. At night they fell asleep without murmur and I stayed up reading and writing as I had when a student, till the early morning hours. I remember thinking: This is what living with children could be—without school hours, fixed routines, naps, the conflict of being both mother and wife with no room for being, simply, myself. Driving home once after midnight from a late drive-in movie, through the foxfire and stillness of a winding Vermont road, with three sleeping children in the back of the car, I felt wide awake, elated; we had broken together all the rules of bedtime, the night rules, rules I myself thought I had to observe in the city or become a "bad mother." We were conspirators, outlaws from the institution of motherhood; I felt enormously in charge of my life. Of course the institution closed down on us again, and my own mistrust of myself as a "good mother" returned, along with my resentment of the archetype. But I knew even then that I did not want my sons to act for me in the world, any more than I wished for them to kill or die for their country. I wanted to act, to live, in myself and to love them for their separate selves.

3

> Does this sense of personal worth, this enthusiasm for one's own personality [as in Whitman and Richard Jefferies] belong only to great self-expressive souls? or to a mature period of life I have not yet attained? or may I perhaps by shut off from it by eternal law because I am a woman, and lonely? It seems to me the one priceless gift of this life:—of all blessings on earth I would choose to have a man-child who possessed it.[25]

The fathers have of course demanded sons; as heirs, field-hands, cannon-fodder, feeders of machinery, images and extensions of themselves; their immortality. In societies systematically practicing female infanticide, women might understandably wish for boys rather than face the prospect of nine months of pregnancy whose outcome would be treated as a waste product. Yet, under the realities of organized male territoriality and aggression, when women produce sons, they are literally working for the army. It may be easier to repress this knowledge, or to believe that one's own child will escape death at war, than to face the routine murder of a female infant. In a society riddled with sanctions against women, a mother may instinctively place more value—let us say more hope—on a son, just as some Afro-Americans, before the growth of "black pride," felt constrained to value the child with the lightest skin and most Caucasoid features. The sense of the unlived, the unachieved in a woman's own life, may unconsciously express itself, as in the passage quoted above from the youthful notebooks of Ruth Benedict (who was later to marry, hope for children she never had, finally leave her marriage and become a distinguished anthropologist and a feminist of a kind).

"To have a man-child who possessed it." And so we come upon ground still lying in the shadow of Freud. Within the last forty years, Freud's work has been both revised and vulgarized, so that acceptance or rejection of "Freudianism" is frequently based on selected aspects of his work, filtered through other minds. (We should not underestimate the power of films, plays, jokes.) No one aspect of his theory has been more influential than the so-called Oedipus complex. Women who have never read Freud are raising their sons in the belief that to show them physical affection is to be "seductive," that to influence their sons against forms of masculine behavior they as women abhor, is to "castrate" them or to become "the 'devouring,' 'domineering' creature that their sons will have to reject in order to grow up mentally healthy," or that they, and they alone, are responsible if their sons become "unnecessarily [*sic*] homosexual."[26]

Freud was unquestionably a pioneer along certain lines: for example, in positing the idea that the emotionally afflicted are not simply moral criminals, and that unconscious impulses contribute to ordinary human actions. Primitive as his dream-analysis may seem to us today, he did reestablish recognition of the dream as a significant event, to which attention must be paid, after several centuries of a "science" of medicine which had denied its validity. But Freud was also a man, terribly limited both by his culture and his gender. Karen Horney, one of his most searching early critics, pointed out the narrowly biological and mechanistic foundations of his thought, his reduction of psychological qualities to anatomical causes, and his inherently dualistic thinking, in which instinct and "ego," feminine and masculine, passivity and activity, are seen as polar opposites. In particular she assailed his view that we go on throughout life repeating or regressing backward into events of childhood; a view which she rightly felt to deny the organic development of a person, the qualitative changes we go through in the process of a life.

Horney accepted the Oedipus complex, though with serious qualifications: unlike Freud she did not believe that a child's intense sexual feelings toward parents are biologically determined, therefore universal; she saw them as the result of concrete situations experienced by some, but not all, children.[27] Her critique was extremely daring and courageous at a time when the ubiquitous Oedipus complex, repressed or active, was believed to be at the center of psychic life. Her divergences from Freud caused her to be excommunicated two years later from the ·powerful New York Psychoanalytic Institute. But for us, her views do not press far enough.

For the male child, Freud believed the Oedipus complex to consist of the process whereby a little boy first experiences strong sexual feelings for his mother, then learns to detach and differentiate himself from her, to identify as a male with his father instead of perceiving him as a rival, and finally to go on to a point where his erotic instincts can be turned toward a woman other than his mother. Freud thought that the boy's infantile sexual feelings for his mother create anxiety in him that his jealous father will punish him by castration. The ideal resolution of the Oedipus complex is for the boy to give up his attachment to his mother, and to internalize and identify with his father, whom he recognizes as superior in power. The price of keeping his penis, then, is to adopt his father, in Freudian terminology, as "super-ego"—in short, to acknowledge the supremacy of patriarchal law, the discipline of the instincts, exogamy, and the incest taboo.

Freud suggested a range of possibilities in this early crisis: the boy might actually be threatened with castration as punishment for masturbation; jealous fathers might actually use circumcision (symbolic castration) against pubescent sons; but also, these events might simply take place in fantasy.[28]

The fundamental assumption here is that the two-person mother-child relationship is by nature regressive, circular, unproductive, and that culture depends on the son-father relationship. All that the mother can do for the child is perpetuate a dependency which prevents further development. Through the resolution of the Oedipus complex, the boy makes his way into the male world, the world of patriarchal law and order. Civilization—meaning, of course, patriarchal civilization—requires the introduction of the father (whose presence has so far not been essential since nine months before birth) as a third figure in the interrelationship of mother and child. The

Oedipus complex thus becomes, in Juliet Mitchell's phrase, "the entry into human culture." But it is distinctively the father who represents not just authority but culture itself, the super-ego which controls the blind thrashings of the "id." Civilization means identification, not with the mother but with the father.

Freud also held that the little girl experiences her lack of a penis as "castration"; that, to become a woman, she must substitute pregnancy and a baby for the missing male organ. Given this assumption, it is not surprising that he should have invested the mother-son relationship with this "libidinal," unconscious quality: the son is not only a baby, he possesses the penis the mother has craved. (It is, however, difficult to understand how Freud also imagined the relationship of mother and son to be free from ambivalence and "egoistic considerations.")

Over and over, this view of the impulse to motherhood has been challenged by women analysts. Not only Horney, but Clara Thompson and Frieda Fromm-Reichmann urged that if the small girl wishes for a penis at all, it is only because she sees privilege and favor bestowed on people who have this single distinguishing feature. They perceived the penis as a metaphor, the wish for a child as a wholly different kind of impulse.

But even as we challenge or refute Freud's structure, the questions arise: How *does* the male child differentiate himself from his mother, and does this mean inevitably that he must "join the army," that is, internalize patriarchal values? Can the mother, in patriarchy, represent culture, and if so, what does this require of her? Above all, what does separation from the mother mean for the son?

It means, of course, in the first place, physical birth, leaving the warm, weightless dream of the amniotic sac. It means the gradual process through which the baby discovers that the mother's breast, her face, her body's warmth, belong to another person, do not exist purely for him, can disappear and return, will respond to his crying, his smiles, his physical needs, but increasingly, not always in perfect rhythm with his desires and pangs. It means a dual process, in which the mother first absents herself—momentarily or longer—from the child, then later he experiments with games of hide-and-seek, and finally, on his own legs, is able to wander away from her for short distances. It means weaning, learning that others beside his mother can take care of him, that he is safe in his mother's absence. Undoubtedly the child feels anxiety and desolation at each of these stages, the fear that security, tenderness, reliability may have departed forever. A third person, other persons, are obviously necessary to relieve this anxiety, to dry his tears of abandonment, to reassure him that all care and love are not embodied solely in one person, his mother, and to make it possible for him to accept her separateness and his own. But more often than not that third person has also been a woman: a grandmother, aunt, older sister, nurse. She may, in fact, give more care and cherishing than the mother has been able to give; she may become, emotionally, the mother. As for male figures, the child's experience is that they are less physical, less cherishing, more intermittent in their presence, more remote, more judgmental, more for-themselves, than the women who are around him. Male or female, the child learns early that gender has something to do with emotional attunement to others.

Yet finally he must be taken over by these male figures. Tribal societies have always required a "second birth" of the young boy at puberty into the male group. "In the initiation rites . . . the young men are as it were swallowed up by the tutelary spirit of this masculine world and are reborn as children of the spirit rather than of the mother; they are sons of heaven, not just sons of earth. This spiritual rebirth signifies the birth of the 'higher man' who, even on the primitive level, is associated with consciousness, the ego, and will power. . . . The man's world, representing 'heaven,' stands for law and tradition, for the gods of aforetime, so far as they were masculine gods."[29] The event is often attended by animal castration and sacrifice, symbolic wounds, ordeal. But whatever the ritual to be enacted, the child-with-a-penis is expected to bond himself with others who have penises. It hardly matters, then, if the son grows up in a so-called matriarchal family of strong women, or one in which the mother is head of the household. He must still—according to this view—come to terms with the Fathers, the representatives of law and tradition, the wagers of aggression, the creators and purveyors of the dominant culture.

And his mother, whatever her deepest instincts tell her, is expected to facilitate this. My grandmother often described, and still with pain, how my father—an undersized, slender Jewish boy—was sent off to military school at the age of about ten. "The uniform was too big for him . . . I can see him to this day, the smallest of all the boys, looking so scared on that platform waiting for that train." But she sent him off, for a "better education" and to become a man; what choice did she have, in Birmingham, Alabama, in the early twentieth century?

The third term in the so-called Oedipal triangle is, in fact, patriarchal power. Any attempt to salvage the Oedipus complex as a theory of human development must begin here. The anthropologist Sherry Ortner offers the possibility that, even though Freud assumed that the "Oedipal process" takes place in a biological family, there is a more basic underlying theory of socialization which is independent of any specific society or gender-roles. "It is a powerful and . . . ultimately dialectical theory; the person evolves through a process of struggle with and . . . integration . . . of symbolic figures of love, desire and authority." Ortner suggests that this structure would exist even if a child were reared equally by two or more parents, male and female or of the same sex, who shared in nurturance and authority; although, as she points out, "even where the nuclear family has been experimentally broken up, as in the Kibbutz for example, the nursery attendants have always been wholly or predominantly female."[30]*

Rereading Freud, and some Freudians (notably Juliet Mitchell, who is more a Freudian than either a Marxist or a feminist), wending through such concepts as *penis envy, castration,* the child (especially the son) as *penis-substitute,* what finally leaves the strongest impression is a tone-deafness in the language. This may well result from the psychoanalysts' desire to feel that they are dealing with memory, dream, fantasy, on a "scientific" level; that is, in the false sense of science as the

---

* And state authority has been wholly or predominantly male: for example, Israel, the Soviet Union, Cuba, the Republic of China. That Golda Meir or Indira Gandhi are women does not alter the maleness of that authority, which emanates, finally, from and through male institutions.

opposite of poetry.* A penis, a breast, obviously have imaginative implications beyond their biological existence (just as
an eye, an ear, the lungs, the vulva, or any other part of the
body which we inhabit intellectually and sensually). Yet these
implications go unexplored; the density and resonance of the
physical image gets lost in the abstract reductiveness of the
jargon. Even the much-evoked penis, in Freudian theory, seems
a poor thing, divested of the dimensionality it possessed as a
symbol of generative power, the *herm*, the Great Mother's appur-
tenance in prepatriarchal cults. This limitation—which comes,
as Karen Horney suggests, from Freud's rigidly biological and
dualistic approach—is particularly notable where the figure of
the mother (and hence of woman) is involved, in the dreams
and fantasies of men.

Juliet Mitchell reiterates that we should not fault Freud for
what he did not attempt: an analysis of the social conditions
which, as he himself acknowledged, contribute to feminine
psychology.[31] Robert Jay Lifton, a psychiatrist, has been quoted
as saying that "every great thinker has at least one blind spot:
Freud's was women."[32] But in fact there is no such thing as an
intellectual "blind spot" surrounded by an outlook of piercing
lucidity—least of all when that spot happens to cover the immense and complex dimensions in which women exist, both for
ourselves and in the minds of men. Freud need not have been a
feminist in order to have had a deeper sense of the resonance
and chargedness of the figure of the woman—especially as
mother—in patriarchal thinking. But, even in terms of his
own proclaimed methods and goals, he, as it were, lost his
nerve and drew back where women were concerned. And this
affected not simply his attitudes toward women but, of necessity, his speculations and observations about men, and about
the significance of the penis for both sexes. The Freudian view
of the son is saturated with the Freudian hostility—and sentimentality—toward the mother.

It was Freud himself, of course, who emphasized the extent
to which, in "everyday life," the double meaning, the loss of
memory, the slip of the tongue, express what we do not con-

---

* I do not mean that science and poetry are the same thing; only that they
need be in no way opposed.

sciously take responsibility for meaning. Elizabeth Janeway calls
attention to his repeated use of the phrase, "the *fact* of castration," referring to the little girl. "We must assume that this
slip is meaningful, and indeed I believe that it leads us to the
heart of Freud's dilemma about the female sex."[33] Janeway suggests that although "little girls have not 'in fact' been cas-
trated," Freud *was* well aware—though he never chose to in-
vestigate it—that women have suffered intense thwarting and
deprivation as social beings. In short, Freud meant female castration as a metaphor. But precisely because he did not pursue
the psychic meaning of this *social* mutilation of women (which
would have forced him to go deeper into male psychology, also)
his work, both on women and on men, lacks a kind of truth
which has been called political and which I would call poetic
and scientific as well.

4

Every culture invents its special version of the mother-son relationship. The mockery (and sentimentalization, its obverse)
leveled at the Jewish-American mother by her sons, in fiction,
theatre, film, and anecdote, has its roots both in Yahwist
misogynist tradition and in the situation of the Jewish woman
and man in assimilationist America. The Jewish woman suffered extreme reduction in the process of becoming "American"; she rapidly lost her role as mediator with the outside
world, woman of business, entrepreneur, manager of the family and its fortunes, strategist of survival, to become an "American" wife to her "American" husband. Since his prestige now
depended on being the aggressive breadwinner and achiever instead of the other-worldly Talmudic student, his assertion of
masculinity in transatlantic terms demanded (or seemed to demand) her dwindling into home-enclosed motherhood.[34]

It is interesting to compare Freud's idyll of the "perfect" and
"unambivalent" mother-son relationship with the resentment
and contempt for the mother reflected in such novels as Philip
Roth's *Portnoy's Complaint*, or in popular nonbooks such as
Dan Greenburg's *How To Be a Jewish Mother*. Yet, the idyll
and the actuality have been held in a strange kind of double

vision in Jewish-American culture; the mother is either senti-
mentalized, or ruthlessly caricatured; she is too loud, too pushy,
too full of vitality (sexuality?), or asexual to the point of re-
pressiveness; she suffers, in Freud's phrase, from "housewife
psychosis"; she bullies her children with guilt and unwanted
food; at intervals she is dignified by mourning or the lighting
of Sabbath candles.

Pauline Bart has depicted some of the human damages inflicted on these women in her study of depression in middle-
aged women.[35] And depression there is in plenty, revealed in
forms ranging from the high-pitched voice and nervous laugh of
self-derogation to the year-after-year reliance on sleeping-pills
and tranquilizers. But there is also a smoldering energy and re-
silience in the domesticated Jewish woman which—from a
woman's point of view—commands respect, however it has
been abused or derogated by this particular subculture.* She is
a survivor-woman, a fighter with tooth and claw and her own
nervous system, who, like her black sisters, has borne the
weight of a people on her back. Yet she has lived between her
sons' dependency and denigration on the one hand, and her
own guilt-feelings and repressed rage, on the other.

The black mother has been charged by both white and black
males with the "castration" of her sons through her so-called
matriarchal domination of the family, as breadwinner, decision-
maker, and rearer of children in one. Needless to say, her
"power" as "matriarch" is drastically limited by the bonds of
racism, sexism, and poverty. What is misread as power here is
really survival-strength, guts, the determination that her children's lives shall come to something even if it means driving
them, or sacrificing her own pride in order to feed and clothe
them. In attributing to the black mother a figurative castration of her sons, white male racism, which has literally cas-
trated thousands of black men, reveals yet again its inextricable
linkage with sexism.

* "Traits that enabled Jewish women to keep their families together in the
shtetl and to ease their transition to the New World are the very same
ones the processes of assimilation . . . were bent on exorcising. . . . Their
bowls of chicken soup have become philters of hemlock" (Charlotte Baum,
Paula Hyman, and Sonya Michel, *The Jewish Woman in America* [New
York: Dial Press, 1975], pp. 244–51).

5

"If you want to know more about femininity, enquire from your own experience of life, or turn to the poets, or wait until science can give you deeper and more coherent information." Thus, in an edgy yet candid acknowledgment of his own limitations, Freud ended his essay, "On Femininity."

In the forty-odd years since he wrote those words, a great deal has happened. We have begun to accumulate, through the work of scientists like Mary Jane Sherfey, Masters and Johnson, Niles Newton, Alice Rossi, new information about female biology and sexuality and their relation to psychology;[36] the women's movement has unearthed and stimulated new descriptions of female experience by women; and women poets, certainly, have spoken.

One aspect of female experience which is changing—albeit gradually—is the expressed desire for sons. Undoubtedly there are and will long continue to be women who, for all the reasons given earlier, will still prefer sons, and still have higher expectations for their male children. But as some women come closer to shaping their own lives, there are signs that the overvaluation of the son *as a male* is undergoing changes as well.

Many women are expressing the sense that at this moment in human history it is simply better to be a woman; that the broadening and deepening of the demand for women's self-determination has created a largeness of possibility, a scope for original thought and activism, above all a new sense of mutual aims and sharing among women; that we are living on the edge of immense changes which we ourselves are creating. In addition, many women have felt that the first outrush of anger they experienced in coming to feminism, the bursting of the floodgates of years, involved them in painful contradictions with their male children as part of the male caste. "You cannot alienate the child from his culture. My sons are developing many features that are most distasteful to me. They have contempt for women . . . I love them [her sons]. I cannot get myself to look at them as my enemy."[37] Whatever this woman's confusions, she is expressing a conflict which is not unique.

The fear of alienating a male child from "his" culture seems to go deep, even among women who reject that culture for themselves every day of their lives. In the early sixties I recall a similar uneasiness, among some mothers who called themselves pacifists, that to forbid toy machine guns and hand grenades was to "alienate" their sons from playmates, even perhaps to "emasculate" them. (Perhaps those mothers, too, instinctively knew the gun was phallic, that it stood for more than simple killing; perhaps they simply feared being accused, as mothers so often are accused, of castrating their children.) But the feminist mothers' fear of alienating a son from "his" culture goes even deeper.

What do we fear? That our sons will accuse us of making them into misfits and outsiders? That they will suffer as we have suffered from patriarchal reprisals? Do we fear they will somehow lose their male status and privilege, even as we are seeking to abolish that inequality? Must a woman see her child as "the enemy" in order to teach him that he need not imitate a "macho" style of maleness? How does even a mother genuinely love a son who has contempt for women—or is this that bondage, misnamed love, that so often exists between women and men? It is indeed a painful contradiction when a mother who has herself begun to break female stereotypes sees her young sons apparently caught in patterns of TV violence, football, what Robert Reid has described as "the world of male-animal posturing, from which one male can emerge as dominant."[38] It is all too easy to accept unconsciously the guilt so readily thrust upon any woman who is seeking to broaden and deepen her own existence, on the grounds that this must somehow damage her children. That guilt is one of the most powerful forms of social control of women; none of us can be entirely immune to it.

A woman whose rage is under wraps may well foster a masculine aggressiveness in her son; she has experienced no other form of assertiveness. She may allow him literally to strike her, to domineer over her, in his small maleness, out of a kind of double identification: this young, posturing male animal is one with the entire male realm that has victimized her; but also, he is a piece of *her*, a piece that can express itself unchecked; and for this he is forgiven his *khamstvo* (a Russian word which combines "coarseness, truculence, bestiality and brutality" and which Soviet women have used about their men).[39]

Elizabeth Cady Stanton, a leader of the nineteenth-century American women's suffrage movement and the mother of five sons,* acknowledged the burdens of mothering her sons, and the essential ironies:

> I have so much care with all these boys on my hands. . . . How much I do long to be free from housekeeping and children . . . but it may be well for me to understand all the trials of woman's lot, that I may more eloquently proclaim them when the time comes . . .

> . . . tomorrow the sun will shine and my blessed baby will open his sweet blue eyes, crow and look so lovingly on me that I shall live again joyfully . . .

> When I think of all the wrongs that have been heaped upon womankind, I am ashamed that I am not forever in a condition of chronic wrath, stark mad, skin and bone, my eyes a fountain of tears, my lips overflowing with curses, and my hand against every man and brother! Ah, how I do repent me of the male faces I have washed, the mittens I have knit, the trousers mended, the cut fingers and broken toes I have bound up![40]

But it is absurd to think that women on the path of feminism wish to abandon their sons, emotionally or otherwise. Rather, the mother-son relationship—like all relationships—is undergoing revaluation, both in the light of the mother's changing relationship to male ideology, and in terms of her hopes and fears for her sons. If we wish for our sons—as for our daughters —that they may grow up unmutilated by gender-roles, sensitized to misogyny in all its forms, we also have to face the fact that in the present stage of history our sons may feel profoundly alone in the masculine world, with few if any close relationships with other men (as distinct from male "bonding" in defense of male privilege). When the son ceases to be the mother's outreach into the world, because she is reaching out into it herself, he

* One son, Theodore, collaborated with a sister in editing the two volumes of Stanton's writings. He also wrote his own book on *The Woman Question in Europe*.

ceases to be instrumental for her and has the chance to become a person.

I have been asked, sometimes with genuine curiosity, sometimes with veiled hostility, "What do your sons think about all this?" ("All this" being feminism in general, my own commitment to women in particular.) When asked with hostility the implication is that a feminist must be man-hating, castrating; that "all this" must of course be damaging to my children; it is a question meant to provoke guilt. (My only answer, obviously, is, "You'll have to ask them.") But the less our energy and power, as women, is expended on making our sons into our instruments, our agents in a system which has tried to keep us powerless, the less our sons need live under the burden of their mother's unlived lives.

The poet Sue Silvermarie writes of her young son, not as a compensation for male power and privilege, but as a source of unexpected revelation of the depth of what she calls "the motherbond":

My deep preference for women made mothering a male seem contradictory. But it is my very preference which now generates insight into the motherbond. The bond so easily blurred by everyday role-tasks. . . . What comes clear is the passion—the series of love-poems that poured from me while I carried him . . . the strength that let me defy all those who called him illegitimate . . . the moment of holding him to my breast in the hospital room and looking up to see my own mother at the foot of the bed with tears in her eyes . . . the feeling that when I am right with him, my life is lucid, but when our relationship is muddled, clouds cover my days. It is when I use this kind of perspective that his gender pales into insignificance. . . . Resentment gone, I can love him freely. I am more important to myself than is anyone else, I need not sacrifice my integrity, but neither must I sacrifice my son's. The passion of the motherbond demands whole persons.

But this mother also acknowledges, in her poem, "To a Boy-Child," the possibility of a time of confusion and separation:

> i tremble to see your temptations.
> how clear for me what losing you would mean.

> how confusing for you
> little man. already
> you're lured by what passes for power,
> and is, by half.
> what do I do with your guns?
> outlaws, you're playing, and I think
> it is i who am out of the law,
> it is you within it,
> approved,
> who grows blind to its bars . . .[41]

Surely here the "penis" becomes the obverse of the mother's fulfillment. Passionately loving her child as a small human being, she has nothing to gain from the mere fact of his maleness. She fears the *price* of the penis for him—the boy's acceptance of (and within) patriarchal law. But neither does she wish her son were a girl; she affirms both the complexity and the pain of the world of gender.

In a different vein, Robin Morgan addresses her son:

> Little heart, little heart,
> You have sung in me like the spiral alder-bud.
> You, who gave birth to this mother
> comprehend, for how much longer? my mysteries.
> Son of my cellular reincarnation, you alone know
> the words that awaken me when I play dead
> in our game. You alone wave
> at the wisp through which I see you.
> You understand . . .
>
> Still, I have grieved before the time, in preparation
> for my dolor, at how you will become
> a grown male child, tempted by false gods . . .
> You have clung to me like a spiderling
> to the back of the *Lycosa lenta*; wolf-spider mother,
> I have waited, wherever you fell off,
> for you to scramble on before proceeding.
>
> But you have come five-fold years
> and what I know now is nothing
> can abduct you fully from the land where you were born . .
>
> . . . there is no erasing this:
> the central memory of what we are

to one another, the grove of ritual.
I have set my seal upon you.

I say:
you shall be a child of the mother
as of old, and your face will not be turned from me . . .[42]

It may be objected that these mothers, too, want to make their sons instrumental, in the sense of rearing them in anti-masculinist values. But there is a distinction between heaping our thwarted energies on our sons, and hoping to unlock possibilities for them even as we are doing it for ourselves. I sense in Morgan's poem a hope and longing, expressed—perhaps optimistically—as conviction; in Silvermarie's a greater diffidence as to the outcome, but in both a recognition that the son will have to make choices between "the male group" and his own humanity.

We come back to the question of separation. For the son to remain a "child of the mother" in Morgan's sense is not for him to remain childish, dependent, the receiver rather than the giver of nurture, an eternal boy. In a seeming paradox, it is the "sons of the fathers" who persist in searching everywhere for the woman with whom they can be infantile, the embodiment of demand, the primitive child, Stanley Kowalski howling for his wife. The world of the fathers, the male group, is too obsessed with aggression and defense to sanction and give solace to fear, self-doubt, ordinary mortal weakness, and tears. The son of the fathers learns contempt for himself in states of suffering, and can reveal them only to women, whom he must then also hold in contempt, or resent for their knowledge of his weakness. The "son of the mother" (the mother who first loves herself) has a greater chance of realizing that strength and vulnerability, toughness and expressiveness, nurturance and authority, are not opposites, not the sole inheritance of one sex or the other. But this implies a new understanding of the love between mother and son.

Vulgar psychoanalytic opinion has it that the "son of the mother" becomes homosexual, either in flight from the power of women, or in protest against the traditional male role. In fact, we know next to nothing about the influences and accidents which lead to erotic love for one's own sex. And of heterosexuality, we know only that it has had a biological function, and that enormous social pressure has appeared to be necessary to maintain it, an institutionalized compulsion far beyond the present biological needs of the species. Why men choose men instead of women for sexual gratification, or as life-partners, is a question which cannot be answered simplistically in terms of fifth-century Athens; nor in terms of the "effeminizing" of sons by mothers who want to "hold on" to them. (Goethe and Freud, neither of them famous as homosexuals, were both sons of the mother in the sense of being preferred and cherished.) A man may well seek the love of other men in reaction to his father's *khamstvo,* his gross abuse of women as sexual objects; or he may try to replace a father who was chiefly absent. The spectrum of male homosexuality—ranging from the homosexual who genuinely likes and cares about women to the drag queen's contemptuous parody of female oppression, is known as yet only in its superficial aspects. I believe that all men to some degree dread strong women, but I have had no experience which suggests that dread to be greater in homosexuals than in men who call themselves "straight." The systems men have created are homogeneous systems, which exclude and degrade women or deny our existence; and the most frequent rationalization for our exclusion from those systems is that we are or ought to be mothers. Both straight and homosexual men take refuge in those systems. Yet the fear that our strength, or our influence, will "make our sons into homosexuals" still haunts even women who do not condemn homosexuality as such, perhaps because the power of patriarchal ideology still makes it seem a better fate for the boy to grow into a "real man."

6

What do we want for our sons? Women who have begun to challenge the values of patriarchy are haunted by this question. We want them to remain, in the deepest sense, sons of the mother, yet also to grow into themselves, to discover new ways of being men even as we are discovering new ways of being women. We could wish that there were more fathers—not one, but many—to whom they could also be sons, fathers with the sensitivity and commitment to help them into a manhood in which they would not perceive women as the sole sources of nourishment and solace. These fathers barely exist as yet; one exceptional individual here and there is a sign of hope, but still only a personal solution. Nor, as Jane Lazarre has pointed out, is the tokenly "involved" father even an individual solution. Until men are ready to share the responsibilities of full-time, universal child-care as a social priority, their sons and ours will be without any coherent vision of what nonpatriarchal manhood might be.[43] The pain, floundering, and ambivalence our male children experience is not to be laid at the doors of mothers who are strong, nontraditional women; it is the traditional fathers who—even when they live under the same roof—have deserted their children hourly and daily. We have to recognize, at this moment of history, as through centuries past, that most of our sons are—in the most profound sense—virtually fatherless.

Even if contraception were perfected to infallibility, so that no woman need ever again bear an unwanted child; even if laws and customs change—as long as women and women only are the nurturers of children, our sons will grow up looking only to women for compassion, resenting strength in women as "control," clinging to women when we try to move into a new mode of relationship. As long as society itself is patriarchal—which means antimaternal—there can never be enough mothering for sons who have to grow up under the rule of the Fathers, in a public "male" world separate from the private "female" world of the affections.

We need to understand that there is a difference between handing our sons over to patriarchy, on its terms, "travaillant pour l'armée," figuratively or literally allowing them to victimize us as tokens of their manhood; and helping them to separate from us, to become themselves. Esther Harding cites the recurrent myth of "the sacrifice of the son": Attis, Adonis, Horus, Osiris. In these myths, the son on reaching manhood is sacrificed "by the edict and consent of his mother." She observes that this myth has always been treated from the son's point of view, as "the need . . . to sacrifice his own childishness and dependence." She examines it from the point of view of the mother: "She loves him, and, in the myths, must always sacrifice him." A decisive "no" must be said where all was "yes" before: indulgence, protectiveness, compliance, pure motherliness.

For the mother as much as for the son, lifelong mothering is a denial of her own wholeness. Harding suggests that a continuing maternal protectiveness is an unwillingness to face the harshness of life, for herself as much as for her child. She further sees the "sacrifice of the son" as needing to take place, by extension, between women and men in general:

> It is no accident that the sacrifice . . . is represented by castration, for the most fundamental demand for satisfaction that man makes upon woman is the demand for satisfaction of his sexuality. It is in this realm that he feels . . . most helpless to cope with his own need, except by demanding that the woman serve him. This childish demand on his part and the equally undeveloped maternal wish to give on hers, may serve on a low level . . . to produce an alliance between a man and a woman which passes for relationship. But when a necessity arises for something more mature in the situation between them . . . the man may be compelled to recognize that the woman is something more than the reciprocal of his need. . . . When she refuses any longer to mother him, no longer repressing her own needs in her determination to fulfill his, he will find himself faced with the necessity of meeting the reality of the situation. . . . The loss of the phallus refers to the necessity for the man to give up his demand that the woman satisfy his sexual and emotional needs as if she were his mother.[44]

Harding is saying that the maternal emotions can hold the mother in arrest as much as the son. But maternal altruism is the one quality universally approved and supported in women. The son may be ritually passed over into manhood, or his later difficulties may be blamed on his mother's excessive love and protectiveness, but *she* gets little support in her efforts to achieve a separation.

Harding, like other Jungians, fails to give full weight to the pressure on all women—not only mothers—to remain in a "giving," assenting, maternalistic relationship to men. The cost of refusing to do so, even in casual relationships or conversations, is often to be labeled "hostile," a "ball-breaker," a "castrating bitch." A plain fact cleanly spoken by a woman's tongue is not infrequently perceived as a cutting blade directed at a man's genitals.

And women too reinforce in each other a "mothering" attitude toward men. Often one woman's advice to another on relationships with men will be worded in terms of the treatment of children. "[Our] attitude can influence men's perception of themselves, so that they conform to it. In other words—as in dealing with children—if you say to a child 'You're mean!' he or she will agree, internalize your judgment, and get mean!" a sensitive and learned woman writes to me. In fact, one of the most insidious patterns between the sexes is the common equation, by women, of man with child. It is infantilizing to men, and it has meant a trapping of female energy which can hardly be calculated.

Mary Daly has noted that men perceive the new presence of women to each other as an absence.[45] This is the real separation they dread—that women should not be waiting there for them when they return from the male group, the hierarchies, the phallic world. This fear of women communing with each other, when not expressed as ridicule or contempt, often takes the overt forms of "Don't leave me!"—the man beseeching the woman who is finding her spiritual and political community with other women. "Any really creative vision of new ways, of a new society, ought to and will have to include men," a troubled friend writes to me, on the letterhead of one of the most sexist institutions in the United States. He fears a loss of "humanity" when women speak and listen to women. I suspect that what he really fears is the absence of humanity among men, the cerebral divisions of the male group, the undeveloped affections between man and man, the ruthless pursuit of goals, the defensive male bonding which goes only skin-deep. Underneath it all I hear the cry of the man-child: "Mother! Don't leave me!"

And, men fear the loss of privilege. It is all too evident that the majority of "concerned" or "profeminist" men secretly hope that "liberation" will give them the right to shed tears while still exercising their old prerogatives. Frantz Fanon de-

scribes the case of a European police inspector engaged in tor-
turing Algerian revolutionaries, who suffered from mental disorder and pain so serious that his family life became gravely
disturbed, and who came for psychiatric treatment.

> This man knew perfectly well that his disorders were directly
> caused by the kind of activity that went on inside the rooms
> where interrogations were carried out. . . . As he could not
> see his way to stopping torturing people (that made nonsense
> to him for in that case he would have to resign) he asked me
> without beating about the bush to help him go on torturing
> Algerian patriots without any prickings of conscience, without
> any behavior problems, and with complete equanimity.[46]

Men are increasingly aware that their disorders may have something to do with patriarchy. But few of them wish to resign
from it. The women's movement is still seen in terms of the
mother-child relationship: either as a punishment and abandonment of men for past bad behavior, or as a potential healing of
men's pain by women, a new form of maternalism, in which
little by little, through gentle suasion, women with a new
vision will ease men into a more humane and sensitive life. In
short, that women will go on doing for men what men cannot
or will not do for each other or themselves.

The question, "What do we want for our sons?" ultimately
does become, what do we want for men and what will we demand of them? (As I write these words, most women in the
world are far too preoccupied with the immediate effects of
patriarchy on their lives—too-large families, inadequate or non-
existent child-care, malnutrition, enforced seclusion, lack of
education, inadequate wages due to sex discrimination—to
demand anything, or to ask this question; but that fact does
not render the question either reactionary or trivial.) The question of first priority is, of course, what do we want for ourselves? But, whether we are childed or childless, married, divorced, lesbian, celibate, token women, feminists, or separatists,
the other question is still with us.

If I could have one wish for my own sons, it is that they
should have the courage of women. I mean by this something
very concrete and precise: the courage I have seen in women
who, in their private and public lives, both in the interior world

of their dreaming, thinking, and creating, and the outer world of patriarchy, are taking greater and greater risks, both psychic and physical, in the evolution of a new vision. Sometimes this involves tiny acts of immense courage; sometimes public acts which can cost a woman her job or her life; often it involves moments, or long periods, of thinking the unthinkable, being labeled, or feeling, crazy; always a loss of traditional securities. Every woman who takes her life into her own hands does so knowing that she must expect enormous pain, inflicted both from within and without. I would like my sons not to shrink from this kind of pain, not to settle for the old male defenses, including that of a fatalistic self-hatred. And I would wish them to do this not for me, or for other women, but for themselves, and for the sake of life on the planet Earth.

In 1890 Olive Schreiner related a parable in which a woman is trying to cross a deep, fordless river into the land of freedom. She wants to carry with her the male infant suckling at her breast, but she is told, No, you will lose your life trying to save him; he must grow into a man and save himself, and then you will meet him on the other side.[47] We infantilize men and deceive ourselves when we try to make these changes easy and unthreatening for them. We are going to have to put down the grown-up male children we have carried in our arms, against our breasts, and move on, trusting ourselves and them enough to do so. And, yes, we will have to expect their anger, their cries of "Don't leave me!", their reprisals.

This is not the place, nor am I the person, to draw blueprints for the assimilation of men in large numbers into a comprehensive system of child-care, although I believe that would be the most revolutionary priority that any male group could set itself. It would not only change the expectations children—and therefore men—have of women and men; nor would it simply break down gender-roles and diversify the work-patterns of both sexes; it would change the entire community's relationship to childhood. In learning to give care to children, men would have to cease being children; the privileges of fatherhood could not be toyed with, as they now are, without an equal share in the full experience of nurture. I can see many difficulties and dangers in integrating men into the full child-rearing process; looming first is the old notion that child-care, because it has been women's work, is passive, low-level, nonwork; or that it is simply "fun." Close behind this comes the undeveloped capacity for sympathetic identification in men. I also believe that many women would prefer that even in a comprehensive day-care system, women remain the prime carers for children—for a variety of reasons, not all of them short-sighted or traditional. Women, at all events, must and will take the leadership in demanding, drafting, and implementing such a profound structural and human change. In order to do so we will have to possess more consciously our own realms of unconscious, preverbal knowledge as mothers, biological or not. Perhaps for a long time men will need a kind of compensatory education in the things about which their education as males has left them illiterate.

Meanwhile, in the realm of personal relationships, if men are to begin to share in the "work of love" we will have to change our ways of loving them. This means, among other things, that we cease praising and being grateful to the fathers of our children when they take some partial share in their care and nurture. (No woman is considered "special" because she carries out her responsibilities as a parent; not to do so is considered a social crime.) It also means that we cease treating men as if their egos were of eggshell, or as if the preservation of a masculine ego at the expense of an equal relationship were even desirable. It means that we begin to expect of men, as we do of women, that they can behave like our equals without being applauded for it or singled out as "exceptional"; and that we refuse them the traditional separation between "love" and "work."

They will not, for a long time, see this as a new form of love. We will be told we are acting and speaking out of hatred; that we are becoming "like them"; that they will perish emotionally without our constant care and attention. But through centuries of suckling men emotionally at our breasts we have also been told that we were polluted, devouring, domineering, masochistic, harpies, bitches, dykes, and whores.

We are slowly learning to discredit these recitals, including the one that begins, "Mothers are more real than other women."

IX MOTHERHOOD AND DAUGHTERHOOD

Mother
I write home
I am alone and
give me my body back.
—Susan Griffin

A folder lies open beside me as I start to write, spilling out references and quotations, all relevant probably, but none of which can help me to begin. This is the core of my book, and I enter it as a woman who, born between her mother's legs, has time after time and in different ways tried to return to her mother, to repossess her and be repossessed by her, to find the mutual confirmation from and with another woman that daughters and mothers alike hunger for, pull away from, make possible or impossible for each other.

The first knowledge any woman has of warmth, nourishment, tenderness, security, sensuality, mutuality, comes from her mother. That earliest enwrapment of one female body with another can sooner or later be denied or rejected, felt as choking possessiveness, as rejection, trap, or taboo; but it is, at the beginning, the whole world. Of course, the male infant also first knows tenderness, nourishment, mutuality from a female body. But institutionalized heterosexuality and institutionalized motherhood demand that the girl-child transfer those first feelings of dependency, eroticism, mutuality, from her first woman to a man, if she is to become what is defined as a "normal" woman —that is, a woman whose most intense psychic and physical energies are directed towards men.*

I saw my own mother's menstrual blood before I saw my own. Hers was the first female body I ever looked at, to know what women were, what I was to be. I remember taking baths with her in the hot summers of early childhood, playing with her in the cool water. As a young child I thought how beautiful she was; a print of Botticelli's Venus on the wall, half-smiling, hair flowing, associated itself in my mind with her. In early adolescence I still glanced slyly at my mother's body, vaguely imagining: I too shall have breasts, full hips, hair between my thighs—whatever that meant to me then, and with all the ambivalence of such a thought. And there were other thoughts: I too shall marry, have children—but *not like her*. I shall find a way of doing it all differently.

My father's tense, narrow body did not seize my imagination, though authority and control ran through it like electric filaments. I used to glimpse his penis dangling behind a loosely tied bathrobe. But I had understood very early that he and my mother were different. It was his voice, presence, style, that seemed to pervade the household. I don't remember when it was that my mother's feminine sensuousness, the reality of her body, began to give way for me to the charisma of my father's assertive mind and temperament; perhaps when my sister was just born, and he began teaching me to read.

My mother's very name had a kind of magic for me as a child: Helen. I still think it one of the most beautiful of names. Reading Greek mythology, while very young, I somehow identified Helen my mother with Helen of Troy; or perhaps even more with Poe's "Helen," which my father liked to quote:

> Helen, thy beauty is to me
> Like those Nicean barks of yore,
> That gently, o'er a perfumed sea,

* At the risk of seeming repetitious, I will note here, again, that the *institution* of heterosexuality, with its social rewards and punishments, its role-playing, and its sanctions against "deviance," is not the same thing as a human experience freely chosen and lived.

The weary, wayworn wanderer bore
To his own native shore . . .

She was, Helen my mother, *my* native shore of course; I think
that in that poem I first heard my own longings, the longings
of the female child, expressed by a male poet, in the voice of
a man—my father.

My father talked a great deal of beauty and the need for perfection. He felt the female body to be impure; he did not like
its natural smells. His incorporeality was a way of disengaging
himself from that lower realm where women sweated, excreted,
grew bloody every month, became pregnant. (My mother became aware, in the last months of pregnancy, that he always
looked away from her body.) He was perhaps very Jewish in
this, but also very southern: the "pure" and therefore bloodless
white woman was supposed to be a kind of gardenia, blanched
by the moonlight, staining around the edges when touched.

But the early pleasure and reassurance I found in my mother's
body was, I believe, an imprinting never to be wholly erased,
even in those years when, as my father's daughter, I suffered
the obscure bodily self-hatred peculiar to women who view
themselves through the eyes of men. I trusted the pleasures I
could get from my own body even at a time when masturbation
was an unspeakable word. Doubtless my mother would have actively discouraged such pleasures had she known about them.
Yet I cannot help but feel that I finally came to love my own
body through first having loved hers, that this was a profound
matrilineal bequest. I knew I was not an incorporeal intellect.
My mind and body might be divided, as if between father and
mother; but *I had both.*

Mothers and daughters have always exchanged with each
other—beyond the verbally transmitted lore of female survival
—a knowledge that is subliminal, subversive, preverbal: the
knowledge flowing between two alike bodies, one of which has
spent nine months inside the other. The experience of giving
birth stirs deep reverberations of her mother in a daughter;
women often dream of their mothers during pregnancy and
labor. Alice Rossi suggests that in first breast-feeding her own
child a woman may be stirred by the remembered smell of her

own mother's milk. About menstruation, some daughters feel a womanly closeness with their mothers even where the relationship is generally painful and conflicted.[1]

2

It is hard to write about my own mother. Whatever I do write, it is my story I am telling, my version of the past. If she were to tell her own story other landscapes would be revealed. But in my landscape or hers, there would be old, smoldering patches of deep-burning anger. Before her marriage, she had trained seriously for years both as a concert pianist and a composer. Born in a southern town, mothered by a strong, frustrated woman, she had won a scholarship to study with the director at the Peabody Conservatory in Baltimore, and by teaching at girls' schools had earned her way to further study in New York, Paris, and Vienna. From the age of sixteen, she had been a young belle, who could have married at any time, but she also possessed unusual talent, determination, and independence for her time and place. She read—and reads—widely and wrote—as her journals from my childhood and her letters of today reveal—with grace and pungency.

She married my father after a ten years' engagement during which he finished his medical training and began to establish himself in academic medicine. Once married, she gave up the possibility of a concert career, though for some years she went on composing, and she is still a skilled and dedicated pianist. My father, brilliant, ambitious, possessed by his own drive, assumed that she would give her life over to the enhancement of his. She would manage his household with the formality and grace becoming to a medical professor's wife, though on a limited budget; she would "keep up" her music, though there was no question of letting her composing and practice conflict with her duties as a wife and mother. She was supposed to bear him two children, a boy and a girl. She had to keep her household books to the last penny—I still can see the big blue gray ledgers, inscribed in her clear, strong hand; she marketed by streetcar, and later, when they could afford a car, she drove my father to and from his laboratory or lectures, often awaiting him for hours. She raised two children, and taught us all our lessons, including music. (Neither of us was sent to school until the fourth grade.) I am sure that she was made to feel responsible for all our imperfections.

My father, like the transcendentalist Bronson Alcott, believed that he (or rather, his wife) could raise children according to his unique moral and intellectual plan, thus proving to the world the values of enlightened, unorthodox child-rearing. I believe that my mother, like Abigail Alcott, at first genuinely and enthusiastically embraced the experiment, and only later found that in carrying out my father's intense, perfectionist program, she was in conflict with her deep instincts as a mother. Like Abigail Alcott, too, she must have found that while ideas might be unfolded by her husband, their daily, hourly practice was going to be up to her. (" 'Mr. A. aids me in general principles, but nobody can aid me in the detail,' she mourned. . . . Moreover her husband's views kept her constantly wondering if she were doing a good job. 'Am I doing what is right? Am I doing enough? Am I doing too much?' " The appearance of "temper" and "will" in Louisa, the second Alcott daughter, was blamed by her father on her inheritance from her mother.[2]) Under the institution of motherhood, the mother is the first to blame if theory proves unworkable in practice, or if anything whatsoever goes wrong. But even earlier, my mother had failed at one part of the plan: she had not produced a son.

For years, I felt my mother had chosen my father over me, had sacrificed me to his needs and theories. When my first child was born, I was barely in communication with my parents. I had been fighting my father for my right to an emotional life and a selfhood beyond his needs and theories. We were all at a draw. Emerging from the fear, exhaustion, and alienation of my first childbirth, I could not admit even to myself that I wanted my mother, let alone tell her how much I wanted her. When she visited me in the hospital neither of us could uncoil the obscure lashings of feeling that darkened the room, the tangled thread running backward to where she had labored for three days to give birth to me, and I was not a son. Now, twenty-six years later, I lay in a contagious hospital with my allergy, my skin covered with a mysterious rash, my lips and eyelids swollen, my body bruised and sutured, and, in a cot beside my bed, slept the perfect, golden, male child I had brought forth. How could I have interpreted her feelings when I could not begin to decipher my own? My body had spoken all too eloquently, but it was, medically, just my body. I wanted her to mother me again, to hold my baby in her arms as she had once held me; but that baby was also a gauntlet flung down: *my son*. Part of me longed to offer him for her blessing; part of me wanted to hold him up as a badge of victory in our tragic, unnecessary rivalry as women.

But I was only at the beginning. I know now as I could not possibly know then, that among the tangle of feelings between us, in that crucial yet unreal meeting, was her guilt. Soon I would begin to understand the full weight and burden of maternal guilt, that daily, nightly, hourly, *Am I doing what is right? Am I doing enough? Am I doing too much?* The institution of motherhood finds all mothers more or less guilty of having failed their children; and my mother, in particular, had been expected to help create, according to my father's plan, a perfect daughter. This "perfect" daughter, though gratifyingly precocious, had early been given to tics and tantrums, had become permanently lame from arthritis at twenty-two; she had finally resisted her father's Victorian paternalism, his seductive charm and controlling cruelty, had married a divorced graduate student, had begun to write "modern," "obscure," "pessimistic" poetry, lacking the fluent sweetness of Tennyson, had had the final temerity to get pregnant and bring a living baby into the world. She had ceased to be the demure and precocious child or the poetic, seducible adolescent. Something, in my father's view, had gone terribly wrong. I can imagine that whatever else my mother felt (and I know that part of her *was* mutely on my side) she also was made to feel blame. Beneath the "numbness" that she has since told me she experienced at that time, I can imagine the guilt of Everymother, because I have known it myself.

But I did not know it yet. And it is difficult for me to write of my mother now, because I have known it too well. I struggle to describe what it felt like to be her daughter, but I find myself divided, slipping under her skin; a part of me identifies too much with her. I know deep reservoirs of anger toward her still exist: the anger of a four-year-old locked in the closet (my father's orders, but my mother carried them out) for childish misbehavior; the anger of a six-year-old kept too long at piano practice (again, at his insistence, but it was she who gave the lessons) till I developed a series of facial tics. (As a mother I know what a child's facial tic is—a lancet of guilt and pain running through one's own body.) And I still feel the anger of a daughter, pregnant, wanting my mother desperately and feeling she had gone over to the enemy.

And I know there must be deep reservoirs of anger in her; every mother has known overwhelming, unacceptable anger at her children. When I think of the conditions under which my mother became a mother, the impossible expectations, my father's distaste for pregnant women, his hatred of all that he could not control, my anger at her dissolves into grief and anger *for* her, and then dissolves back again into anger at her: the ancient, unpurged anger of the child.

My mother lives today as an independent woman, which she was always meant to be. She is a much-loved, much-admired grandmother, an explorer in new realms; she lives in the present and future, not the past. I no longer have fantasies— they are the unhealed child's fantasies, I think—of some infinitely healing conversation with her, in which we could show all our wounds, transcend the pain we have shared as mother and daughter, say everything at last. But in writing these pages, I am admitting, at least, how important her existence is and has been for me.

For it was too simple, early in the new twentieth-century wave of feminism, for us to analyze our mothers' oppression, to understand "rationally"—and correctly—why our mothers did not teach us to be Amazons, why they bound our feet or simply left us. It was accurate and even radical, that analysis; and yet, like all politics narrowly interpreted, it assumed that consciousness knows everything. There was, is, in most of us, a girl-child still longing for a woman's nurture, tenderness, and approval, a woman's power exerted in our defense, a woman's smell and touch and voice, a woman's strong arms around us in moments of fear and pain. Any of us would have longed for a mother who had chosen, in Christabel Pankhurst's words, that "reckoning the cost [of her suffragist activism] in advance, Mother prepared to pay it, for women's sake."[3] It was not enough to *understand* our mothers; more than ever, in the effort to touch our own strength as women, we *needed* them. The cry of that female child in us need not be shameful or regressive; it is the germ of our desire to create a world in which strong mothers and strong daughters will be a matter of course.

We need to understand this double vision or we shall never understand ourselves. Many of us were mothered in ways we cannot yet even perceive; we only know that our mothers were in some incalculable way on our side. But if a mother had deserted us, by dying, or putting us up for adoption, or because life had driven her into alcohol or drugs, chronic depression or madness, if she had been forced to leave us with indifferent, uncaring strangers in order to earn our food money, because institutional motherhood makes no provision for the wage-earning mother; if she had tried to be a "good mother" according to the demands of the institution and had thereby turned into an anxious, worrying, puritanical keeper of our virginity; or if she had simply left us because she needed to live without a child—whatever our rational forgiveness, whatever the individual mother's love and strength, the child in us, the small female who grew up in a male-controlled world, still feels, at moments, wildly unmothered. When we can confront and unravel this paradox, this contradiction, face to the utmost in ourselves the groping passion of that little girl lost, we can begin to transmute it, and the blind anger and bitterness that have repetitiously erupted among women trying to build a movement together can be alchemized. Before sisterhood, there was the knowledge—transitory, fragmented, perhaps, but original and crucial—of mother-and-daughterhood.

3

This cathexis between mother and daughter—essential, distorted, misused—is the great unwritten story. Probably there is nothing in human nature more resonant with charges than the flow of energy between two biologically alike bodies, one of

which has lain in amniotic bliss inside the other, one of which
has labored to give birth to the other. The materials are here
for the deepest mutuality and the most painful estrangement.
Margaret Mead offers the possibility of "deep biochemical
affinities between the mother and the female child, and con-
trasts between the mother and the male child, of which we now
know nothing."[4] Yet this relationship has been minimized and
trivialized in the annals of patriarchy. Whether in theological
doctrine or art or sociology or psychoanalytic theory, it is the
mother and son who appear as the eternal, determinative dyad.
Small wonder, since theology, art, and social theory have been
produced by sons. Like intense relationships between women in
general, the relationship between mother and daughter has been
profoundly threatening to men.

A glance at ancient texts would suggest that daughters barely
existed. What the son means to the father is abundantly expressed, in the Upanishads:

> [The woman] nourishes her husband's self, the son, within
> her. . . . The father elevates the child even before the birth,
> and immediately after, by nourishing the mother and by per-
> forming ceremonies. When he thus elevates the child . . . he
> really elevates his second self, for the continuation of these
> worlds. . . . This is his second birth.

Aten, or Atum, is hailed in the Egyptian hymn:

> Creator of seed in women,
> Thou who makes fluid into man,
> Who maintainest the son in the womb of the mother. . . .

And Jewish traditional lore has it that a female soul is united
with a male sperm, resulting in, of course, a "man-child."[5]

Daughters have been nullified by silence, but also by infanticide, of which they have everywhere been the primary victims.
"Even a rich man always exposes a daughter." Lloyd deMause
suggests that the statistical imbalance of males over females
from antiquity into the Middle Ages resulted from the routine
practice of killing off female infants. Daughters were destroyed
not only by their fathers, but by their mothers. A husband of
the first century B.C. writes to his wife as a matter of course: "If,

as well may happen, you give birth to a child, if it is a boy let it live; if it is a girl, expose it."⁶* Given the long prevalence of this practice, it is no wonder if a mother dreaded giving birth to a female like herself. While the father might see himself as "twice-born" in his son, such a "second birth" was denied the mothers of daughters.

In *To the Lighthouse* Virginia Woolf created what is still the most complex and passionate vision of mother-daughter schism in modern literature. It is significantly, one of the very few literary documents in which a woman has portrayed her mother as a central figure. Mrs. Ramsay is a kaleidoscopic character, and in successive readings of the novel, she changes, almost as our own mothers alter in perspective as we ourselves are changing. The feminist scholar Jane Lilienfeld has pointed out that during Virginia's early years her mother, Julia Stephen, expended almost all her maternal energies in caring for her husband and his lifework, the *Dictionary of National Biography*. Both Virginia and her sister Vanessa were later to seek each other for mothering, and Lilienfeld suggests that Leonard Woolf was to provide Virginia with the kind of care and vigilance that her mother had given her father.⁷ In any case, Mrs. Ramsay, with her "strange severity, her extreme courtesy" her attentiveness to others' needs (chiefly those of men), her charismatic attractiveness, even as a woman of fifty who had borne eight children—Mrs. Ramsay is no simple idealization. She is the "delicious fecundity . . . [the] fountain and spray of life [into which] the fatal sterility of the male plunged itself"; at the same time that "she felt this thing that she called life terrible, hostile, and quick to pounce on you if you gave it a chance."

She perceives "without hostility, the sterility of men," yet as Lilienfeld notes, she doesn't like women very much, and her life is spent in attunement to male needs. The young painter Lily Briscoe, sitting with her arms clasped around Mrs. Ramsay's knees, her head on her lap, longs to become one with her, in

* It can be argued that, just as infanticide in general was a form of population control and even of eugenics (twins, infants who were undersized, malformed, or otherwise abnormal were destroyed, whatever their sex), female infanticide was a way of limiting births, since females were seen primarily as breeders. Still, the implicit devaluation of the female was hardly a message to be lost on women.

"the chambers of the mind and heart of the woman who was, physically, touching her. . . . Could loving, as people called it, make her and Mrs. Ramsay one? for it was not knowledge but unity that she desired, not inscriptions on tablets, nothing that could be written in any language known to men, but intimacy itself . . ."

Yet nothing happens. Mrs. Ramsay is not available to her. And since Woolf has clearly transcribed herself into Lily Briscoe, the scene has a double charge: the daughter seeking intimacy with her own mother, the woman seeking intimacy with another woman, not her mother but toward whom she turns those passionate longings. Much later she understands that it is only in her work that she can "stand up to Mrs. Ramsay" and her "extraordinary power." In her work, she can reject the grouping of Mrs. Ramsay and James, "mother and son," as a pictorial subject. Through her work, Lily is independent of men, as Mrs. Ramsay is not. In the most acute, unembittered ways, Woolf pierces the shimmer of Mrs. Ramsay's personality; she needs men as much as they need her, her power and strength are founded on the dependency, the "sterility" of others.

It is clear that Virginia the daughter had pondered Julia her mother for years before depicting her in *To the Lighthouse*. Again, that fascinated attention is ascribed to Lily Briscoe:

> Fifty pairs of eyes were not enough to get around that one woman with, she thought. Among them, must be one that was stone blind to her beauty. One wanted some most secret sense, fine as air, with which to steal through keyholes and surround her where she sat knitting, talking, sitting silent in the window alone; which took to itself and treasured up like the air which held the smoke of the steamer, her thoughts, her imaginations, her desires. What did the hedge mean to her, what did the garden mean to her, what did it mean to her when a wave broke?[8]

And this, precisely, is what Virginia the artist achieved; but the achievement is testimony not merely to the power of her art but to the passion of the daughter for the mother, her need above all to understand this woman, so adored and so unavailable to her; to understand, in all complexity, the differences that separated her mother from herself.

The woman activist or artist born of a family-centered mother may in any case feel that her mother cannot understand or sympathize with the imperatives of her life; or that her mother has preferred and valued a more conventional daughter, or a son. In order to study nursing, Florence Nightingale was forced to battle, in the person of her mother, the restrictive conventions of upper-class Victorian womanhood, the destiny of a life in drawing rooms and country houses in which she saw women going mad "for want of something to do."[9] The painter Paula Modersohn-Becker was, throughout her life, concerned—and fearful—that her mother might not accept the terms of her life. Writing in 1899 of her struggles with her work, she says: "I write this especially for mother. I think she feels that my life is one long continuous egoistic drunken joyousness." On leaving her husband she writes: "I was so fearful that you might have been angry. . . . And now you are so good to me. . . . You, my dearest mother, stay by me and bless my life." And, the year before her own death in childbirth:

> . . . I am in continuous tumult, always . . . only sometimes resting, then moving again towards a goal . . . I beg of you to keep this in mind when at times I seem unloving. It means that all my strength is concentrated towards one thing only. I do not know whether this should be called egotism. If so, it is the most noble.

> I put my head in the lap from which I came forth, and thank you for my life.[10]

Emily Dickinson's famous statement that "I never had a mother" has been variously interpreted; but surely she meant in part that she felt herself deviant, set apart, from the kind of life her mother lived; that what most concerned her, her mother could not understand. Yet when her mother suffered a paralytic stroke in 1875, both Dickinson sisters nursed her tenderly until her death in 1882, and in a letter of that year Emily Dickinson writes:

> . . . the departure of our Mother is so bleak a surprise, we are both benumbed . . . only the night before she died, she was happy and hungry and ate a little Supper I made her with so much enthusiasm, I laughed with delight . . .

Wondering with sorrow, how we could spare our lost Neighbors
[her correspondents] our first Neighbor, our Mother, quietly
stole away.

Plundered of her dear face, we scarcely know each other, and
feel as if wrestling with a Dream, waking would dispel . . .

And the daughter's letter ends with the poet's cry: "Oh, Vision
of Language!"[11]

"Between Sylvia and me existed—as between my own mother
and me—a sort of psychic osmosis which, at times, was very
wonderful and comforting; at other times an unwelcome in-
vasion of privacy." This is Aurelia Plath's description of the
relationship between herself and her daughter Sylvia, from the
other side. The intensity of the relationship seems to have
disturbed some readers of Plath's *Letters Home*, an outpour-
ing chiefly to her mother, written weekly or oftener, first
from college and later from England. There is even a tendency
to see this mother-daughter relationship as the source of Sylvia
Plath's early suicide attempt, her relentless perfectionism and
obsession with "greatness." Yet the preface to *Letters Home*
reveals a remarkable woman, a true survivor; it was Plath's
father who set the example of self-destructiveness. The letters
are far from complete* and until many more materials are released, efforts to write Plath biography and criticism are ques-
tionable at best. But throughout runs her need to lay in her
mother's lap, as it were, poems and prizes, books and babies, the
longing for her mother when she is about to give birth, the effort
to let Aurelia Plath know that her struggles and sacrifices to
rear her daughter had been vindicated. In the last letters Sylvia
seems to be trying to shield herself and Aurelia, an ocean away,
from the pain of that "psychic osmosis." "I haven't the strength
to see you for some time," she writes, explaining why she will not
come to America after her divorce. "The horror of what you saw
and what I saw you see last summer is between us and I cannot
face you again until I have a new life . . ." (October 9, 1962).
Three days later: "Do tear up my last one . . . I have [had] an
incredible change of spirit. . . . Every morning, when my sleep-

* There are many elisions and omissions, since publication had to be
approved by Ted Hughes, Sylvia's husband.

ing pill wears off, I am up about five, in my study with coffee, writing like mad—have managed a poem a day before break-fast. . . . Terrific stuff, as if domesticity had choked me. . . . Nick [her son] has two teeth, stands, and is an *angel* . . ." (October 12, 1962).[12]

Psychic osmosis. Desperate defenses. The power of the bond often denied because it cracks consciousness, threatens at times to lead the daughter back into "those secret chambers . . . be-coming, like waters poured into one jar, inextricably the same, one with the object one adored . . ."[13] Or, because there is no indifference or cruelty we can tolerate less, than the indifference or cruelty of our mothers.

In *The Well of Loneliness*, a novel by now discredited for its pathological-tragic view of lesbianism (yet still popularly viewed as *the* novel on the subject), Radclyffe Hall suggests an almost preternatural antipathy between Anna Gordon and her lesbian daughter Stephen. It is Stephen's father who—through having read Krafft-Ebbing—"understands" her, and treats her as he might a tragically maimed son. Her mother views her from the first as a stranger, an interloper, an alien creature. Radclyffe Hall's novel is painful as a revelation of the author's self-rejection, her internalizing of received opinions against her own instincts. The crux of her self-hatred lies in her imagining no possible relationship between Anna the mother and Stephen the daughter. Yet there is one passage in which she suggests the longing for and possibility of connection between mother and daughter—a connection founded on physical sensation:

The scents of the meadows would move those two strangely. . . . Sometimes Stephen must tug at her mother's sleeve sharply—intolerable to bear that thick fragrance alone!

One day she had said: "Stand still or you'll hurt it—it's all round us—it's a white smell, it reminds me of you!" And then she had flushed, and had glanced up quickly, rather frightened in case she should find Anna laughing.

But her mother had looked at her curiously, gravely, puzzled by this creature who seemed all contradictions. . . . Anna had been stirred, as her child had been stirred, by the breath of the meadowsweet under the hedges; for in this way they were one,

the mother and daughter . . . could they only have divined it,
such simple things might have formed a link between them . . .

They had gazed at each other as though asking for something
. . . the one from the other; then the moment had passed—
they had walked on in silence, no nearer in spirit than before.[14]

A woman who feels an unbridgeable gulf between her mother
and herself may be forced to assume that her mother—like
Stephen's—could never accept her sexuality. But, despite the
realities of popular ignorance and bigotry about lesbians, and
the fear that *she* has somehow "damaged" her daughter in the
eyes of society, the mother may at some level—mute, indirect,
oblique—want to confirm that daughter in her love for women.
Mothers who have led perfectly traditional, heterosexual lives
have welcomed their daughters' women lovers and supported
their domestic arrangements, though often denying, if asked,
the nature of the relationship. A woman who fully and gladly
accepts her love for another woman is likely to create an
atmosphere in which her mother will not reject her. But that
acceptance has first to be found in ourselves; it does not come as
an act of will.

For those of us who had children, and later came to recognize
and act upon the breadth and depth of our feelings for women,
a complex new bond with our mothers is possible. The poet
Sue Silvermarie writes:

I find now, instead of a contradiction between lesbian and
mother, there is an overlapping. What is the same between my
lover and me, my mother and me, and my son and me is the
motherbond—primitive, all-encompassing, and paramount.

In loving another woman I discovered the deep urge to both be
a mother to and find a mother in my lover. At first I feared the
discovery. Everything around me told me it was evil. Popular
Freudianism cursed it as a fixation, a sign of immaturity. But
gradually I came to have faith in my own needs and desires.
. . . Now I treasure and trust the drama between two loving
women, in which each can become mother and each become
child.

It is most clear during lovemaking, when the separation of
everyday life lifts for awhile. When I kiss and stroke and enter

my lover, I am also a child re-entering my mother. I want to return to the womb-state of harmony, and also to the ancient world. I enter my lover but it is she in her orgasm who returns. I see on her face for a long moment, the unconscious bliss that an infant carries the memory of behind its shut eyes. Then when it is she who makes love to me . . . the intensity is also a pushing out, a borning! She comes in and is then identified with the ecstasy that is born. . . . So I too return to the mystery of my mother, and of the world as it must have been when the motherbond was exalted.

Now I am ready to go back and understand the one whose body actually carried me. Now I can begin to learn about her, forgive her for the rejection I felt, yearn for her, ache for her. I could never want her until I myself had been wanted. By a woman. Now I know what it is to feel exposed as a newborn, to be pared down to my innocence. To lie with a woman and give her the power of my utter fragility. To have that power be cherished. Now that I know, I can return to her who could not cherish me as I needed. I can return without blame, and I can hope that she is ready for me.[15]

In studying the diaries and letters of American women of thirty-five families, from the 1760s to the 1880s, the historian Carroll Smith-Rosenberg has traced a pattern—indeed, a network—of close, sometimes explicitly sensual, long-lasting female friendships characteristic of the period. Tender, devoted, these relationships persisted through separations caused by the marriage of one or both women, in the context of a "female world" distinctly separate from the larger world of male concerns, but in which women held a paramount importance in each others' lives.

Smith-Rosenberg finds

. . . an intimate mother-daughter relationship . . . at the heart of this female world. . . . Central to these relationships is what might be described as an apprenticeship system . . . mothers and other older women carefully trained daughters in the arts of housewifery and motherhood . . . adolescent girls temporarily took over the household . . . and helped in childbirth, nursing and weaning . . .

Daughters were born into a female world. . . . As long as the mother's domestic role remained relatively stable and few viable alternatives competed with it, daughters tended to accept their mother's world and to turn automatically to other women for support and intimacy . . .

One could speculate at length concerning the absence of that mother-daughter hostility today considered almost inevitable to an adolescent's struggle for autonomy. . . . It is possible that taboos against female aggression . . . were sufficiently strong to repress even that between mothers and their adolescent daughters. Yet these letters seem so alive and the interest of daughters in their mothers' affairs so vital and genuine that it is difficult to interpret their closeness exclusively in terms of repression and denial.[16]

What the absence of such a female world meant on the newly opening frontier can be grasped from the expressions of loneliness and nostalgia of immigrant women from Europe, who had left such networks of friends, mothers, and sisters far behind. Many of these women remained year-in, year-out on the homesteads, waiting eagerly for letters from home, fighting a peculiarly female battle with loneliness. "If I only had a few good women friends, I would be entirely satisfied. Those I miss," writes a Wisconsin woman in 1846. Instead of giving birth and raising children near her mother or other female relatives, the frontier mother had no one close to her with whom to share her womanly experiences; if cholera or diphtheria carried off a child or children, she would have to face the rituals of death and mourning on her own. Loneliness, unshared grief, and guilt often led to prolonged melancholy or mental breakdown.[17] If the frontier offered some women a greater equality and independence, and the chance to break out of more traditional roles, it also, ironically, deprived many of the emotional support and intimacy of a female community; it tore them from their mothers.

It may also seem ironic that the growth of nineteenth-century feminism, the false "liberation" (to smoke cigarettes and sleep around) of the twentieth-century flapper, the beginnings of new options for women as birth control gained in acceptance and use, may have had the initial effect of weakening the mother-daughter tie (and with it, the network of intense female friendships based on a common life-pattern and common expectancies). By the 1920s, and with the increasing pervasiveness of Freudian thought, intense female friendships could be tolerated between schoolgirls as "crushes," but were regarded as regressive and neurotic if they persisted into later life.*

4

"Matrophobia" as the poet Lynn Sukenick has termed it[18] is the fear not of one's mother or of motherhood but of *becoming one's mother*. Thousands of daughters see their mothers as having taught a compromise and self-hatred they are struggling to win free of, the one through whom the restrictions and degradations of a female existence were perforce transmitted. Easier by far to hate and reject a mother outright than to see beyond her to the forces acting upon her. But where a mother is hated to the point of matrophobia there may also be a deep underlying pull toward her, a dread that if one relaxes one's guard one will identify with her completely. An adolescent daughter may live at war with her mother yet borrow her clothes, her perfume. Her style of housekeeping when she leaves home may be a negative image of her mother's: beds never made, dishes unwashed, in unconscious reversal of the immaculately tended house of a woman from whose orbit she has to extricate herself.

While, in Grace Paley's words, "her son the doctor and her son the novelist" blame and ridicule the "Jewish mother," Jewish daughters are left with all the panic, guilt, ambivalence, and self-hatred of the woman from whom they came and the woman they may become. "Matrophobia" is a late-arrived strain in the life of the Jewish daughter. Jewish women of the *shtetl* and ghetto and of the early immigrant period supported their

* A woman of my mother's generation told me that her husband had effectively dampened her intimate friendship with another woman by telling her he was sure the woman was a lesbian. A hundred years before, their friendship would have been taken for granted, even to the husband's leaving the conjugal bed when a wife's woman friend came to visit, so that the two women could share as many hours, day and night, as possible. (See Carroll Smith-Rosenberg, "The Female World of Love and Ritual: Relations between Women in Nineteenth-Century America," *Signs*, Vol. 1, No. 1, pp. 10, 26.)

Talmud-studying men, raised children, ran the family business, trafficked with the hostile gentile world, and in every practical and active way made possible the economic and cultural survival of the Jews. Only in the later immigrant generations, with a greater assimilationism and pressure for men to take over the economic sphere, were women expected to reduce themselves to perfecting the full-time mother-housewife role already invented by the gentile middle class.

"My mother would kill me if I didn't marry." "It would kill my mother if I didn't marry." In the absence of other absorbing and valued uses for her energy, the full-time "homemaker" has often sunk, yes, into the overinvolvement, the martyrdom, the possessive control, the chronic worry over her children, caricatured in fiction through the "Jewish mother." But the "Jewish mother" is only one creation of the enforced withdrawal of nineteenth- and twentieth-century women from all roles save one.

Matrophobia can be seen as a womanly splitting of the self, in the desire to become purged once and for all of our mothers' bondage, to become individuated and free. The mother stands for the victim in ourselves, the unfree woman, the martyr. Our personalities seem dangerously to blur and overlap with our mothers'; and, in a desperate attempt to know where mother ends and daughter begins, we perform radical surgery.

> When her mother had gone, Martha cupped her hands protestingly over her stomach, and murmured to the creature within it that nothing would deform it, freedom would be its gift. She, Martha, the free spirit, would protect the creature from her, Martha, the maternal force; the maternal Martha, that enemy, would not be allowed to enter the picture.[19]

Thus Doris Lessing's heroine, who has felt devoured by her own mother, splits herself—or tries to—when she realizes she, too, is to become a mother.

But even women with children, can exist in an uneasy wariness such as Kate Chopin depicts in *The Awakening* (1899):

> . . . Mrs. Pontellier was not a mother-woman. The mother-women seemed to prevail that summer at Grand Isle. It was easy to know them, fluttering about with extended, protecting

wings when any harm, real or imaginary, threatened their precious brood. They were women who idolized their children, worshipped their husbands, and esteemed it a holy privilege to efface themselves as individuals and grow wings as ministering angels.[20]

Edna Pontellier, seeking her own pleasure and self-realization (though still entirely through men) is seen as "inadequate" as a mother, although her children are simply more independent than most. Cora Sandel sets her heroine, Alberta, against an archetypal mother-woman, Jeanne. Alberta is a writer, "haunted in recent years [by the fear] of not appearing sufficiently motherly and domesticated." She feels both reproached and wearied by the efficient, energetic Jeanne, who maintains an eye on everyone:

> "Don't forget your strengthening medicine, Pierre. Then you must lie down for awhile. You'll work all the better for it. Marthe, you've scratched yourself; don't touch anything before I've put iodine on it. You ought to look in at Mme. Poulain, Alberta, before she sells the rest of those sandshoes. . . . I don't think Tot should be in the sun for such a long time, Alberta . . .[21]

Thus, women who identify themselves primarily as mothers may seem both threatening and repellent to those who do not, or who feel unequal to the mother-role as defined by Chopin. Lily Briscoe, too, rejects this role: She does not want to *be* Mrs. Ramsay, and her discovery of this is crucial for her.

5

The loss of the daughter to the mother, the mother to the daughter, is the essential female tragedy. We acknowledge Lear (father-daughter split), Hamlet (son and mother), and Oedipus (son and mother) as great embodiments of the human tragedy; but there is no presently enduring recognition of mother-daughter passion and rapture.

There was such a recognition, but we have lost it. It was expressed in the religious mystery of Eleusis, which constituted the spiritual foundation of Greek life for two thousand years.

Based on the mother-daughter myth of Demeter and Korê, this rite was the most forbidden and secret of classical civilization, never acted on the stage, open only to initiates who underwent long purification beforehand. According to the Homeric hymn to Demeter of the seventh century B.C., the mysteries were established by the goddess herself, on her reunion with her daughter Korê, or Persephone, who had been raped and abducted, in one version of the myth by Poseidon as lord of the underworld, or, in a later version, by Hades or Pluto, king of death. Demeter revenges herself for the loss of her daughter by forbidding the grain—of which she is queen—to grow.

When her daughter is restored to her—for nine months of the year only—she restores fruitfulness and life to the land for those months. But the Homeric hymn tells us that Demeter's supreme gift to humanity, in her rejoicing at Korê's return, was not the return of vegetation, but the founding of the sacred ceremonies at Eleusis.

The Elcusinian mysteries, inaugurated somewhere between 1400 and 1100 B.C., were considered a keystone to human spiritual survival. The Homeric hymn says:

> Blessed is he among men on earth who has beheld this. Never will he who has had no part in [the Mysteries] share in such things. He will be a dead man, in sultry darkness.*

Pindar and Sophocles also distinguish between the initiate and "all the rest," the nonbeatified. And the Roman Cicero is quoted as saying of the Mysteries: "We have been given a reason not only to live in joy but also to die with better hope." The role played by the Mysteries of Eleusis in ancient spirituality has been compared to that of the passion and resurrection of Christ. But in the resurrection celebrated by the Mysteries, it is a mother whose wrath catalyzes the miracle, a daughter who rises from the underworld.

The rites of Eleusis were imitated and plagiarized in many parts of the ancient world. But the unique and sacred place, the *only* place where the true vision might be experienced, was

---

* The above rendering is from C. Kerenyi's book *Eleusis*. For a verse translation of the entire hymn to Demeter, see Thelma Sargent, *The Homeric Hymns* (New York: Norton, 1973), pp. 2–14.

the shrine at Eleusis itself. This was the site of the "Virgin's Well" or fountain where Demeter is supposed to have sat, grieving for the loss of Korê, and where she returned to establish the ceremonies. This sanctuary was destroyed, after two thousand years, when the Goths under Alaric invaded Greece in 396 A.D.

But for two thousand years, once a year in September, the *mystai* or initiands underwent purification by sea bathing, then walked in procession, carrying torches and bundles of myrtle, to Eleusis, where they finally had access to the "vision"—"the state of having seen." Pigs (animals sacred to the Great Mother) were slaughtered in sacrifice to Demeter, and eaten in her honor as a first stage in initiation. Only initiands and hierophants were allowed into the innermost shrine, where Korê appeared, called up by the voice of a thundering gong. There, in a great blaze of light, the queen of the dead, Persephone, appeared with her infant son, a sign to human beings that "birth in death *is* possible . . . if they had faith in the Goddess." The real meaning of the Mysteries was this reintegration of death and birth, at a time when patriarchal splitting may have seemed about to sever them entirely.

At the end of the ceremonies, according to C. Kerenyi, whose study of Eleusis I have drawn on for most of the above, the hierophant turned to the initiates and showed them a cut-off ear of grain:

> All who had "seen" turned, at the sight of this "concrete thing", as though turning back from the hereafter into this world, back to the world of tangible things, including grain. The grain *was* grain and not more, but it may well have summed up for the [initiates] everything that Demeter and Persephone had given to mankind: Demeter food and wealth, Persephone birth under the earth. To those who had seen Korê at Eleusis this was no mere metaphor.[22]

A marble relief of the fifth century B.C., found at Eleusis, portrays the goddesses Demeter and Korê, and between them the figure of a boy, Triptolemus. Triptolemus is the "primordial man," who must come to Demeter for her gift of the grain. According to one myth, he is converted from a violent, warlike way of life to a peaceful, agrarian one, through his initiation at Eleusis. He is supposed to have disseminated three command- ments: "Honor your parents," "Honor the gods with fruits," and "Spare the animals." But Kerenyi makes clear that Triptole- mus is not an essential figure at Eleusis.[23] Demeter as "tranquilly- enthroned" grain-goddess had existed in the archaic past, giver of fruits to man. But in her aspect as Goddess of the Mysteries she became much more: "she herself in grief and mourning entered upon the path of initiation and turned toward *the core of the Mysteries, namely, her quality as her daughter's mother.*" (Emphasis mine.)[24]

The separation of Demeter and Korê is an unwilling one; it is neither a question of the daughter's rebellion against the mother, nor the mother's rejection of the daughter. Eleusis seems to have been a final resurgence of the multiple aspects of the Great Goddess in the classical-patriarchal world. Rhea, the mother of Demeter, also appears in some of the myths; but also, Korê herself becomes a mother in the underworld.[25] Jane Harrison considered the Mysteries to be founded on a much more ancient women's rite, from which men were excluded, a possi- bility which tells us how endangered and complex the mother- daughter cathexis was, even before recorded history. Each daughter, even in the millennia before Christ, must have longed for a mother whose love for her and whose power were so great as to undo rape and bring her back from death. And every mother must have longed for the power of Demeter, the efficacy of her anger, the reconciliation with her lost self.

6

A strange and complex modern version of the Demeter-Korê myth resides in Margaret Atwood's novel, *Surfacing.* Her nar- rator—a woman without a name, who says of herself that she "can't love," "can't feel"—returns to the island in Canada where she and her family lived during World War II. She is searching for her father, who had been living there alone and has mysteriously disappeared. Her mother is dead. With her lover, and another couple, David and Anna—all more or less hippies in the American style, though professing hatred for all things Yankee—she returns to the place where her childhood was spent. She searches for clues to her father's whereabouts, in the surrounding woods and the neglected cabin. She finds old albums and scrapbooks of her childhood, saved by her mother; her mother's old leather jacket still swings from a hanger. She also finds sketches of Indian pictographs, made by her father. Her hippie friends are restless and bored in the primitive setting of the island, although they constantly express disgust with American technological imperialism. But it's the men in the novel—Canadian as well as Yankee—who are destroying the natural world, who kill for the sake of killing, cut down the trees; David brutally dominates Anna, sex is exploitative. Finally the narrator learns that her father's body has been found in the lake, drowned, evidently, while attempting to photograph some Indian wall-paintings. The others in her party are picked up by boat to return to civilization; she remains, determined to get back into connection with the place and its powers. She crawls naked through the woods, eating berries and roots, seeking her vision. Finally she returns to the cabin and its overgrown, half-wild garden, and there

. . . I see her. She is standing in front of the cabin, her hand stretched out, she is wearing her grey leather jacket; her hair is long, down to her shoulders, in the style of thirty years ago, before I was born; she is turned half away from me. I can see only the side of her face. She doesn't move, she is feeding them: one perches on her wrist, another on her shoulder.

I've stopped walking. At first I feel nothing except a lack of surprise: that is where she would be, she has been standing there all along. Then as I watch and it doesn't change I'm afraid, I'm cold with fear, I'm afraid it isn't real, paper doll cut by my eyes, burnt picture, if I blink she will vanish.

She must have sensed it, my fear. She turns her head quietly and looks at me, past me, as though she knows something is there but she can't quite see it . . .

I go up to where she was. The jays are there in the trees, cawing at me; there are a few scraps on the feeding-tray still, they've knocked some to the ground. I squint up at them, trying to see her, trying to see which one she is.

Later, she has a vision of her father in the same place:

> He has realized he was an intruder; the cabin, the fences, the
> fires and paths were violations; now his own fence excludes him,
> as logic excludes love. He wants it ended, the borders abolished,
> he wants the forest to flow back into the places his mind
> cleared: reparation . . .
>
> He turns toward me and it's not my father. It is what my father
> saw, the thing you meet when you've stayed here too long
> alone . . .
>
> I see now that although it isn't my father, it is what my father
> has become. I knew he wasn't dead . . .

Atwood's last chapter begins:

> This above all, to refuse to be a victim. Unless I can do that I
> can do nothing. I have to recant, give up the old belief that I
> am powerless and because of it nothing I can do will ever hurt
> anyone. . . . The word games, the winning and losing games
> are finished, at the moment there are no others but they will
> have to be invented. . . .[26]

She is no "free woman," no feminist; her way of dealing with
male-identification, the struggle with a male culture, has been
to numb herself, to believe she "can't love." But *Surfacing* is
not a programmatic novel. It is the work of a poet, filled with
animistic and supernatural materials. The search for the father
leads to reunion with the mother, who is at home in the wilderness, Mistress of the Animals. In some obscure, subconscious
way, Atwood's narrator begins to recognize and accept her own
power through her moment of vision, her brief, startling visitation from her mother. She has worked her way back—through
fasting and sacrifice—beyond patriarchy. She cannot stay there:
the primitive (her father's solution, the male—ultimately the
fascist—solution) is not the answer; she has to go and live out
her existence in this time. But she has had her illumination: she
has seen her mother.

7

The woman who has felt "unmothered" may seek mothers all
her life—may even seek them in men. In a women's group

recently, someone said: "I married looking for a mother"; and a number of others in the group began agreeing with her. I myself remember lying in bed next to my husband, half-dreaming, half-believing, that the body close against mine was my mother's.* Perhaps all sexual or intimate physical contact brings us back to that first body. But the "motherless" woman may also react by denying her own vulnerability, denying she has felt any loss or absence of mothering. She may spend her life proving her strength in the "mothering" of others—as with Mrs. Ramsay, mothering men, whose weakness makes her feel strong, or mothering in the role of teacher, doctor, political activist, psychotherapist. In a sense she is giving to others what she herself has lacked; but this will always mean that she needs the neediness of others in order to go on feeling her own strength. She may feel uneasy with equals—particularly women.

Few women growing up in patriarchal society can feel mothered enough; the power of our mothers, whatever their love for us and their struggles on our behalf, is too restricted. And it is the mother through whom patriarchy early teaches the small female her proper expectations. The anxious pressure of one female on another to conform to a degrading and dispiriting role can hardly be termed "mothering," even if she does this believing it will help her daughter to survive.

Many daughters live in rage at their mothers for having accepted, too readily and passively, "whatever comes." A mother's victimization does not merely humiliate her, it mutilates the daughter who watches her for clues as to what it means to be a woman. Like the traditional foot-bound Chinese woman, she passes on her own affliction. The mother's self-hatred and low expectations are the binding-rags for the psyche of the daughter. As one psychologist has observed:

* Simone de Beauvoir says of her mother that: "Generally speaking, I thought of her with no particular feeling. Yet in my sleep (although my father only made very rare and then insignificant appearances) she often played a most important part: she blended with Sartre, and we were happy together. And then the dream would turn into a nightmare: why was I living with her once more? How had I come to be in her power again? So our former relationship lived on in me in its double aspect—a subjection that I loved and hated" (*A Very Easy Death* [New York: Warner Paperback, 1973], pp. 119–20).

When a female child is passed from lap to lap so that all the males in the room (father, brother, acquaintances) can get a hard-on, it is the helpless mother standing there and looking on that creates the sense of shame and guilt in the child. One woman at the recent rape conference in New York City testified that her father put a series of watermelon rinds in her vagina when she was a child to open it up to his liking, and beat her if she tried to remove them. Yet what that woman focuses her rage on today is that her mother told her, "Never say a word about it to anyone."

Another young girl was gang-raped in her freshman year of high school and her mother said to her, "You have brought disgrace on the family. You are no good anymore." . . . When she talks about these things now, the pain is as great as if it all happened yesterday.[27]

It is not simply that such mothers feel both responsible and powerless. It is that they carry their own guilt and self-hatred over into their daughters' experiences. The mother knows that if raped *she* would *feel* guilty; hence she tells her daughter she *is* guilty. She identifies intensely with her daughter, but through weakness, not through strength. Freudian psychoanalysis has viewed the rage of daughters toward their mothers as resentment for not having been given a penis. Clara Thompson, however, remarked, in a suprisingly early political view of "penis envy" that "the penis is the sign of the person in power in one particular competitive set-up in this culture, that between man and woman. . . . So, the attitude called penis envy is similar to the attitude of any underprivileged group toward those in power."[28] A contemporary psychoanalyst points out that the daughter's rage at her mother is more likely to arise from her mother having relegated her to second-class status, while looking to the son (or father) for the fulfillment of her own thwarted needs.[29] But even where there is no preferred brother or father, a daughter can feel rage at her mother's powerlessness or lack of struggle—because of her intense identification and because in order to fight for herself she needs first to have been both loved and fought for.*

* Nancy Chodorow cites examples of communities—among the Rajput and Brahmins in India—where, although sons are considered more de-

The nurture of daughters in patriarchy calls for a strong sense of *self*-nurture in the mother. The psychic interplay between mother and daughter can be destructive, but there is no reason why it is doomed to be. A woman who has respect and affection for her own body, who does not view it as unclean or as a sex-object, will wordlessly transmit to her daughter that a woman's body is a good and healthy place to live. A woman who feels pride in being female will not visit her self-depreciation upon her female child. A woman who has used her anger creatively will not seek to suppress anger in her daughter in fear that it could become, merely, suicidal.

All this is extremely difficult in a system which has persistently stolen women's bodies and egos from us. And what can we say of mothers who have not simply been robbed of their egos but who—alcoholic, drugged, or suicidal—are unavailable to their daughters? What of a woman who has to toil so hard for survival that no maternal energy remains at the end of the day, as she numbly, wearily picks up her child after work? The child does not discern the social system or the institution of motherhood, only a harsh voice, a dulled pair of eyes, a mother who does not hold her, does not tell her how wonderful she is. And what can we say of families in which the daughter feels that it was her father, not her mother, who gave her affection and support in becoming herself? It is a painful fact that a nurturing father, who replaces rather than complements a mother, *must be loved at the mother's expense*, whatever the reasons for the mother's absence. He may be doing his best, giving everything that a man can give, but the mother is twice-lost, if love for him takes the place of love for her.

"I have always gotten more support from men than from

---

sirable, mothers show a special attachment to their daughters, and she comments that "people in both groups say that this is out of sympathy for the future plight of their daughters, who will have to leave their natal family for a strange and usually oppressive postmarital household" ("Family Structure and Feminine Personality," in M. Z. Rosaldo and L. Lamphère, eds., *Woman, Culture and Society* [Stanford, Calif.: Stanford University Press, 1974], p. 47). But this kind of female bonding, though far preferable to rejection or indifference, arises from identification with the daughter's future victimization. There is no attempt on the mothers' part to change the cycle of repetitions into which the daughters' lives are being woven.

women": a cliché of token women, and an understandable one, since we do identify gratefully with anyone who seems to have strengthened us. But who has been *in a position* to strengthen us? A man often lends his daughter the ego-support he denies his wife; he may use his daughter as stalking-horse against his wife; he may simply feel less threatened by a daughter's power, especially if she adores him. A male teacher may confirm a woman student while throttling his wife and daughters. Men have been able to give us power, support, and certain forms of nurture, as individuals, when they chose; but the power is always stolen power, withheld from the mass of women in patriarchy. And, finally, I am talking here about a kind of strength which can only be one woman's gift to another, the bloodstream of our inheritance. Until a strong line of love, confirmation, and example stretches from mother to daughter, from woman to woman across the generations, women will still be wandering in the wilderness.

8

What do we mean by the nurture of daughters? What is it we wish we had, or could have, as daughters; could give, as mothers? Deeply and primally we need trust and tenderness; surely this will always be true of every human being, but women growing into a world so hostile to us need a very profound kind of loving in order to learn to love ourselves. But this loving is not simply the old, institutionalized, sacrificial, "mother-love" which men have demanded: we want courageous mothering. The most notable fact that culture imprints on women is the sense of our limits. The most important thing one woman can do for another is to illuminate and expand her sense of actual possibilities. For a mother, this means more than contending with the reductive images of females in children's books, movies, television, the schoolroom. It means that the mother herself is trying to expand the limits of her life. *To refuse to be a victim*: and then to go on from there.

Only when we can wish imaginatively and courageously for ourselves can we wish unfetteredly for our daughters. But finally, a child is not a wish, nor a product of wishing. Women's lives—in all levels of society—have been lived too long in both depression and fantasy, while our active energies have been trained and absorbed into caring for others. It is essential, now, to begin breaking that cycle. Anyone who has read the literature in the obstetrician's waiting-room knows the child-care booklets which, at some point, confess that "you may get a fit of the blues" and suggest "having your husband take you to dinner in a French restaurant, or going shopping for a new dress." (The fiction that most women have both husbands and money is forever with us.) But the depressive mother who now and then allows herself a "vacation" or a "reward" is merely showing her daughters both that the female condition is depressing, and that there is no real way out.

As daughters we need mothers who want their own freedom and ours. We need not to be the vessels of another woman's self-denial and frustration. The quality of the mother's life—however embattled and unprotected—is her primary bequest to her daughter, because a woman who can believe in herself, who is a fighter, and who continues to struggle to create livable space around her, is demonstrating to her daughter that these possibilities exist. Because the conditions of life for many poor women demand a fighting spirit for sheer physical survival, such mothers have sometimes been able to give their daughters something to be valued far more highly than full-time mothering. But the toll is taken by the sheer weight of adversity, the irony that to fight for her child's physical survival the mother may have to be almost always absent from the child, as in Tillie Olsen's story, "I Stand Here Ironing."[30] For a child needs, as that mother despairingly knew, the care of someone for whom she is "a miracle."

Many women have been caught—have split themselves—between two mothers: one, usually the biological one, who represents the culture of domesticity, of male-centeredness, of conventional expectations, and another, perhaps a woman artist or teacher, who becomes the countervailing figure. Often this "counter-mother" is an athletics teacher who exemplifies strength and pride in her body, a freer way of being in the world; or an unmarried woman professor, alive with ideas, who represents the choice of a vigorous work life, of "living alone and liking it." This splitting may allow the young woman to fantasize alternately living as one or the other "mother," to test out two different identifications. But it can also lead to a life in which she never consciously resolves the choices, in which she alternately tries to play the hostess and please her husband as her mother did, and to write her novel or doctoral thesis. She has tried to break through the existing models, but she has not gone far enough, usually because nobody has told her how far there is to go.

The double messages need to be disentangled. "You can be anything you really want to be" is a half-truth, whatever a woman's class or economic advantages. We need to be very clear about the missing portion, rather than whisper the fearful subliminal message: "Don't go too far." A female child needs to be told, very early, the practical difficulties females have to face in even trying to imagine "what they want to be." Mothers who can talk freely with their daughters about sex, even teaching them to use contraception in adolescence, still leave them in the dark as to the expectations and stereotypes, false promises and ill-faith, awaiting them in the world. "You can be anything you really want to be"—*if* you are prepared to fight, to create priorities for yourself against the grain of cultural expectations, to persist in the face of misogynist hostility. Interpreting to a little girl, or to an adolescent woman, the kinds of treatment she encounters because she is female, is as necessary as explaining to a nonwhite child reactions based on the color of her skin.*

It is one thing to adjure a daughter, along Victorian lines, that her lot is to "suffer and be still," that woman's fate is determined. It is wholly something else to acquaint her honestly with the jeopardy all women live under in patriarchy, to let her know by word and deed that she has her mother's support, and moreover, that while it *can* be dangerous to move, to speak, to act, each time she suffers rape—physical or psychic—in silence, she is putting another stitch in her own shroud.

---

* A woman recently described in my hearing how her friend's daughter had been on the verge of dropping out of architecture school because of the harassment she encountered there as a woman. It was her mother who

9

I talk with a brilliant and radical thinker, a woman scholar of my generation. She describes her early feelings when she used to find herself at conferences or parties among faculty wives, most of whom had or would have children, she the only unmarried woman in the room. She felt, then, that her passionate investigations, the recognition accorded her work, still left her the "barren" woman, the human failure, among so many women who were mothers. I ask her, "But can you imagine how some of them were envying you your freedom, to work, to think, to travel, to enter a room as yourself, not as some child's mother or some man's wife?" Yet even as I speak, I know: the gulf between "mothers" and "nonmothers" (even the term is pure negation, like "widow," meaning *without*) will be closed only as we come to understand how *both* childbearing and childlessness have been manipulated to make women into negative quantities, or bearers of evil.

In the interstices of language lie powerful secrets of the culture. Throughout this book I have been thrown back on terms like "unchilded," "childless," or "child-free"; we have no familiar, ready-made name for a woman who defines herself, by choice, neither in relation to children nor to men, who is self-identified, who has chosen herself. "Unchilded," "childless," simply define her in terms of a lack; even "child-free" suggests only that she has refused motherhood, not what she is about *in and of herself*. The notion of the "free woman" is strongly tinged with the suggestion of sexual promiscuity, of "free love," of being "free" of man's ownership; it still defines the woman by her relationships with men. The ancient meaning of the word "virgin" (she-who-is-unto-herself) is obscured by connotations of the "undeflorated" or intact hymen, or of the Roman Catholic Virgin Mother, defined entirely by her relationship to God the Son. "Amazon" suggests too narrowly the warrior-maiden who has renounced all ties with men except for procreation: again, definition through relatedness. Neither is "lesbian" a satisfactory term here; not all self-identified women would call

---

urged her to stay, to fight a political battle against sexism, and get the training she wanted.

themselves lesbians; and moreover, numberless lesbians are mothers of children.

There can be no more simplistic formula for women than to escape into some polarization such as "Mothers or Amazons," "matriarchal clan or guerilleres." For one thing, in the original matriarchal clan *all* females, of whatever age, were called "mothers"—even little girls. Motherhood was a social rather than a physical function. "Women . . . were sisters to one another and mothers to all the children of the community without regard to which individual mother bore any child. . . . Aborigines describe themselves as . . . 'brotherhoods' from the standpoint of the male and 'motherhoods' from the standpoint of the female."[31] And everywhere, girl-children as young as six have cared for younger siblings.

The "childless woman" and the "mother" are a false polarity, which has served the institutions both of motherhood and heterosexuality. There are no such simple categories. There are women (like Ruth Benedict) who have tried to have children and could not. The causes may range from a husband's unacknowledged infertility to signals of refusal sent out from her cerebral cortex. A woman may have looked at the lives of women with children and have felt that, given the circumstances of motherhood, she must remain childless if she is to pursue any other hopes or aims.* As the nineteenth-century feminist Margaret Fuller wrote in an undated fragment:

> I have no child and the woman in me has so craved this experience, that it seems the want of it must paralyze me. But now as I look on these lovely children of a human birth, what slow and neutralizing cares they bring with them to the mother! The children of the muse come quicker, with less pain and disgust, rest more lightly on the bosom.†

A young girl may have lived in horror of her mother's child-worn existence and told herself, once and for all, *No, not for*

---

* There are enough single women now adopting children, enough unmarried mothers keeping their children, to suggest that if mothering were not an enterprise so riddled with oppression, many "childless" women would choose to have children of their own.

† She was later to bear a child, in Italy, to a man ten years younger than herself, and to die in the wreck of the ship on which she, the child, and the father were returning to America.

me. A lesbian may have gone through abortions in early relationships with men, love children, yet still feel her life too insecure to take on the grilling of an adoption or the responsibility of an artificial pregnancy. A woman who has chosen celibacy may feel her decision entails a life without children. Ironically, it is precisely the institution of motherhood, which, in an era of birth control, has influenced women against becoming mothers. It is simply too hypocritical, too exploitative of mothers and children, too oppressive.

But is a woman who bore a baby she could not keep a "childless" woman? Am I, whose children are grown-up, who come and go as I will, unchilded as compared to younger women still pushing prams, hurrying home to feedings, waking at night to a child's cry? What makes us mothers? The care of small children? The physical changes of pregnancy and birth? The years of nurture? What of the woman who, never having been pregnant, begins lactating when she adopts an infant? What of the woman who stuffs her newborn into a bus-station locker and goes numbly back to her "child-free" life? What of the woman who, as the eldest girl in a large family, has practically raised her younger sisters and brothers, and then has entered a convent?

The woman struggling to cope with several young children, a job, and the unavailability of decent child-care and schooling, may feel pure envy (and rage) at the apparent freedom and mobility of the "child-free" woman (I have). The woman without children of her own may see, like Margaret Fuller, the "dull and neutralizing cares" of motherhood *as it is lived in the bondage of a patriarchal system* and congratulate herself on having stayed "free," not having been "brainwashed into motherhood." But these polarizations imply a failure of imagination.

ⁱ Throughout recorded history the "childless" woman has been regarded (with certain specific exceptions, such as the cloistered nun or the temple virgin) as a failed woman, unable to speak for the rest of her sex,* and omitted from the hypocritical and palliative reverence accorded the mother. "Childless" women

* See for example Albert Memmi's criticism of Simone de Beauvoir's *The Second Sex*: she is suspect because she did not exercise what Memmi glibly describes as her "woman's right" to bear children (*Dominated Man* [Boston: Beacon, 1968], pp. 150–51).

have been burned as witches, persecuted as lesbians, have been refused the right to adopt children because they were unmarried. They have been seen as embodiments of the great threat to male hegemony: the woman who is not tied to the family, who is disloyal to the law of heterosexual pairing and bearing. These women have nonetheless been expected to serve their term for society as missionaries, nuns, teachers, nurses, maiden aunts; to give, rather than sell their labor if they were middle-class; to speak softly, if at all, of women's condition. Yet ironically, precisely because they were not bound to the cycle of hourly existence with children, because they could reflect, observe, write, such women in the past have given us some of the few available strong insights into the experience of women in general. Without the unacclaimed research and scholarship of "childless" women, without Charlotte Brontë (who died in her first pregnancy), Margaret Fuller (whose major work was done before her child was born), without George Eliot, Emily Brontë, Emily Dickinson, Christina Rossetti, Virginia Woolf, Simone de Beauvoir—we would all today be suffering from spiritual malnutrition as women.

The "unchilded" woman, if such a term makes any sense, is still affected by centuries-long attitudes—on the part of both women and men—towards the birthing, child-rearing function of women. Any woman who believes that the institution of motherhood has nothing to do with *her* is closing her eyes to crucial aspects of her situation.

Many of the great mothers have not been biological. The novel *Jane Eyre,* as I have tried to show elsewhere, can be read as a woman-pilgrim's progress along a path of classic female temptation, in which the motherless Jane time after time finds women who protect, solace, teach, challenge, and nourish her in self-respect.[32] For centuries, daughters have been strengthened and energized by nonbiological mothers, who have combined a care for the practical values of survival with an incitement toward further horizons, a compassion for vulnerability with an insistence on our buried strengths.* It is precisely this

* Mary Daly has suggested to me that the "nonbiological mother" is really a "spirit-sister" (a phrase which affirms her in terms of what she is rather than what she isn't).

that has allowed us to survive; not our occasional breakthroughs into tokendom, not our "special cases," although these have been beacons for us, illuminations of what ought to be.

We are, none of us, "either" mothers or daughters; to our amazement, confusion, and greater complexity, we are both. Women, mothers or not, who feel committed to other women, are increasingly giving each other a quality of caring filled with the diffuse kinds of identification that exist between actual mothers and daughters. Into the mere notion of "mothering" we may carry, as daughters, negative echoes of our own mothers' martyrdom, the burden of their valiant, necessarily limited efforts on our behalf, the confusion of their double messages. But it is a timidity of the imagination which urges that we can be "daughters"—therefore free spirits—rather than "mothers" —defined as eternal givers. Mothering and nonmothering have been such charged concepts for us, precisely because *whichever we did has been turned against us.*

To accept and integrate and strengthen both the mother and the daughter in ourselves is no easy matter, because patriarchal attitudes have encouraged us to split, to polarize, these images, and to project all unwanted guilt, anger, shame, power, freedom, onto the "other" woman. But any radical vision of sisterhood demands that we reintegrate them.

10

As a child raised in what was essentially the South, Baltimore in the segregated 1930s, I had from birth not only a white, but a black mother. This relationship, so little explored, so unexpressed, still charges the relationships of black and white women. We have not only been under slavery, lily white wife and dark, sensual concubine; victims of marital violation on the one hand and unpredictable, licensed rape on the other. We have been mothers and daughters to each other; and although, in the last few years, black and white feminists have been moving toward a still-difficult sisterhood, there is little yet known, unearthed, of the time when we were mothers and daughters. Lillian Smith remembers:

I knew that my old nurse who had cared for me through long months of illness, who had given me refuge when a little sister took my place as the baby of the family, who soothed me, fed me, delighted me with her stories and games, let me fall asleep on her warm, deep breast, was not worthy of the passionate love I felt for her but must be given instead a half-smiled-at affection . . . I knew but I never believed it that the deep respect I felt for her, the tenderness, the love, was a childish thing which every normal child outgrows . . . and that some- how—though it seemed impossible to my agonized heart—I too must outgrow these feelings. . . . I learned to cheapen with tears and sentimental talk of "my old mammy" one of the pro- found relationships of my life.[33]

My black mother was "mine" only for four years, during which she fed me, dressed me, played with me, watched over me, sang to me, cared for me tenderly and intimately. "Child- less" herself, she *was* a mother. She was slim, dignified, and very handsome, and from her I learned—nonverbally—a great deal about the possibilities of dignity in a degrading situation. After my sister's birth, though she still worked from time to time in the house, she was no longer my care-giver. Another nurse came, but she was not the same to me; I felt she belonged to my sister. Twenty years later, when I left my parents' house, expecting never to return, my black mother told me: "Yes, I understand how you have to leave and do what you think is right. I once had to break somebody's heart to go and live my life." She died a few years later; I did not see her again.

And, yes: I know what Lillian Smith describes, the confusion of discovering that a woman one has loved and been cherished by is somehow "unworthy" of such love after a certain age. That sense of betrayal, of the violation of a relationship, was for years a nameless thing, for no one yet spoke of racism, and even the concept of "prejudice" had not yet filtered into my childhood world. It was simply "the way things were," and we tried to repress the confusion and the shame.

When I began writing this chapter I began to remember my black mother again: her calm, realistic vision of things, her physical grace and pride, her beautiful soft voice. For years, she had drifted out of reach, in my searches backward through time, exactly as the double silence of sexism and racism intended her to do. She was meant to be utterly annihilated.

But, at the edge of adolescence, we find ourselves drawing back from our natural mothers as if by a similar edict. It is toward men, henceforth, that our sensual and emotional energies are intended to flow. The culture makes it clear that neither the black mother, nor the white mother, nor any of the other mothers, are "worthy" of our profoundest love and loyalty. Women are made taboo to women—not just sexually, but as comrades, cocreators, coinspiritors. In breaking this taboo, we are reuniting with our mothers; in reuniting with our mothers, we are breaking this taboo.

X VIOLENCE: THE HEART OF MATERNAL DARKNESS

I know of streets of houses where there are large factories built, taking the whole of the daylight away from the kitchen, where the woman spends the best part of her life. On top of this you get the continual grinding of machinery all day. Knowing that it is mostly women and girls who are working in these factories gives you the feeling that their bodies are going round with the machinery. The mother wonders what she has to live for; if there is another baby coming she hopes it will be dead when it is born. The result is she begins to take drugs. I need hardly tell you the pain and suffering she goes through if the baby survives, or the shock it is to the mother when she is told there is something wrong with the baby. She feels she is to blame if she has done this without her husband knowing, and she is living in dread of him. All this tells on the woman physically and mentally; can you wonder at women turning to drink? If the child lives to grow up you find it hysterical and with very irritable, nasty ways. . . . When you see all this it is like a sting at your heart when you know the cause of it all and no remedy . . .

—*Maternity: Letters from Working-Women*, Collected by the Women's Cooperative Guild, 1915

On June 11, 1974, "the first hot day of summer," Joanne Michulski, thirty-eight, the mother of eight children ranging from eighteen years to two months of age, took a butcher knife, decapitated and chopped up the bodies of her two youngest on the neatly kept lawn of the suburban house where the family lived outside Chicago. This "bizarre incident," as her husband called it, created an enormous stir in the surrounding community. Full pages in the local press were devoted to "human interest" reporting of the background of Ms. Michulski's act. Columns headed "IT NEED NOT HAVE HAPPENED," "WHY DO MOTHERS KILL? THEY ARE KILLING THEMSELVES," "THE POLICE ROLE IN MENTAL CASES: STRICTLY LIMITED," "WALK-IN CLINIC CAN'T HELP EMERGENCIES" attempted to explain, exonerate, psychologize; the local newspapers ran an interview with Victor Michulski in which "HUSBAND TELLS OF TORTURED LIFE." Ms. Michulski was charged with voluntary manslaughter but found innocent by reason of insanity, and was committed to a state hospital. Her husband sued for divorce.

The history of Joanne Michulski, as described by her husband, her neighbors, by psychiatric caseworkers, by the clergy and police, had been as follows: None of her eight children were "wanted" children. After the birth of each child, she had gone into deep depression; after the third was born, she discussed using contraceptives with her husband. He "talked about a vasectomy, but just never had it done." She planned to take oral contraceptives, but according to him she never did so. In her depressions she lay on the couch, "saying and doing nothing" for long periods. Michulski, described as a "trim, dapper man," said that his wife had never been known to use violence toward her children, and that "she seemed to show extreme love to the smallest of the children at all times." He described her as "a fairly good wife and mother; not the best." The minister who lived next door said that she seemed "quietly desperate from the moment the family moved into the home" in 1959. Her women neighbors found her "withdrawn"; she did not drive and her husband was absent from home for long periods. The neighboring pastor also reported that while her husband kept the outside of the house neat, the inside was "a mess." She "rarely cooked. Her refrigerator was never cleaned." But the children always seemed "well cared-for." Her husband took the children out to eat several times a week; she had developed a

habit of standing up in the kitchen while the family sat in the
dining room. She began to talk out loud to herself and had
periods of screaming—not at the children, but at "imaginary
people." According to the pastor, "I never saw her lay a hand
on her children. . . . She was like a mother bear where their
safety or reputation was concerned. She did react violently,
however."*

Between 1961 and 1966 the county probation department
was in contact with the family. Joanne Michulski was three
times voluntarily admitted to mental hospitals: once for her
"real blue spells" as her husband termed them; once because of
her fear that "X-rays" or "laser beams" were being projected
into her home; once for "heart pains" which were treated as
psychosomatic. During one of these periods Michulski placed
the children in foster homes. On later discovering that one of
his daughters had been abused in a foster home, Michulski resolved never to break up the family again.

At home again, Joanne Michulski's spells of disturbance
lengthened, but in between she was "easy to get along with,"
according to her husband. In general, it seemed that she was
better when her husband was around, and that her bouts of
rage, fear, and shouting took place when she was left alone
with the children. Aware that the situation was deteriorating,
Michulski stuck to his decision to "keep the family together"—
that is, to leave his wife all day long responsible for eight children. At no point do news accounts or interviews suggest that
there was any attempt to get household help, or to offer her any
respite from her existence as "wife and mother." And perhaps
she would have refused.[1]

Throughout history numberless women have killed children
they knew they could not rear, whether economically or emotionally, children forced upon them by rape, ignorance, poverty,
marriage, or by the absence of, or sanctions against, birth control and abortion. These terrible, prevalent acts have to be
distinguished from infanticide as a deliberate social policy, prac-

---

* This pastor opened his interview with a reporter: "I am a Christian man."
The interview ends: "My wife and I respected her the same way we would
a vicious dog."

ticed by peoples everywhere, against female or malformed children, twins, or the first-born.

Legal, systematic infanticide was practiced in Sparta, in Rome, by the Arabs, in feudal Japan, in India, in traditional China, and it has always been a form of population control in preliterate societies. "In the Old Testament are preserved clear traces of the parental sacrifice of the first fruit of the womb not only to Baal but to Yahweh."[2] Males have been spared as warriors: "The old Vikings extended a spear to the newborn boy. If the child seized it, it was allowed to live."[3] Although sickly and malformed infants of both sexes were killed or exposed, and twins perceived as monsters or as the product of a double impregnation by two different fathers, female children (and their mothers) have borne the brunt of official infanticidal practice, for various reasons; chiefly the expense of "marrying off" daughters, and contempt for female life. Under Christianity, infanticide was forbidden as a policy, but it continued nonetheless to be practiced as an individual act, in which women, raped or seduced and then branded with their "sin," and under pain of torture or execution, have in guilt, self-loathing, and blind desperation done away with the newborns they had carried in their bodies.

The Church had much to do with creating the crime of individual maternal infanticide, by pronouncing all children born out of wedlock "illegitimate." Until the eighteenth century or later bastards were largely excluded from participation in trades and guilds, could not inherit property, and were essentially without the law. Since the "sin" of the child's father was more difficult to prove, it was on the unmarried mother that the full penalty fell; as the eternally guilty party, she was considered by the Church to be "the root of the whole sex problem."[4]

Maternal infanticide was "the most common crime in Western Europe from the Middle Ages down to the end of the eighteenth century."[5]* In the Middle Ages the punishments

---

* Rape, by the way, is almost unmentioned as a cause of illegitimate pregnancy; the term usually employed is "seduction," implying that the father had promised marriage and then deserted the mother. Yet, as Susan Brownmiller has documented, rape has been taken for granted as a part of war. Outside wars, rape has gone on throughout history; as Brownmiller points out, "*Thou shalt not rape* was conspicuously missing from the Ten

were drastic: The woman found guilty of infanticide might be buried alive, impaled through the heart with a pointed stick, or burnt at the stake. "In Zittau . . . the infanticide was stuffed into a black sack together with a dog, a cat, a rooster or a viper. The sack had to remain under water for six hours, and the choir boys sang, Aus tiefer Noth schrei ich zu Dir." (*Out of great trouble I cry to Thee.*) Since, in the minds of the clergy, women who followed the old pagan religion were believed to have intercourse with the devil, an unmarried mother was often assumed to be a witch.[6]

Toward the end of the eighteenth century infanticide began to obsess the minds of legislators, rulers, and writers. Oscar Werner says that the plight of Goethe's Gretchen in *Faust* was, far from being unusual, "the most popular literary theme" in Germany between 1770 and 1800.[7] It now began to be recognized in Europe that the woman who murdered her infant was no callous criminal, but a desperate person. Maria Theresa of Austria and Catherine the Great of Russia both established foundling homes and maternity clinics to receive the children of illegitimate pregnancies, and Frederick the Great was concerned that the laws regulating infanticide should be made more consistent and humane. But it has to be emphasized that, historically, to bear a child out of wedlock has been to violate the property laws that say a woman and her child must legally belong to some man, and that, if they do not, they are at best marginal people, vulnerable to every kind of sanction. The rape victim has paid the cost at every level. And within wedlock,

---

Commandments" (*Against Our Will* [New York: Simon and Schuster, 1975], pp. 19, 30–113). Even Frederick the Great acknowledged an "unmarried soldiery" was responsible for the high rate of infanticide in Prussia in the eighteenth century, although he implied that rapes took place because of pent-up lust, a male theory that is slowly dying hard today. (See Oscar Werner, *The Unmarried Mother in German Literature* [New York: Columbia University Press, 1917], pp. 36–37.) Werner does note (p. 32) that, in the Middle Ages, "in looking through the archives one seldom finds a case where the seducer is mentioned. When he was found out he was punished severely. The reason he was so seldom punished is to be found in the fact that the courts always accepted the man's denial in preference to the woman's accusation. It was a war against the unmarried mother and not against the unmarried father." This is of course a rationalization of the much deeper assumption of women's sexual guilt.

women have been legally powerless to prevent their husbands' use of their bodies, resulting in year-in, year-out pregnancies. In a tenement, or hovel already crowded with undernourished and ailing children, the new infant, whose fate was already almost certainly death, might be "accidentally" or unconsciously suffocated, lain upon in bed, allowed to drown, or simply left unfed.*

In the Massachusetts Bay Colony, at least two women, unnerved by the stress of living with a covenant theology which offered to men, but not to women, a direct relationship with God and knowledge of his will, chose the certainty of damnation over the anxiety and helplessness of their situation by attempting, or actually committing, infanticide. Though translated into theological terms (since theology was the language of Puritan life) their acts were statements of revolt against both a patriarchal religion (which promised the priesthood of all believers but extended it only to men) and a patriarchal family system. One woman, Dorothy Talbye, tried to kill not just her children but her husband, after announcing that "it was so revealed" to her by God.[8]

The Victorian period abounds with cases of the seduction (read "rape") of servant girls by their employers; if they refused sex, they would be fired, and many were fired anyway for getting pregnant. Disraeli admitted in 1845 that "infanticide is practised as extensively and as legally in England as it is on the banks of the Ganges."[9] Queen Victoria, however, supported the abolition of capital punishment for this crime.[10]

In America, Elizabeth Cady Stanton rose to the defense of women charged with infanticide, and associated it with "the triple cord of a political, religious, and social serfdom—that have made [woman] a pliant, pitiable victim to the utter perversion of the highest and holiest sentiments of her nature."[11] She managed to obtain a governor's pardon for one woman, Hester Vaughan, who, at age twenty, deserted by her hus-

---

* "The sacrifice of the wage-earner's children was caused by the mother's starvation; vainly she gave her own food to the children, for then she was unable to suckle the baby and grew too feeble for her former work." In such circumstances, the baby might well be consciously sacrificed. (Alice Clark, *The Working Life of Women in the Seventeenth Century* [London: Routledge & Sons, 1919], p. 87.)

hand, had been "seduced" by her employer and fired when he found she was pregnant. She gave birth in an unheated garret in midwinter; later she was found in a critical condition and the baby was dead. She was imprisoned, without proof, for infanticide. Stanton, in addressing the New York legislature on this case, demanded that women should have the right to a jury of their peers—i.e., of women—and that equal moral standards should be enforced for men and women.[12]

In 1973 the *New York Times* headlined an epidemic of infanticide in Japan; according to reports, a newborn infant was found stuffed into a railway-station coin locker on an average of every ten days, sometimes with a note expressing contrition and guilt. In Tokyo alone during a single year 119 babies had been deserted. The *Times* failed to associate these deaths with the repeal of the liberal abortion laws and the limiting of available contraceptives to the diaphragm, measures which were reported in the same month (December 1973) by the newsletter of Boston Female Liberation.[13]

But Stanton's was the first feminist voice to be heard on behalf of women who, battered by patriarchal laws and practices, had taken the most desperate and emphatic way they knew to make a clear statement.

2

Joanne Michulski's statement was also clear and desperate. She spoke, after her arrest, of "a sacrifice." If we assume that any word of hers is simply the raving of a "paranoid-schizophrenic" we shall not hear what she was saying. A sacrifice is "the act of offering something to a deity in propitiation or homage; especially the ritual slaughter of an animal or person for this purpose"; it is also "the forfeiture of something highly valued." Joanne Michulski had endured the violence of the institution of motherhood for nineteen years, and it seems that the most precious thing in her life was, in fact, her children. ("There never was a question of her interest or love for her children," a caseworker observed. "She just couldn't handle the situation.") Particularly, her husband said, she always showed "extreme love toward the smallest ones." These were the two she killed and mutilated.

Much of the speculation in the newspapers had to do with whether the county mental health services and the laws surrounding commitment had failed this family. But what could traditional psychiatry have done for Joanne Michulski? It could have tried to "adjust" her to motherhood, or it could have incarcerated her. But, as a group of twelve women pointed out in a letter published in a local newspaper, the expectations laid on her and on millions of women with children are "insane expectations." Instead of recognizing the institutional violence of patriarchal motherhood, society labels those women who finally erupt in violence as psychopathological.

Here are a few statements by psychiatrists on the subject of women who in one way or another attempt to resist the demands of the institution:

> The very fact that a woman cannot tolerate pregnancy, or is in intense conflict about it, or about giving birth to a child, is an indication that the pre-pregnant personality of this woman was immature and in that sense can be labelled as psychopathological. . . . The problem centers around unresolved oedipal situations. . . . Since pregnancy and birth are the overt proofs of femininity, the exaggerated castrative factors become overwhelmingly threatening. Identification with the mother is predominant and hostile. Receptivity in the feminine sexual role appears as debasing. Competition with the male is always at a high pitch. . . . Pregnancy as a challenge of femininity is unacceptable to them.[14]

> With sterilization the woman voluntarily surrenders a portion of her femininity. . . . Some women with unresolved hostility for their mother thereby hope to appease that same hated and hating mother and to obtain forgiveness for their wish for Father and Father's child.[15]

> [Vasectomy] frequently is requested as a contraceptive measure. It seldom, if ever, can be so considered. Some emotionally sick women would like to castrate their husbands, and manage for this reason to force their own equally emotionally sick mates to request vasectomies.[16]

I am not offering the naive proposition that existing methods of birth control, or a twice-weekly baby-sitter, could have "solved" Joanne Michulski's "problems." Why didn't she use the pill? it can be asked. For all we know, a few doses made her feel continually nauseated. And, as we now know, it could have killed her. Perhaps she felt the hopelessness of any control of her life which is indoctrinated into so many women. Motherhood without autonomy, without choice, is one of the quickest roads to a sense of having lost control.* Because only her husband, her neighbors, psychiatric workers, the clergy, and the police have spoken for her, because her rage and despair communicated itself in metaphors, in violence turned first inward, then upon what she loved, we will never know the small details which built over the years toward her honorable, unendurable suffering.

A woman in depression does not usually welcome sex. We can assume that although Ms. Michulski accepted the violence of the institution of marriage, which guarantees a man his "conjugal rights" so that he cannot be considered the rapist of his wife, she did not wish to have sex at the cost of bearing children. *She knew* she had had enough children by the time the third was born. Once she had children at all, she was faced with the double violence of marital rape (a woman regarded as her husband's physical property is a raped woman) and of institutionalized motherhood. Let us look at the aspects of that institution which converged in this woman's life.

There is no safe, infallible method of birth control. Had the Michulskis been Catholic (they were Lutheran) there would have been grave sanctions against using any method whatever. But non-Catholics are better off only to a degree. Christopher Tietze, a biostatistician involved in the movement for population control, has said that the hazards to a woman's health are far less with the diaphragm, condom, foam, or rhythm methods, but these methods require medically safe, legal, abortion as a back-up if they are to be regarded as genuinely effective. The

---

* Some women express this by furiously and incessantly cleaning house, which they know will be immediately disorganized by small children; others, by letting the house go utterly to pieces since any kind of order seems hopeless.

pill and the IUD, though they have a higher rate of prevention, are physically dangerous and potentially lethal. The IUD causes exceptionally heavy menses, severe cramps (20 percent of IUD users request removal of the device within a year), irritation of pelvic infections, and perforation of the uterus. The pill is known to cause blood-clotting, heart attack, stroke, gall bladder and kidney disease, and cancer of the breast and possibly of other organs. Both it and the IUD have still-unexplored long-term hazards. Even some of the jellies used with the diaphragm contain a mercury compound known to cause birth defects if pregnancy does occur.[17] It is improbable that a problem which affected as many men in the sensitive genital area, as contraception affects women, would be considered solvable by methods so dangerous, even deadly, and so undependable.

We know the judgments from within the psychiatric establishment against women who do not wish to become mothers. We have to connect these voices with others reaching far back in history. Soranus of Ephesus, the Greek gynecologist, would have had abortion permitted for only three reasons: (1) "to maintain feminine beauty"; (2) to avoid danger to the mother's life if her uterus should be "too small" for the fetus; (3) to control population as urged by Plato in the *Republic* and Aristotle in the *Politics*.[18] St. Augustine regarded abortion as "the work of minds characterized by 'lustful cruelty' or 'cruel lust.' "[19] Christian theologians through the ages have engaged in hair-splitting debates. If a pregnant woman is attacked by a bull, may she run for her life even though running may cause her to abort? Yes, said the sixteenth-century Jesuit Tomàs Sanchez. If a woman conceives out of wedlock, and her male relatives would kill her if they found out, may she destroy the fetus to save her life? Yes, again, said Sanchez.[20] Within the Catholic Church opinion has swayed back and forth as to when a fetus is "ensouled," a controversy which began with Tertullian, a self-confessed loather of female sexuality and also the first to say in effect that "abortion is murder." The early Christian theologians, still cleaving to Aristotle, believed that abortion was murder only if the fetus (if male) was within forty days of conception and (if female) within eighty to ninety days, the time when "ensoulment" was presumed to occur for each sex.

(We can only guess at how the gender of the fetus was supposed to be determined.) By 1588, Pope Sixtus V, a fanatic Counter-Reformation cleanser of the Church, declared all abortion murder, with excommunication as its punishment. His successor, finding the sanctions unworkable, revoked them in 1591, except for abortions performed later than forty days from conception. By 1869, Pius IX decided the time was ripe to swing back to the decision of Sixtus V: All abortion was again declared murder.[21] This is at present the official, majority Catholic position. In spite of it, Catholic women comprise over 20 percent of all abortion patients.[22]

The arguments against and for abortion range from attempts to determine biologically or legally when the fetus becomes a "person" to exercises in the most abstract logic and ethics.[23] I shall not attempt here to enumerate the range of arguments; Mary Daly has already provided an overview from a feminist perspective. She notes that

> . . . abortion is hardly the "final triumph" envisaged by all or the final stage of the revolution. There are deep questions beneath and beyond this, such as: Why should women be in situations of unwanted pregnancy at all? Some women see abortion as a necessary measure for themselves but no one sees it as the fulfillment of her highest dreams. Many would see abortion as a humiliating procedure. Even the abortifacient pills, when perfected, can be seen as a protective measure, a means to an end, but hardly as the total embodiment of liberation. Few if any feminists are deceived in this matter, although male proponents of the repeal of abortion laws tend often to be short-sighted in this respect, confusing the feminist revolution with the sexual revolution.[24]

The demand for legalized abortion, like the demand for contraception, has been represented as a form of irresponsibility, a refusal by women to confront their moral destiny, a trivialization or evasion of great issues of life and death. The human facts, however, are hardly frivolous. Here are some of the methods resorted to by women who have been denied legal, safe, low-cost abortion: self-abortion by wire coat-hangers, knitting needles, goose quills dipped in turpentine, celery stalks, drenching the cervix with detergent, lye, soap, Ultra-Jel (a commercial preparation of castor oil, soap, and iodine), drinking purgatives or mercury, applying hot coals to the body. The underworld "cut-rate" abortionists, often alcoholic, disenfranchised members of the medical profession, besides operating in septic surroundings and performing unnecessary curettages on poor women who cannot afford a pregnancy test, frequently rape or sexually molest their patients; well-to-do women have been forced to travel thousands of miles to receive a medically safe abortion.[25]

Clearly, the first violence done in abortion is on the body and mind of the pregnant woman herself. Most people, women and men alike, find it difficult to perform even a minor operation upon themselves, from giving themselves an injection to lancing an infected finger or removing a splinter. It is nothing less than grim, driven desperation which can impel a woman to insert an unbent coat-hanger into her most sensitive parts, to place her body in the hands of a strange man with unverified credentials, or to lie down without anesthesia on a filthy kitchen table, knowing that in so doing she risks illness, grilling by the police, and death. Some women are able to speak later of such experiences in a measured, almost indifferent way; no one should be deceived by this attempt to distance or minimize the trauma. An illegal or self-induced abortion is no casual experience. It is painful, dangerous, and cloaked in the guilt of criminality.

Even when performed in a hospital, under the law, abortion is often packaged with sterilization as a kind of punishment for the crime of wishing not to be pregnant, just as women who request simple tubal ligation as sterilization are frequently given only the option of hysterectomy.[26] The sadism of the underworld abortionist and that of the hospital to which a hemorrhaging woman turns herself in after an incomplete self-inflicted abortion are not so different after all.

To become pregnant with an unwanted child is itself no light experience. There have been efforts to show that abortion, legal or not, is harder psychically on women who have borne children than on a woman who has borne none. A recent Swedish study of nearly five hundred women concluded, however, that no such generalization was possible.[27] Each woman reacts to pregnancy, wanted or not, and to abortion, even the easiest and most legal, in her own way. Guilt about abortion can serve as the channel for other, older feelings of guilt, of needing to atone; it can also be the result of lifelong exposure to the idea that abortion is murder.* If a woman feels her guilt or depression as a kind of punishment, she may try to disavow such feelings. It is crucial, however, in abortion as in every other experience (especially in the realm of sexuality and reproduction) that women take seriously the enterprise of finding out what we *do* feel, instead of accepting what we have been told we must feel. One woman's depression may actually be anger at the man who got her pregnant; another woman may be angry at her treatment by the abortionist or the hospital; another may wish to have a child, know her situation renders it impossible, and genuinely mourn the loss.

No free woman, with 100 percent effective, nonharmful birth control readily available, would "choose" abortion. At present, it is certainly likely that a woman can—through many causes—become so demoralized as to use abortion as a form of violence against herself—a penance, an expiation. But this needs to be viewed against the ecology of guilt and victimization in which so many women grow up. In a society where women entered sexual intercourse willingly,† where adequate contraception was a genuine social priority, there would be no "abortion issue." And in such a society there would be a vast diminishment of female self-hatred—a psychic source of many unwanted pregnancies.

---

* A Boston women's group, COPE, originally begun as a support group for women in pregnancy or in postchildbirth depression, has started two post-abortion discussion groups to enable women to sort out their feelings rather than repress them. "The most important thing . . . is that the woman who's upset over her abortion shouldn't feel like she's crazy or 'sick'. She's been through an unpleasant experience and she has a right to support" (Karen Lindsay, "COPE-ing with the Aftermath of Abortion," *Boston Phoenix*, January 14, 1975).

† The pressure on women to "fulfill their conjugal duties" deserves a chapter of its own in the history of rape. As the wives of working-men quoted in Chapter II make clear, husbands have used many kinds of pressure besides brute physical force to get the use of their wives' bodies. One of these women writes that "no amount of State help can help the sufferings of mothers until men are taught many things in regard to the right use of the organs of reproduction, and until he realizes that the wife's body belongs to herself, and until the marriage relations takes a higher sense of

Abortion is violence: a deep, desperate violence inflicted by a woman upon, first of all, herself. It is the offspring, and will continue to be the accuser, of a more pervasive and prevalent violence, the violence of rapism.

3

From a thoughtful woman's point of view, no ethical ideal has deserved our unconditional respect and adherence, because in every ethics crimes against women are mysteriously unnamed or glossed over. We have always been outside the (manmade) law, although we have been much more stringently punished than men for breaking the law, as in the case of prostitution and adultery.

The absence of respect for women's lives is written into the heart of male theological doctrine, into the structure of the patriarchal family, and into the very language of patriarchal ethics. This is the underlying deceitfulness and hypocrisy of the Catholic or "Right-to-Life" argument against abortion. It is a fiction—not just an "unexamined assumption"—that respect for human life has been an ideal, or, as John Noonan phrases it, "an almost absolute value in history." Women, upon whom most of the burden of respect for life has been placed, know that it is not. We know too much at firsthand about the violence of the warrior, the rapist, the institutional violence of political and social systems in which we have little part, but which affect our bodies, our children, our aging parents: the violence which over centuries we have been told is the way of the world, but which we exist to mitigate and assuage.*

---

morality and bare justice. And what I imply not only exists in the lower strata of society, but is just as prevalent in the higher. . . . Very much injury and suffering comes to the mother and child through the father's ignorance and interference" (*Maternity: Letters from Working Women* [London: 1915], pp. 27–28).

* I have written elsewhere of the impression made on me by two films, released at about the same time: Marcel Ophul's *The Sorrow and the Pity* and Francis Ford Coppola's *The Godfather*. In each of these—one a documentary of French collaboration with and resistance to Nazism in

Neither the theologians, nor the Right-to-Lifers, nor the fertility experts, nor the ecologists, have acknowledged that, where "humanity" and "humanistic values" are concerned, women are not really part of the population. It is not enough that the ecologically-minded, or the Society of Friends, or the planners of Planned Parenthood or Zero Population Growth, concerned for "the quality of life on the planet," happen at this time to support the decontrol of abortion. Abortion legislation has always come and gone with the rhythms of economic and military aggression, the desire for cheap labor, or for greater consumerism. In pre-Christian Rome a husband could order or permit his wife to have an abortion in one pregnancy, and forbid her to in another. We have seen the vacillations of official church policy. In the Soviet Union, the first modern country to legalize abortion (in 1920), virtual abortion factories were provided at first by the state. These were abolished and abortion declared illegal when it became clear that a confrontation was building with Nazi Germany. After World War II, with a new emphasis on consumerism, abortion was again legalized to encourage wives to stay in the labor force and earn a second family income. Throughout, by continuing a half-hearted and ineffective program of birth-control information, the Soviet Union has in effect forced abortion on many women who would have preferred not to conceive at all.[28] In Japan, as we have seen, a liberal abortion law was rescinded, and birth-control pills made virtually unavailable, when the birth rate began to decline and the supply of cheap labor was threatened.

The situation in China has been described by the fertility expert Carl Djerassi as "approaching Nirvana"—not, it would seem, for women but for epidemiologists. "China probably has already, or certainly will have within another two years or so, more women on oral contraceptives than any other country. In addition or in contrast to many women in North America and Europe, Chinese women are much less mobile, their jobs and

---

World War II, the other a dramatization of a best-selling novel about a Mafioso "family"—the men hold their councils of war, while the women, as if symbolically, listen at doorways, silently serve drinks and food, watching the faces of the men with acute anxiety and alertness. It is they who will later hold those men and their children in their arms, whatever crimes they have committed against life.

residences are changed rarely, and the potential for local record-keeping at the site of job and/or residence is unsurpassed." (Birth-control information is not available to students, even at the university level, and is officially disseminated only to married couples; early marriage and premarital intercourse are socially unacceptable.)

"Chinese achievements in fertility control during the past decade are extremely impressive and provide lessons from which most of the world could learn," Djerassi claims. Among these lessons is the fact that "the Chinese *modus operandi* appears to be more flexible than that in the United States . . . animal toxicity requirements do not exceed 6–12 months (as compared to U.S. requirements of up to ten years) . . . the decision to undertake clinical testing is carried out in 'discussions' between the laboratory scientists, clinicians and representatives of the health authorities. . . . The rationale for this *ad hoc* procedure is 'to alleviate human suffering as quickly as possible.' "

Moreover, "subjects for clinical experimentation are obtained by 'making propaganda' among women in nearby Street Committees. The volunteers know that they are participating in an experiment in which they might become pregnant (abortion is, of course, available as a back-up procedure), but they are aware that this is 'science for the revolutionary cause' and hence are willing to undertake the necessary risks." Djerassi himself is slightly skeptical about the conflict between "as quickly as possible" and the safety of the women experimented on, and even about the "extent of real informed consent of the patient (rather than revolutionary zeal)."[29] But however much the Chinese woman benefits today by the possibility of limiting her family to at most two children, the same *modus operandi* may easily be applied, at some further time, to enlarging the size of the population. "The revolutionary cause" can just as easily require that contraceptives become limited, that abortion no longer be available, and that, as presently in the Soviet Union, medals be awarded to women producing more than ten children.

The *New York Times* noted on March 17, 1975, that the Argentine government, hoping to double its population by the end of the twentieth century, had recently prohibited the dissemination of birth-control information and severely restricted the sale of contraceptives. As set forth in the Peronist magazine *Las Bases*, the motives are unambiguous:

> . . . when the year 2000 is at hand, we will have over-populated neighbors with great food problems, and we, on the contrary, will have three million kilometers of land, practically unpopulated. We will not have the arms to work this immense and rich territory, and if we do not do it there will be others who will. . . . We must start from the basis that the principal work of a woman is to have children.

These words have a familiar ring. In the early part of the twentieth century, as contraception became more popular, both in England and America panic arose lest the middle and upper classes, to whom methods were most available, were "breeding themselves out," while the "lower"—therefore "unfit"—masses were still producing large families. (Poor women, as we have seen, were vocal about the need to limit their families, but abstinence or self-inflicted abortion were the chief methods they knew.) Apart from the social-Darwinist fallacy inherent in these polemics (the idea that poor people are poor because they are unfit, rather than because the rich take care to protect their wealth), the arguments have a fascinating honesty about the "true meaning and purpose" of motherhood. Rarely, whether from the Christian or the Freudian, the fascist or the Maoist Fathers, do we get so pure and clear a description of the institution of motherhood as from obscure pamphlets like the Reverend George W. Clark's *Race Suicide—England's Peril*, published in 1917 by the Duty and Discipline Movement.

Reverend Clark begins by declaring that the loss of human life through birth control is more terrible than the lives lost in war. (It is worth remembering that the 1914–1918 World War was considered to have destroyed the "flower of manhood" in the British upper classes. Never mind the ordinary soldier; it was only the "best and brightest" that had been ravaged in the trench warfare of that "war to end all wars.") Clark is perfectly honest about his fear that middle- and upper-class restrictions on the size of families, while the "physically and mentally inferior" continue to breed, will prove a disaster for British society. He divides his sermon into three heads: (1) Limitation [of family] Threatens Our Empire; (2) Limitation Threatens Our Trade ("the merchant with one son has not the same inducement to launch out in new enterprise as his German competitor with two or more sons"); (3) National Defense is Imperilled by Limitation. He concludes with this appeal to the mothers:

> No other service woman can render the State can compensate for her failure in this, the one function God and Nature have assigned to her, and to her alone. Everything else man can do. This is woman's function and her glory. For this she was sent into the world. Her best years must be spent in the nursery, or the nation perishes. In the noblest periods of a nation's history the ablest women are ambitious of bearing distinguished sons. Only in periods of decadence do women seek in barrenness to be distinguished themselves . . .[30]*

Vous travaillez pour l'armée, madame. There is no guarantee, under socialism or "liberal" capitalism, Protestantism, "humanism," or any existing ethics, that a liberal policy will not become an oppressive one, so long as women do not have absolute decision-power over the use of our bodies. We have seen federal conservation programs give way to the lumbering, pipe-lining, and stripping of wilderness lands. We have also seen the laws and opinions regarding birth control and abortion fluctuate throughout history, according to the requirements of military aggression, the labor market, or cultural climates of puritanism or "sexual liberation," patriarchally controlled.

---

* Recently two American feminists reported from the East Berlin World Congress of Women for International Women's Year that report after report, working paper after working paper presented at this male-dominated gathering expressed the view that women's major value is as "the bearers of future generations" and in their "dual social function as mothers and bearers." "Hardly ever during the entire Congress was it pointed out that women are human beings first and foremost and deserve their rights for that and no other reason" (Laura McKinley, Diana Russell *et al.*, "The 'Old Left' Divided in Berlin over the 'Woman Question,'" *Majority Report*, March 6–20, 1976, pp. 10–12).

4

When we think of an institution, we can usually see it as embodied in a building: the Vatican, the Pentagon, the Sorbonne, the Treasury, the Massachusetts Institute of Technology, the Kremlin, the Supreme Court. What we cannot see, until we become close students of the institution, are the ways in which power is maintained and transferred behind the walls and beneath the domes, the invisible understandings which guarantee that it shall reside in certain hands but not in others, that information shall be transmitted to this one but not to that one, the hidden collusions and connections with other institutions of which it is supposedly independent. When we think of the institution of motherhood, no symbolic architecture comes to mind, no visible embodiment of authority, power, or of potential or actual violence. Motherhood calls to mind the home, and we like to believe that the home is a private place. Perhaps we imagine row upon row of backyards, behind suburban or tenement houses, in each of which a woman hangs out the wash, or runs to pick up a tear-streaked two-year-old; or thousands of kitchens, in each of which children are being fed and sent off to school. Or we think of the house of our childhood, the woman who mothered us, or of ourselves. We do not think of the laws which determine how we got to these places, the penalties imposed on those of us who have tried to live our lives according to a different plan, the art which depicts us in an unnatural serenity or resignation, the medical establishment which has robbed so many women of the act of giving birth, the experts—almost all male—who have told us how, as mothers, we should behave and feel. We do not think of the Marxist intellectuals arguing as to whether we produce "surplus value" in a day of washing clothes, cooking food, and caring for children, or the psychoanalysts who are certain that the work of motherhood suits us by nature. We do not think of the power stolen from us and the power withheld from us, in the name of the institution of motherhood.

When we think of motherhood, we are supposed to think of Renoir's blooming women with rosy children at their knees,

Raphael's ecstatic madonnas, some Jewish mother lighting the candles in a scrubbed kitchen on Shabbos, her braided loaf lying beneath a freshly ironed napkin. We are not supposed to think of a woman lying in a Brooklyn hospital with ice packs on her aching breasts because she has been convinced she could not nurse her child; of a woman in Africa equally convinced by the producers of U.S. commercial infant formula that her ample breast-milk is inadequate nourishment; of a girl in her teens, pregnant by her father; of a Vietnamese mother gang-raped while working in the fields with her baby at her side; of two women who love each other struggling to keep custody of their children against the hostility of exhusbands and courts. We are not supposed to think of a woman trying to conceal her pregnancy so she can go on working as long as possible, because when her condition is discovered she will be fired without disability insurance; or of the women whose children have gone unnourished because they had to hire themselves out as wet-nurses; of the slave who, severed from her own child, has rocked and tended the children of her masters; of the woman who passes for "childless," who remembers giving birth to a baby she was not allowed to touch and see because she might love it and wish to keep it. We are not supposed to think of what infanticide feels like, or fantasies of infanticide, or day after wintry day spent alone in the house with ailing children, or of months spent in sweatshop, prison, or someone else's kitchen, in anxiety for children left at home with an older child, or alone. Men have spoken, often, in abstractions, of our "joys and pains." We have, in our long history, accepted the stresses of the institution as if they were a law of nature.

The institution of motherhood cannot be touched or seen: in art perhaps only Käthe Kollwitz has come close to evoking it. It must go on being evoked, so that women never again forget that our many fragments of lived experience belong to a whole which is not of our creation. Rape and its aftermath; marriage as economic dependence, as the guarantee to a man of "his" children; the theft of childbirth from women; the concept of the "illegitimacy" of a child born out of wedlock; the laws regulating contraception and abortion; the cavalier marketing of dangerous birth-control devices; the denial that work done by women at home is a part of "production"; the chaining of women in links of love and guilt; the absence of social benefits for mothers; the inadequacy of child-care facilities in most parts of the world; the unequal pay women receive as wage-earners, forcing them often into dependence on a man; the solitary confinement of "full-time motherhood"; the token nature of fatherhood, which gives a man rights and privileges over children toward whom he assumes minimal responsibility; the psychoanalytic castigation of the mother; the pediatric assumption that the mother is inadequate and ignorant; the burden of emotional work borne by women in the family—all these are connecting fibers of this invisible institution, and they determine our relationship to our children whether we like to think so or not.

Because we have all had mothers, the institution affects all women, and—though differently—all men. Patriarchal violence and callousness are often visited through women upon children —not only the "battered" child but the children desperately pushed, cajoled, manipulated, the children dependent on one uncertain, weary woman for their day-in, day-out care and emotional sustenance, the male children who grow up believing that a woman is nothing so much as an emotional climate made to soothe and reassure, or an emotional whirlwind bent on their destruction.

I come back, as we must, to Joanne Michulski. Desperation surely grew upon her, little by little. She loved, she tried to love, she screamed and was not heard, because there was nothing and no one in her surroundings who saw her plight as unnatural, as anything but the "homemaker's" usual service to the home. She became a scapegoat, the one around whom the darkness of maternity is allowed to swirl—the invisible violence of the institution of motherhood, the guilt, the powerless responsibility for human lives, the judgments and condemnations, the fear of her own power, the guilt, the guilt, the guilt. So much of this heart of darkness is an undramatic, undramatized suffering: the woman who serves her family their food but cannot sit down with them, the woman who cannot get out of

bcd in the morning, the woman polishing the same place on the
table over and over, reading labels in the supermarket as if they
were in a foreign language, looking into a drawer where there
is a butcher knife. The scapegoat is also an escape-valve:
through her the passions and the blind raging waters of a suppressed knowledge are permitted to churn their way so that
they need not emerge in less extreme situations as lucid rebellion. Reading of the "bad" mother's desperate response to an
invisible assault on her being, "good" mothers resolve to become better, more patient and long-suffering, to cling more
tightly to what passes for sanity. The scapegoat is different from
the martyr; she cannot teach resistance or revolt. She represents a terrible temptation: to suffer uniquely, to assume that
I, the individual woman, am the "problem."

> Does motherhood release rage and cruelty in anyone except
> me and "sick" child batterers? . . . My children, when they
> were about a year old, released in me terrifying fantasies of
> torture and cruelty. They did it by being children, with normal
> childish traits of persistence, nagging, crying, curiosity.

> Fantasy films unwind in my brain . . . I . . . seize a child by
> the heels, swing it round, and smash its head into the wall,
> watching the blood and brains flow down. . . . Sometimes
> . . . I leave them in the house alone and just run away. . . .
> After the fantasy films run out I look at my babies and realize I
> could never do those things . . . I love my children too much.
> Then I am able to be tender and gentle with them once again.

> But I really have, in anger (not rage: that makes me turn in-
> ward or destroy *things*, not children) kicked at their legs,
> spanked, pulled hair, and pushed them to the floor. . . . I
> understand how the battered children become that way . . .

> I am ashamed to admit I . . . really have hit and kicked my
> little children. . . . I spend so much time in self-hate . . .
> (Autobiography of a student in a class in "Women's
> Biography," California State College at Sonoma) [31]

Self-hatred of the mother in anger, the woman in anger. She
does not look beyond her individual anger hurled at the indi-

vidual child, even when, like Tillie Olsen's Anna, she herself is
the target of her husband's violence:

> For several weeks Jim Holbrook had been in an evil mood.
> . . . He had nothing but blows for the children, and he struck
> Anna too often to remember . . .

> Anna too became bitter and brutal. If one of the children was
> in her way, if they did not obey her instantly, she would hit at
> them in a blind rage, as if it were some devil she was exorcising.
> Afterward, in the middle of her work, regret would cramp her
> heart at the memory of the tear-stained little face. " 'Twasn't
> them I was beating up on. Somethin just seems to get into me
> when I have somethin to hit." [32]

In her prose-poem *Momma*, the poet Alta places her finger
on the raw nerve of motherhood: loving our children, defending them, as did Joanne Michulski, "like a mother bear," we
still find in them the nearest targets for our rage and frustration:

> a child with untameable curly hair. i call her kia,
> pine nut person, & her eyes so open as she watches me try
> to capture her,
> as I try to
> name her . . .

> what of yesterday when she chased the baby in my room
>   and i screamed
> OUT OUT GET OUT & she ran
> right out but the baby stayed
> unafraid. what is it like to have
> a child afraid of you. your own
> child, your first child, the one . . .
> who must forgive you if either of you are to survive . . .
> & how right is it to shut her out of the room so i can
>   write about her?
> how human, how loving, how can
> i even try to
> : name her

> maybe they could manage w/out me
> maybe I could steal
> away a little time

in a different room
would they all still love me
when i came back?[33]

What woman, in the solitary confinement of a life at home
enclosed with young children, or in the struggle to mother
them while providing for them single-handedly, or in the conflict of weighing her own personhood against the dogma that
says she is a mother, first, last, and always—what woman has
not dreamed of "going over the edge," of simply letting go,
relinquishing what is termed her sanity, so that she can be
taken care of for once, or can simply find a way to take care of
herself? The mothers: collecting their children at school; sitting
in rows at the parent-teacher meeting; placating weary infants
in supermarket carriages; straggling home to make dinner, do
laundry, and tend to children after a day at work; fighting to
get decent care and livable schoolrooms for their children;
waiting for child-support checks while the landlord threatens
eviction; getting pregnant yet again because their one escape
into pleasure and abandon is sex; forcing long needles into their
delicate interior parts; wakened by a child's cry from their
eternally unfinished dreams—the mothers, if we could look into
their fantasies—their daydreams and imaginary experiences—we
would see the embodiment of rage, of tragedy, of the over-
charged energy of love, of inventive desperation, we would
see the machinery of institutional violence wrenching at the
experience of motherhood.

What is astonishing, what can give us enormous hope and
belief in a future in which the lives of women and children shall
be mended and rewoven by women's hands, is all that we have
managed to salvage, of ourselves, for our children, even within
the destructiveness of the institution: the tenderness, the passion, the trust in our instincts, the evocation of a courage we did
not know we owned, the detailed apprehension of another
human existence, the full realization of the cost and precarious-
ness of life. The mother's battle for her child—with sickness,
with poverty, with war, with all the forces of exploitation and
callousness that cheapen human life—needs to become a com-

mon human battle, waged in love and in the passion for survival. But for this to happen, the institution of motherhood
must be destroyed.

The changes required to make this possible reverberate into
every part of the patriarchal system. To destroy the institution
is not to abolish motherhood. It is to release the creation and
sustenance of life into the same realm of decision, struggle,
surprise, imagination, and conscious intelligence, as any other
difficult, but freely chosen work.

AFTERWORD

. . . there are ways of thinking that we don't know
about. Nothing could be more important or precious
than that knowledge, however unborn. The sense of
urgency, the spiritual restlessness it engenders, cannot
be appeased . . .
                    —Susan Sontag, *Styles of Radical Will*

But what do we do with our lives? There are growing, collective
efforts to meet the institution of motherhood head-on, for
example, the National Welfare Rights Organization, the National Abortion Rights Action League, and numerous special
groups such as Catholics For A Free Choice, the Sisterhood of
Black Single Mothers in New York, and the Lesbian Mothers'
National Defense Fund, based in Seattle. A national organization, MOMMA, with a newspaper and chapters throughout the
country, addresses itself to the problems of single mothers in
general. The Womancare Childbearing Clinic in San Diego,
the Association for Childbirth at Home in Massachusetts, are
among groups working toward greater maternal control of
childbirth. The women's health-care movement, challenging the
ignorance and passivity fostered in women by the male medical
profession, is a spreading force, already having an incalculable
effect on a new generation of women.*

* For a listing of women's health centers and collectives, publications and
films addressed to the issue of "taking our bodies back" (Margaret Lazarus's
phrase) see K. Grimstad and S. Rennie, eds., *The New Woman's Survival
Sourcebook* (New York: Knopf, 1975).

In the four years of writing this book I have seen the issue of motherhood grow from a question almost incidental in feminist analysis to a theme which now seems to possess the collective consciousness of thoughtful women, whether as mothers, as daughters, or both. Various writers have called for a new matriarchalism; for the taking over by women of genetic technology; for the insistence on child-care as a political commitment by all members of a community or by all "child-free" women; communal child-raising; the return to a "village" concept of community in which children could be integrated into the adult life of work; the rearing of children in feminist enclaves to grow up free of gender-imprinting. There is a ripple of interest in "new fatherhood," in the establishing of a basis of proof that men, as well as women, can and should "mother," or for redefinitions of fatherhood which would require a more active, continuous presence with the child.

To seek visions, to dream dreams, is essential, and it is also essential to try new ways of living, to make room for serious experimentation, to respect the effort even where it fails. At the same time, in the light of most women's lives as they are now having to be lived, it can seem naive and self-indulgent to spin forth matriarchal utopias, to "demand" that the technologies of contraception and genetics be "turned over" to women (by whom, and under what kinds of effective pressure?); to talk of impressing "unchilded" women into child-care as a political duty, of boycotting patriarchal institutions, of the commune as a solution for child-rearing. Child-care as enforced servitude, or performed out of guilt, has been all too bitter a strain in our history. If women boycott the laboratories and libraries of scientific institutions (to which we have barely begun to gain access) we will not even know what research and technology is vital to the control of our bodies.* Certainly the commune, in and of itself, has no special magic for women, any more than

---

* It is, rather, essential that women become well informed about current developments in genetics, cloning, and extrauterine reproduction. A two-pronged approach is needed: just as more women are receiving medical training, while other women are educating themselves and each other as lay persons in the fields of health-care and childbirth, so we need women scientists within the institutions, *and* lay women who are knowledgeably monitoring the types of decisions and research that go on there, and disseminating the information they gather.

has the extended family or the public day-care center. Above all, such measures fail to recognize the full complexity and political significance of the woman's body, the full spectrum of power and powerlessness it represents, of which motherhood is simply one—though a crucial—part.

Furthermore, it can be dangerously simplistic to fix upon "nurturance" as a special strength of women, which need only be released into the larger society to create a new human order. Whatever our organic or developed gift for nurture, it has often been turned into a boomerang. About women political prisoners under torture, Rose Styron writes:

> The imagination, the "emotionalism" a woman is classically assigned—the passion she has developed defending her children, the compassion (or insight into human motive and possibility) she has acquired being alert to the needs and demands of her family or community—can make her into a fierce opponent for her tormentors. *It can also make her exceptionally vulnerable* (Emphasis mine).*

This has been true for women in general under patriarchy, whether our opponents are individual men, the welfare system, the medical and psychoanalytic establishments, or the organized network of drug traffic, pornography, and prostitution. When an individual woman first opposes the institution of motherhood she often has to oppose it in the person of a man, the father of her child, toward whom she may feel love, compassion, friendship, as well as resentment, anger, fear, or guilt. The "maternal" or "nurturant" spirit we want to oppose to rapism and the warrior mentality can prove a liability so long as it remains a lever by which women can be controlled through what is most generous and sensitive in us. Theories of female power and female ascendancy must reckon fully with the ambiguities of our being, and with the continuum of our consciousness, the potentialities for both creative and destructive energy in each of us.

I am convinced that "there are ways of thinking that we don't yet know about." I take those words to mean that many women are *even now* thinking in ways which traditional intel-

* "The Hidden Women," in *Women Political Prisoners in the USSR*, Ukrainian National Women's League of America (New York, 1975), pp. 3–4.

lection denies, decries, or is unable to grasp. Thinking is an active, fluid, expanding process; intellection, "knowing" are recapitulations of past processes. In arguing that we have by no means yet explored or understood our biological grounding, the miracle and paradox of the female body and its spiritual and political meanings, I am really asking whether women cannot begin, at last, to *think through the body*, to connect what has been so cruelly disorganized—our great mental capacities, hardly used; our highly developed tactile sense; our genius for close observation; our complicated, pain-enduring, multi-pleasured physicality.

I know no woman—virgin, mother, lesbian, married, celibate —whether she earns her keep as a housewife, a cocktail waitress, or a scanner of brain waves—for whom her body is not a fundamental problem: its clouded meaning, its fertility, its desire, its so-called frigidity, its bloody speech, its silences, its changes and mutilations, its rapes and ripenings. There is for the first time today a possibility of converting our physicality into both knowledge and power. Physical motherhood is merely one dimension of our being. We know that the sight of a certain face, the sound of a voice, can stir waves of tenderness in the uterus. From brain to clitoris through vagina to uterus, from tongue to nipples to clitoris, from fingertips to clitoris to brain, from nipples to brain and into the uterus, we are strung with invisible messages of an urgency and restlessness which indeed cannot be appeased, and of a cognitive potentiality that we are only beginning to guess at. We are neither "inner" nor "outer" constructed; our skin is alive with signals; our lives and our deaths are inseparable from the release or blockage of our thinking bodies.

But the fear and hatred of our bodies has often crippled our brains. Some of the most brilliant women of our time are still trying to think from somewhere outside their female bodies— hence they are still merely reproducing old forms of intellection.* There is an inexorable connection between every aspect

* Even Mary Wollstonecraft, viewing with pain the "passive obedience" and physical weakness she saw in the majority of women around her, remarked that she had been "led to imagine that the few extraordinary

of a woman's being and every other; the scholar reading denies at her peril the blood on the tampon; the welfare mother accepts at her peril the derogation of her intelligence. These are issues of survival, because the woman scholar and the welfare mother are both engaged in fighting for the mere right to exist. Both are "marginal" people in a system founded on the traditional family and its perpetuation.

The physical organization which has meant, for generations of women, unchosen, indentured motherhood, is still a female resource barely touched upon or understood. We have tended either to *become* our bodies—blindly, slavishly, in obedience to male theories about us—or to try to exist in spite of them. "I don't *want* to be the Venus of Willendorf—or the eternal fucking machine." Many women see any appeal to the physical as a denial of mind. We have been perceived for too many centuries as pure Nature, exploited and raped like the earth and the solar system; small wonder if we now long to become Culture: pure spirit, mind. Yet it is precisely this culture and its political institutions which have split us off from itself. In so doing it has also split itself off from life, becoming the death-culture of quantification, abstraction, and the will to power which has reached its most refined destructiveness in this century. It is this culture and politics of abstraction which women are talking of changing, of bringing to accountability in human terms.

The repossession by women of our bodies will bring far more essential change to human society than the seizing of the means of production by workers. The female body has been both territory and machine, virgin wilderness to be exploited and assembly-line turning out life. We need to imagine a world in which every woman is the presiding genius of her own body. In such a world women will truly create new life, bringing forth not only children (if and as we choose) but the visions, and

women who have rushed in eccentrical directions out of the orbit prescribed to their sex, were *male* spirits, confined by mistake in female frames" (A *Vindication of the Rights of Woman*, 1792 [New York: Norton, 1967], p. 70). I am indebted to Barbara Gelpi for drawing this passage to my attention.

the thinking, necessary to sustain, console, and alter human existence—a new relationship to the universe. Sexuality, politics, intelligence, power, motherhood, work, community, intimacy will develop new meanings; thinking itself will be transformed.

This is where we have to begin.

NOTES

I. ANGER AND TENDERNESS

1. Arthur W. Calhoun, A *Social History of the American Family from Colonial Times to the Present* (Cleveland: 1917). See also Gerda Lerner, *Black Women in White America: A Documentary History* (New York: Vintage, 1973), pp. 149–50 ff.

II. THE "SACRED CALLING"

1. Margaret Sanger, *Motherhood in Bondage* (New York: Maxwell Reprint, 1956), p. 234.
2. John Spargo, *Socialism and Motherhood* (New York: 1914).
3. Benjamin F. Riley, *White Man's Burden* (Birmingham, Ala.: 1910), p. 131.
4. Stuart Hampshire, review of Elizabeth Hardwick's *Seduction and Betrayal*, *New York Review of Books*, June 27, 1975, p. 21.
5. Arthur W. Calhoun, A *Social History of the American Family from Colonial Times to the Present* (Cleveland: 1917), I: 67, 87. Julia C. Spruill, *Women's Life and Work in the Southern Colonies* (New York: Norton, 1972), pp. 137–39; first published 1938.
6. Margaret Llewelyn Davies, ed., *Life as We Have Known It* (New York: Norton, 1975), p. 1; first published 1931 by the Hogarth Press, London.
7. Calhoun, *op. cit.*, II: 244.
8. Rev. John S. Abbott, *The Mother at Home, or The Principles of Maternal Duty* (New York: American Tract Society, 1833); this book was a best-seller in its time.
9. Maria J. McIntosh, *Woman in America: Her Work and Her Reward* (New York: Appleton, 1850).
10. Abbott, *op. cit.*, pp. 62–64.
11. Lydia Maria Child, *The Mother's Book* (Boston: 1831), p. 5.

12. Louisa May Alcott, *Little Women* (New York: A. L. Burt, 1911), p. 68.

13. Lillian Krueger, "Motherhood on the Wisconsin Frontier," *Wisconsin, A Magazine of History*, Vol. 29, No. 2, 157–83; Vol. 29, No. 3, 333–46.

14. Stella Davies, *Living Through the Industrial Revolution* (London: Routledge and Kegan, 1966).

15. Margaret Hewitt, *Wives and Mothers in Victorian Industry* (London: Rockliff, 1958), p. 22.

16. *Ibid.*, pp. 153–54.

17. *Maternity: Letters from Working Women*, collected by the Women's Cooperative Guild, with a preface by the Rt. Hon. Herbert Samuel, M.P. (London: G. Bell, 1915), p. 5.

18. *Ibid.*, pp. 27–28.

19. *Ibid.*, p. 49.

20. *Ibid.*, pp. 67–68.

21. *Ibid.*, p. 153.

22. *Ibid.*, p. 47.

23. Calhoun, *op. cit.*, III: 86; Elinor C. Guggenheim, "The Battle for Day Care," *Nation*, May 7, 1973.

24. Hannah Gavron, *The Captive Wife: Conflicts of Housebound Mothers* (London: Routledge and Kegan, 1966), pp. 72–73, 80.

25. Lee Sanders Comer, "Functions of the Family under Capitalism," pamphlet reprinted by the New York Radical Feminists, 1974. Eli Zaretsky, "Capitalism, the Family, and Personal Life," *Socialist Revolution*, January–June 1973, p. 69.

26. Carl Djerassi, "Some Observations on Current Fertility Control in China," *The China Quarterly*, No. 57 (January–March 1974), pp. 40–60.

III. THE KINGDOM OF THE FATHERS

1. Sherry Ortner, "Is Female to Male as Nature Is to Culture?" in Michelle Rosaldo and Louise Lamphère, eds., *Woman, Culture and Society* (Stanford: Stanford University Press, 1974); Hannah Papanek, "Purdah in Pakistan: Seclusion and Modern Occupations for Women," *Journal of Marriage and the Family*, August 1971, p. 520.

2. Alexander Mitscherlich, *Society Without the Father* (New York: Schocken, 1970), pp. 145–47, 159.

3. Brigitte Berger, Introduction to Helen Diner, *Mothers and Amazons* (New York: Anchor Books, 1973), p. xvi.

4. Angela Davis, "Reflections on the Black Woman's Role," *The Black Scholar*, Vol. 3, No. 3. See also Pat Robinson *et al.*, "A

Historical and Critical Essay for Black Women in the Cities," in Toni Cade, ed., *The Black Woman* (New York: Signet, 1970), pp. 198–211.

5. David Schneider and Kathleen Gough, eds., *Matrilineal Kinship* (Berkeley: University of California Press, 1962), p. 5.

6. *Ibid.*, pp. 21–23.

7. Robert Briffault, *The Mothers* (New York: Johnson Reprint, 1969), I: 433–35.

8. Simone de Beauvoir, *The Second Sex*, trans. H. M. Parshley (New York: Knopf, 1953), p. 82.

9. See Ortner, *op. cit.* In a forthcoming book, *Women and Nature*, Susan Griffin explores in depth the evolution and consequences of this splitting.

10. Sigmund Freud, *Collected Papers*, ed. and trans. James Strachey (New York: Basic Books, 1959), Vol. 5.

11. Niles Newton, *Maternal Emotions: a study of women's feelings toward menstruation, pregnancy, childbirth, breast feeding and other aspects of their femininity* (New York: P. B. Hoeber, 1955), p. 24–26.

12. See Linda Thurston, "On Male and Female Principle," *The Second Wave*, Vol. 1, No. 2 (Summer 1971).

13. See Frantz Fanon, *Black Skin, White Masks* (New York: Grove, 1967), pp. 72–73; *The Wretched of the Earth* (New York: Grove, 1968), p. 294; *Toward the African Revolution* (New York: Grove, 1967), pp. 3ff.; Paolo Freire, *The Pedagogy of the Oppressed* (New York: Seabury, 1971), pp. 31ff.; Albert Memmi, *Dominated Man* (Boston: Beacon, 1968), p. 202.

14. See Leslie H. Farber, "I'm Sorry, Dear," in *The Ways of the Will* (New York: Harper and Row, 1968); Albert Memmi, "A Tyrant's Plea," in *Dominated Man, op. cit.*

15. E. M. Forster, *Howards End* (Baltimore: Penguin, 1953), p. 175.

16. Briffault, *op. cit.*, II: 557.

17. De Beauvoir, *op. cit.*, p. 171.

18. Eleanor Flexner, *Century of Struggle* (New York: Atheneum, 1971), p. 46.

19. Olive Schreiner, *The Story of an African Farm* (New York: Fawcett, 1968), pp. 168–69.

20. See Ben Barker-Benfield, "Anne Hutchinson and the Puritan Attitude Toward Women," *Feminist Studies*, Vol. 1, No. 2 (Fall 1972), pp. 65–96.

21. Karen Horney, "The Dread of Woman," in *Feminine Psy-*

chology (New York: Norton, 1967); Wolfgang Lederer, *The Fear of Women* (New York: Grune and Stratton, 1968); Philip Slater, *The Glory of Hera* (Boston: Beacon, 1968).

22. Horney, *op. cit.*, p. 137.

23. Slater, *op. cit.*, p. 72. See also Joan Bamberger, "The Myth of Matriarchy: Why Men Rule in Primitive Society," in Rosaldo and Lamphère, *op. cit.*

24. See my essay, "The Anti-Feminist Woman," *New York Review of Books*, November 30, 1972; Nancy Milford, "Out from Under: A Review of *Woman's Estate* by Juliet Mitchell," *Partisan Review*, Vol. 40, No. 1 (Winter 1973); Jane Alpert, "Mother-Right: A New Feminist Theory," *MS.*, August 1973.

25. See Karen Lindsay, "The Sexual Revolution Is No Joke for Women," *Boston Phoenix*, March 13, 1973; Barbara Seaman, *Free and Female* (New York: Fawcett, 1973), pp. 241–45; "New Evidence against the Pill," *MS.*, June 1975.

26. Barbara Segal, "Today Bucharest, Tomorrow the World," *Off Our Backs*, Vol. 5, No. 1 (January 1975), p. 11.

27. Toni Cade, "The Pill: Genocide or Liberation?" *The Black Woman*, *op. cit.*, pp. 162–69.

28. Al Rutledge, "Is Abortion Black Genocide?" *Essence*, September 1973, p. 86.

29. Jessie Bernard, *The Future of Motherhood* (New York: Dial, 1974), p. 268.

30. Shulamith Firestone, *The Dialectic of Sex* (New York: Bantam, 1972), pp. 197ff.

31. Denis de Rougement, *Love in the Western World* (New York: Anchor Books, 1957); first published 1939.

32. Karl Stern, *The Flight from Woman* (New York: Noonday Press, 1970), p. 305.

33. Herbert Marcuse, *Counterrevolution and Revolt* (Boston: Beacon, 1972), pp. 74–78; Robert Bly, *Sleepers Joining Hands* (New York: Harper and Row, 1972), pp. 29–50.

34. Barbara Charlesworth Gelpi, "The Politics of Androgyny," *Women's Studies*, Vol. 2, No. 2 (1974), pp. 151–61.

35. Philip Slater, *The Pursuit of Loneliness* (Boston: Beacon, 1970), pp. 46–47, 89.

36. De Beauvoir, *op. cit.*, p. 66.

37. Alice Schwartzer, interview with Simone de Beauvoir, *MS.*, July 1972. De Beauvoir opened the first International Tribunal on Crimes Against Women in Brussels: "I greet the beginning of a radical decolonization of women" (ITCAW newsletter, April 8,

1976, Berkeley Women's Center, 2112 Channing Way, Berkeley, Calif. 94704).

IV. THE PRIMACY OF THE MOTHER

1. J. J. Bachofen, *Myth, Religion, and Mother Right*, trans. Ralph Manheim (Princeton, N.J.: Princeton University Press, 1967), p. 207.
2. *Ibid.*, pp. 150, 129.
3. *Ibid.*, pp. 143–44.
4. *Ibid.*, p. 150.
5. *Ibid.*, p. 101.
6. *Ibid.*, pp. 109–10.
7. Robert Briffault, *The Mothers* (New York: Johnson Reprint, 1969), I:v.
8. *Ibid.*, III: 509–10.
9. See, for example, Amy Hackett and Sarah Pomeroy, "Making History: *The First Sex*," *Feminist Studies*, Vol. 1, No. 2 (1972).
10. Jane Harrison, *Mythology* (New York: Harcourt, Brace and World, 1963), p. 43; first published 1924.
11. Erich Neumann, *The Origins and History of Consciousness* (Princeton, N.J.: Princeton University Press, 1971), p. 43; first published 1949.
12. Erich Neumann, *The Great Mother* (Princeton, N.J.: Princeton University Press, 1972), pp. 129–31; first published 1955.
13. Joseph Campbell, *The Masks of God: Primitive Mythology* (New York: Viking, 1972), pp. vi–vii.
14. James Mellaart, *Çatal Hüyük: A Neolithic Town in Anatolia* (New York: McGraw-Hill, 1967), pp. 201–2.
15. Neumann, *The Great Mother*, pp. 135–37; Briffault, *op. cit.*, I: 466–67. See also H. R. Hays, *The Dangerous Sex* (New York: Pocket Books, 1972).
16. Briffault, *op. cit.*, I: 473–74.
17. Kate Millett, *Sexual Politics* (New York: Doubleday, 1970), pp. 210–20.
18. Neumann, *The Great Mother*, p. 288.
19. Briffault, *op. cit.*, II: 513, 490.
20. Otto Rank, "The Creation of the Sexual Self," in *Beyond Psychology*, (New York: Dover, 1958), pp. 202–12.
21. Bronislaw Malinowski, *The Sexual Life of Savages* (New York: Harcourt, Brace and World, 1929), pp. 2, 170–75.
22. Neumann, *The Origins and History of Consciousness*, pp. 49–51.

23. Barbara Seaman, *Free and Female* (New York: Fawcett, 1973), p. 22.

24. Briffault, *op. cit.*, I: 441.

25. Bruno Bettelheim, *Symbolic Wounds: Puberty Rites and the Envious Male* (New York: Collier, 1968).

26. Campbell, *op.cit.*, pp. 30–31, 46, 59–60.

27. Briffault, *op. cit.*, II: 403–6.

28. C. G. Hartley, *The Age of Mother-Right* (New York: Dodd, Mead, 1914), pp. 65–68.

29. Neumann, *The Great Mother*, pp. 280, 290.

30. M. Esther Harding, *Woman's Mysteries* (New York: C. G. Jung Foundation, 1971), p. 70.

31. Mary Douglas, *Purity and Danger: An Analysis of Concepts of Pollution and Taboo* (Baltimore: Pelican, 1970), pp. 166–69.

32. Paula Weideger, *Menstruation and Menopause: The Physiology and Psychology, The Myth and the Reality* (New York: Knopf, 1976), pp. 93–94.

33. Briffault, *op. cit.*, II: 634–40; Harding, *op. cit.*, chs. 8, 9.

34. G. Rachel Levy, *Religious Conceptions of the Stone Age* (New York: Harper Torchbooks, 1963), pp. 52, 157–59. Originally published in England in 1948 as *The Gate of Horn*.

35. Erich Neumann, *The Great Mother, op. cit.*, pp. 217–25.

V. THE DOMESTICATION OF MOTHERHOOD

1. Frederick Engels, *The Origin of the Family, Private Property and the State* (New York: International Publishers, 1971), p. 73.

2. Karen Horney, *Feminine Psychology* (New York: Norton, 1967), pp. 106–18.

3. Eli Zaretsky, *Capitalism, the Family, and Personal Life*. Originally published in *Socialist Revolution*, January–June 1973, pp. 78, 72–73. (Available as a paperback from Harper and Row, N. Y., 1975.)

4. H. R. Hays, *The Dangerous Sex* (New York: Pocket Books, 1972), p. 270; first published 1964.

5. Robin Fox, *Kinship and Marriage* (Baltimore: Penguin, 1967), pp. 27–33.

6. Bruno Bettelheim, *Symbolic Wounds: Puberty Rites and the Envious Male* (New York: Collier, 1968); first published 1954.

7. Joseph Campbell, *The Masks of God: Primitive Mythology* (New York: Viking, 1972), pp. 315ff.; first published 1959.

8. G. Rachel Levy, *Religious Conceptions of the Stone Age* (New York: Harper Torchbooks, 1963), pp. 83–85.

9. *Ibid.*, pp. 27, 86–87, 100.

10. *National Geographic*, Vol. 144, No. 6 (December 1973).

11. Campbell, *op. cit.*, p. 372.

12. Leonard Palmer, *Mycenaeans and Minoans: Aegean Pre-History in the Light of the Linear B Tablets* (New York: Knopf, 1965), p. 347.

13. Levy, *op. cit.*, p. 120; Erich Neumann, *The Great Mother* (Princeton, N.J.: Princeton University Press, 1972), p. 153.

14. Raphael Patai, *Sex and Family in the Bible and the Middle East* (New York: Doubleday, 1959), p. 135.

15. Raphael Patai, *The Hebrew Goddess* (New York: Ktav, 1967), pp. 52, 97–98.

16. Aeschylus, *Oresteia*, trans. Richmond Lattimore (Chicago: University of Chicago Press, 1953), pp. 158, 161.

17. B. Ehrenreich and D. English, *Witches, Midwives and Nurses: A History of Women Healers* (Old Westbury, N.Y.: Feminist Press, 1973), pp. 8–9.

18. E. O. James, *The Cult of the Mother-Goddess* (New York: Praeger, 1959), pp. 47, 138; James Mellaart, *Çatal Hüyük: A Neolithic Town in Anatolia* (New York: McGraw-Hill, 1967), plate 84.

19. Palmer, *op. cit.*, p. 192; Cyril Aldred, *Akhenaton and Nefertite* (New York: Viking, 1973), p. 181.

20. Patai, *The Hebrew Goddess*, pp. 26–27, 52, 97–98.

21. Erich Neumann, *The Origins and History of Consciousness* (Princeton, N.J.: Princeton University Press, 1971), p. 86.

22. Jane Harrison, *Mythology* (New York: Harcourt Brace, 1963), pp. 44ff.

23. Philip Slater, *The Glory of Hera* (Boston: Beacon, 1968).

24. Aldred, *op. cit.*, pp. 11–12; Lewis Mumford, *The City in History* (New York: Harcourt, Brace and World, 1961), p. 13.

25. Jane Harrison, *op. cit.*, pp. 94–95.

26. Slater, *op. cit.*, pp. 137–41.

27. M. Esther Harding, *Woman's Mysteries* (New York: C. G. Jung Foundation, 1971), p. 31.

28. Robert Briffault, *The Mothers* (New York: Johnson Reprint, 1969), I: 131–41.

29. Margaret Mead, *Male and Female: A Study of the Sexes in A Changing World* (New York: Morrow, 1975), p. 229; first published 1949.

30. *Ibid.*, p. 82.

31. Campbell, *op. cit.*, p. 451.

VI. HANDS OF FLESH, HANDS OF IRON

1. A. J. Rongy, *Childbirth, Yesterday and Today* (New York: Emerson, 1937), pp. 62–64.
2. Quoted in R. P. Finney, *The Story of Motherhood* (New York: Liveright, 1937), p. 21.
3. *Ibid.*, pp. 18–20.
4. Irwin Chabon, M.D., *Awake and Aware: Participating in Childbirth through Prophylaxis* (New York: Delacorte, 1966), pp. 46–47.
5. W. F. Mengert, M.D., "The Origins of the Male Midwife," *Annals of Medical History*, Vol. 4, No. 5, pp. 453–65.
6. Rongy, *op cit.*, pp. 18, 33; Harvey Graham, *Eternal Eve: The Mysteries of Birth and the Customs That Surround It* (London: Hutchinson, 1960), p. 12.
7. Rongy, *op. cit.*, p. 33.
8. Finney, *op. cit.*, p. 31; Rongy, *op. cit.*, pp. 76–77.
9. J. W. White, M.D., "4,000 Years of Obstetrics," *American Journal of Surgery*, Vol. 11, No. 3 (March 1931), pp. 564–72.
10. Finney, *op. cit.*, p. 44.
11. Graham, *op. cit.*, pp. 69–70.
12. Finney, *op. cit.*, p. 56.
13. Graham, *op. cit.*, p. 79.
14. Ben Barker-Benfield, "Anne Hutchinson and the Puritan Attitude Towards Women," *Feminist Studies*, Vol. 1, No. 2 (Fall 1972), pp. 65–96; Finney, *op. cit.*, p. 149.
15. B. Ehrenreich and D. English, *Witches, Midwives and Nurses: A History of Women Healers* (Old Westbury, N.Y.: Feminist Press, 1973), pp. 12–15.
16. Rongy, *op. cit.*, p. 84.
17. *Ibid.*, p. 79.
18. Mengert, *op. cit.*, pp. 453–65.
19. Finney, *op. cit.*, p. 101.
20. Graham, *op. cit.*, p. 87.
21. Rongy, *op. cit.*, p. 46.
22. J. L. Miller, "Renaissance Midwifery: The Evolution of Modern Obstetrics 1500–1700," in *Lectures on the History of Medicine: 1862–1932* (Philadelphia: W. B. Saunders, 1933).
23. Louise Bourgeois, *Les Six Couches de Marie de Médicis* (Paris: 1875), pp. 24–27. I am indebted to Richard Howard for the English version of this paragraph.
24. Percival Willughby, *Observations in Midwifery, as also the country midwife's opusculum or vade mecum* (Warwick: H. T. Cooke, 1863), p. 151.

25. Harold Speert, M.D., and Alan Guttmacher, M.D., *Obstetric Practice* (New York: McGraw-Hill, 1956), p. 304.

26. Graham, *op. cit.*, p. 115.

27. *Ibid.*, p. 120.

28. *Ibid.*, pp. 106–22.

29. John Leake, M.D., *A Lecture Introductory to the Theory and Practice of Midwifery* (London: 1773), p. 48.

30. F. Naroll, R. Naroll, and F. M. Howard, "Position of Women in Childbirth: A study in data quality control," *American Journal of Obstetrics and Gynecology*, Vol. 82, No. 4 (October 1961), p. 953.

31. Leake, *op. cit.*, p. 49.

32. Graham, *op. cit.*, p. 146.

33. Elizabeth Nihell, *A Treatise on the Art of Midwifery: Setting Forth Various Abuses Therein, Especially as to the Practice with Instruments* (London: 1760), pp. viii–ix.

34. *Ibid.*, pp. 91–99.

35. *Ibid.*, p. 167n.

36. See Sheila Kitzinger, *The Experience of Childbirth* (Baltimore: Pelican, 1973), p. 12; Janet Brown *et al.*, *Two Births* (New York: Random House, 1972).

37. Finney, *op. cit.*, p. 238.

38. I. P. Semmelweis, "The Etiology, the Concept and the Prophylaxis of Childbed Fever" (1861), in *Medical Classics*, Vol. 5, No. 5 (January 1941), p. 357.

39. Finney, *op. cit.*, pp. 191ff.

40. *Ibid.*, p. 218.

41. O. W. Holmes, "The Contagiousness of Puerperal Fever" (1843), in *Epoch-Making Contributions to Medicine, Surgery and the Allied Sciences* (Philadelphia: 1909).

42. Semmelweis, *op. cit.*, pp. 369–75.

43. *Ibid.*, p. 391.

44. *Ibid.*, p. 395.

45. *Ibid.*, p. 400. See also A. Janik and S. Toulmin, *Wittgenstein's Vienna* (New York: Simon and Schuster, 1973), p. 35.

46. Semmelweis, *op. cit.*, p. 417.

47. Finney, *op. cit.*, p. 223.

VII. ALIENATED LABOR

1. Lawrence Freedman and Vera Ferguson, "The Question of 'Painless Childbirth' in Primitive Cultures," *American Journal of Orthopsychiatry*, Vol. 20 (1950), pp. 368, 370; Margaret Mead,

Male and Female: A Study of the Sexes in a Changing World (New York: Morrow, 1975), p. 277.

2. Nancy Fuller and Brigitte Jordan, "Birth in a Hammock," *Women: A Journal of Liberation*, Vol. 4, No. 3, pp. 24–26.

3. Freedman and Ferguson, *op. cit.*, p. 369.

4. Robert Briffault, *The Mothers* (New York: Johnson Reprint, 1969), I: 458–59.

5. Simone Weil, *Waiting for God* (New York: Putnam, 1951), pp. 117ff.; *Cahiers* (Paris: Librairie Plon, 1953), p. 9.

6. Doris Lessing, *A Proper Marriage* (New York: New American Library, 1970), p. 274.

7. Cora Sandel, *Alberta and Freedom*, trans. Elizabeth Rokkan (London: Peter Owen, 1963), pp. 231, 241; first published 1931.

8. Margaret Mead and Niles Newton, "Pregnancy, Childbirth and Outcome: A Review of Patterns of Culture and Further Research Needs," in S. A. Richardson and A. F. Guttmacher, eds., *Childbearing: Its Social and Psychological Aspects* (Baltimore: Williams and Wilkins, 1967). See also Elsie Clews Parsons on pregnancy taboos in David Meltzer, ed., *Birth* (New York: Ballantine, 1973), pp. 34–38.

9. Mead and Newton, *op. cit.*, p. 148.

10. *Ibid.*, pp. 170–75.

11. Freedman and Ferguson, *op. cit.*, p. 367.

12. Sheila Kitzinger, *The Experience of Childbirth* (Baltimore: Penguin, 1973), pp. 17–25.

13. Leo Tolstoy, *Anna Karenina*, trans. Rosemary Edmonds (Baltimore: Penguin, 1954), pp. 747–48.

14. Leo Tolstoy, *War and Peace*, trans. Louise and Aylmer Maude (New York: Simon and Schuster, 1942), p. 353.

15. Elizabeth Mann Borgese, *The Ascent of Woman* (New York: Braziller, 1963), p. 44.

16. Walter Radcliffe, *Milestones in Midwifery* (Bristol: Wright, 1967), p. 81; R. P. Finney, *The Story of Motherhood* (New York: Liveright, 1937), pp. 169–75.

17. Claire Tomalin, *The Life and Death of Mary Wollstonecraft* (New York: Harcourt, Brace Jovanovich, 1974), p. 226.

18. O. W. Holmes, "The Contagiousness of Puerperal Fever" (1843), in *Epoch-Making Contributions to Medicine, Surgery and the Allied Sciences* (Philadelphia: 1909).

19. H. W. Haggard, *Devils, Drugs and Doctors* (New York and London: Harper and Bros., 1929), p. 116.

20. B. Ehrenreich and D. English, *Complaints and Disorders: The*

Sexual Politics of Sickness (Old Westbury, N.Y.: Feminist Press, 1973), pp. 26–36.

21. Finney, *op. cit.*, pp. 186–90; Sylvia Plath, *The Bell Jar* (New York: Bantam, 1972), p. 53.

22. H. Speert and A. Guttmacher, *Obstetric Practice* (New York: McGraw-Hill, 1956), p. 305.

23. Grantly Dick-Read, *Childbirth Without Fear: The Principles and Practice of Natural Childbirth* (New York: Harper and Row, 1970); first published 1944.

24. Pierre Vellay *et. al.*, *Childbirth Without Pain* (New York: Dutton, 1968), pp. 18–21.

25. K. D. Keele, *Anatomies of Pain* (Oxford: Blackwell, 1957), p. 182.

26. Suzanne Arms, *Immaculate Deception: A New Look at Women and Childbirth in America* (Boston: Houghton Mifflin, 1975), pp. 145–46.

27. Kitzinger, *op. cit.*, pp. 17–25.

28. Vellay, *op. cit.*, pp. 28, 151.

29. Shulamith Firestone, *The Dialectic of Sex* (New York: Bantam, 1972), pp. 198–99.

30. Cora Sandel, *Alberta Alone*, trans. Elizabeth Rokkan (London: Peter Owen, 1965), p. 94; first published 1939.

31. Brigitte Jordan, Department of Anthropology, Michigan State University, "The Cultural Production of Childbirth," 1974 (unpublished).

32. Arms, *op. cit.*, p. 83; Judith Brister, "Vertical Delivery: Childbirth Improved?" *Detroit News*, June 1971.

33. Roberto Caldeyro-Barcia, M.D., director of the Latin American Center for Perinatology and Human Development, and president of the International Federation of Gynecologists and Obstetricians, at a meeting of the American Foundation for Maternal and Child Health, April 9, 1975. (Jane Brody, "Some Obstetrical Methods Criticized," *New York Times*, April 10, 1975.)

34. Jordan, *op. cit.*; see also Fuller and Jordan, *op. cit.*

35. Margaret Mead, *Male and Female*, p. 268.

36. Doris Haire, "The Cultural Warping of Childbirth," International Childbirth Education Association, 1974. Copies of this pamphlet can be obtained by writing to the International Childbirth Education Association Supplies Center, 1414 N.W. 85th St., Seattle, Wash. 98117.

37. Arms, *op. cit.*, p. 279.

38. *Ibid.*, pp. 125–26.

39. *Ibid.*, p. 22.

40. Mary Jane Sherfey, *The Nature and Evolution of Female Sexuality* (New York: Vintage, 1973), pp. 100–101.

41. Niles Newton, "The Trebly Sensuous Woman," *Psychology Today*, issue on "The Female Experience," 1973.

42. Alice Rossi, "Maternalism, Sexuality and the New Feminism," in *Contemporary Sexual Behavior: Critical Issues in the 1970's*, ed. J. Zubin and J. Money (Baltimore: Johns Hopkins University Press, 1973), pp. 145–71.

43. Kathy Linck, "Legalizing a Woman's Right to Choose," in *Proceedings of the First International Childbirth Conference*, 1973, New Moon Communications, Box 3488, Ridgeway Station, Stamford, Conn. 06905.

VIII. MOTHER AND SON, WOMAN AND MAN

1. Alfred Kazin, *A Walker in the City*, quoted in Franz Kobler, ed., *Her Children Call Her Blessed: A Portrait of the Jewish Mother* (New York: Stephen Daye, 1953), p. 234.

2. Sigmund Freud, *New Introductory Lectures on Psychoanalysis*, ed. and trans. James Strachey (New York: Norton, 1961), p. 133; *A General Introduction to Psychoanalysis*, trans. Joan Riviere (New York: Garden City Publishing, 1943), p. 183.

3. Sherry Ortner, "Oedipal Father, Mother's Brother and the Penis: A Review of Juliet Mitchell's *Psycho-Analysis and Feminism*," *Feminist Studies*, Vol. 2, No. 2–3 (1975).

4. Robert Briffault, *The Mothers* (New York: Johnson Reprint, 1969), I :259–64.

5. George Jackson, *Soledad Brother* (New York: Bantam, 1970), pp. 9–10.

6. Franz Kafka, *Letter to His Father* (New York: Schocken, 1966), pp. 45–47.

7. Frederick Leboyer, *Birth Without Violence* (New York: Knopf, 1975), pp. 26–27.

8. Duncan Emrich, *American Folk Poetry* (Boston: Little, Brown, 1974), p. 739.

9. D. H. Lawrence, "The Symbolic Meaning," quoted in Tom Marshall, *The Psychic Mariner: A Reading of the Poems of D. H. Lawrence* (New York: Viking, 1970), p. 53.

10. G. Rachel Levy, *Religious Conceptions of the Stone Age* (New York: Harper Torchbooks, 1963), pp. 53, 157; Erich Neumann, *The Great Mother* (Princeton, N.J.: Princeton University Press, 1972), pp. 256–58.

11. Leslie H. Farber, "He Said, She Said," *Commentary*, March 1972, p. 55.

12. Karen Horney, *Feminine Psychology* (New York: Norton, 1967), pp. 113, 117, 138, 141.

13. Denis de Rougement, *Love in the Western World* (New York: Anchor Books, 1956), pp. 1–45.

14. Rainer Maria Rilke, *The Duino Elegies*. I am indebted to Lilly Engler for the translation of these lines. Rilke, *The Notebooks of Malte Laurids Brigge*, trans. M. D. Herter Norton (New York: Norton, 1949), pp. 120–21.

15. *Letters of Rainer Maria Rilke*, trans. J. B. Greene and M. D. Herter Norton (New York: Norton, 1945), I: 71–72.

16. Vern L. Bullogh, *The Subordinate Sex: A History of Attitudes Toward Women* (Baltimore: Penguin, 1974), p. 29.

17. *Ibid.*, pp. 231–32.

18. *Ibid.*, pp. 173–74.

19. Mary Daly, *The Church and the Second Sex, with a New Post-Christian Introduction by the Author* (New York: Harper Colophon Books, 1975), pp. 149–52.

20. Bullogh, *op. cit.*, pp. 225–26.

21. John S. Haller and Robin M. Haller, *The Physician and Sexuality in Victorian America* (Chicago: University of Illinois Press, 1974), pp. 100–101.

22. Viola Klein, *The Feminine Character: History of an Ideology* (Chicago: University of Illinois Press, 1972), p. 26.

23. Joseph C. Rheingold, M.D., *The Mother, Anxiety and Death: The Catastrophic Death Complex* (London: J. and A. Churchill, 1967), p. 119.

24. James Daugherty, *Abraham Lincoln* (New York: Viking, 1943), p. 160.

25. Margaret Mead, ed., *An Anthropologist at Work: Writings of Ruth Benedict* (New York: Equinox Books, 1973), p. 123.

26. L. van Gelder and C. Carmichael, "But What About Our Sons?" *MS.*, October 1975, pp. 52ff.

27. Karen Horney, *New Ways in Psychoanalysis* (New York: Norton, 1939).

28. Sigmund Freud, *New Introductory Lectures on Psychoanalysis*, pp. 86–87, 129.

29. Erich Neumann, *The Origins and History of Consciousness* (Princeton, N.J.: Princeton University Press, 1971), pp. 142–43; Bruno Bettelheim, *Symbolic Wounds* (New York: Collier, 1962), pp. 118–19.

30. Ortner, *op. cit.*, p. 180.

31. Juliet Mitchell, *Psycho-Analysis and Feminism* (New York: Vintage, 1975).

32. Richard Gilman, "The Feminist Case Against Sigmund Freud," *New York Times Magazine*, January 31, 1971, p. 10.

33. Jean Strouse, ed., *Women and Analysis: Dialogues on Psychoanalytic Views of Femininity* (New York: Grossman, 1974), p. 58.

34. Charlotte Baum, Paula Hyman, and Sonya Michel, *The Jewish Woman in America* (New York: Dial, 1976).

35. Pauline Bart, "Portnoy's Mother's Complaint: Depression in Middle-Aged Women," *Response: A Contemporary Jewish Review*, special issue on "The Jewish Woman," No. 18 (Summer 1973), pp. 129–41.

36. See Mary Jane Sherfey, *The Nature and Evolution of Female Sexuality* (New York: Vintage, 1973); Niles Newton, "The Trebly Sensuous Woman," *Psychology Today*, issue on "The Female Experience," 1973; and Newton, "Interrelationships between sexual responsiveness, birth, and breast feeding," and Alice Rossi, "Maternalism, Sexuality, and the New Feminism," both in J. Zubin and J. Money, eds., *Contemporary Sexual Behavior* (Baltimore: Johns Hopkins University Press, 1973).

37. Van Gelder and Carmichael, *op. cit.*

38. Robert Reid, *Marie Curie* (New York: Dutton Saturday Review, 1974), p. 206.

39. Klein, *op. cit.*, p. 26.

40. Theodore Stanton and Harriet Stanton Blatch, eds., *Elizabeth Cady Stanton as Revealed in Her Letters, Diary and Reminiscences* (New York: Arno, 1969), II: 38–42, 31, 130–31. I am indebted to Elizabeth Shanklin for bringing these passages to my attention.

41. Sue Silvermarie, "The Motherbond," *Women: A Journal of Liberation*, Vol. 4, No. 1, pp. 26–27.

42. Robin Morgan, "The Child," part IV of "The Network of the Imaginary Mother," in *Lady of the Beasts* (New York: Random House, 1976).

43. Jane Lazarre, "On Being a Father in the Year of the Woman," *Village Voice*, September 22, 1975.

44. M. Esther Harding, *Woman's Mysteries* (New York: C. G. Jung Foundation, 1971), pp. 192–94.

45. Mary Daly, *Beyond God the Father: Toward a Philosophy of Women's Liberation* (Boston: Beacon, 1973).

46. Frantz Fanon, *The Wretched of the Earth* (New York: Grove, 1968), pp. 269–70.

47. Olive Schreiner, *Dreams* (Pacific Grove, Calif.: Select Books, 1971), pp. 59–62; first published 1890.

IX. MOTHERHOOD AND DAUGHTERHOOD

Epigraph from "Mother and Child," in *Like the Iris of an Eye*, by Susan Griffin (New York: Harper and Row, 1976).

1. Alice Rossi, "Physiological and Social Rhythms: The Study of Human Cyclicity," special lecture to the American Psychiatric Association, Detroit, Michigan, May 9, 1974; "Period Piece—Bloody but Unbowed," Elizabeth Fenton, interview with Emily Culpeper, *The Real Paper*, June 12, 1974.

2. Charles Strickland, "A Transcendentalist Father: The Child-Rearing Practices of Bronson Alcott," *History of Childhood Quarterly: The Journal of Psycho-History*, Vol. 1, No. 1 (Summer 1973), pp. 23, 32.

3. Midge Mackenzie, ed., *Shoulder to Shoulder* (New York: Knopf, 1975), p. 28.

4. Margaret Mead, *Male and Female* (New York: Morrow, 1975), p. 61.

5. David Meltzer, *Birth* (New York: Ballantine, 1973), pp. 3, 5, 6–8.

6. Lloyd deMause, "The Evolution of Childhood," in deMause, ed., *The History of Childhood* (New York: Harper and Row, 1974), pp. 25–26, 120.

7. Jane Lilienfeld, "Yes, the Lighthouse Looks Like That: Marriage Victorian Style," unpublished paper, presented at the Northeast Victorian Studies Association, Conference on the Victorian Family, April 18–20, 1975, Worcester, Mass.

8. Virginia Woolf, *To the Lighthouse* (New York: Harcourt, Brace, 1927), pp. 58, 92, 126, 79, 294.

9. Cecil Woodham-Smith, *Florence Nightingale* (New York: Grosset and Dunlap, 1951), p. 46.

10. Diaries and letters of Paula Modersohn-Becker, translated by Liselotte Erlanger, unpublished manuscript, quoted by permission of the translator.

11. Thomas Johnson, ed., *The Letters of Emily Dickinson* (Cambridge, Mass.: Harvard University Press, 1958), III: 782.

12. Sylvia Plath, *Letters Home*, ed. Aurelia Plath (New York: Harper and Row, 1975), pp. 32, 466.

13. Virginia Woolf, *op. cit.*, p. 79.

14. Radclyffe Hall, *The Well of Loneliness* (New York: Pocket Books, 1974), p. 32; first published 1928.

15. Sue Silvermarie, "The Motherbond," *Women: A Journal of Liberation,* Vol. 4, No. 1, pp. 26–27.

16. Carroll Smith-Rosenberg, "The Female World of Love and Ritual: Relations between Women in Nineteenth-Century America," *Signs,* Vol. 1, No. 1, pp. 1–29.

17. Lillian Krueger, "Motherhood on the Wisconsin Frontier," *Wisconsin, A Magazine of History,* Vol. 29, No. 3, pp. 336–46.

18. Lynn Sukenick, "Feeling and Reason in Doris Lessing's Fiction," *Contemporary Literature,* Vol. 14, No. 4, p. 519.

19. Doris Lessing, *A Proper Marriage* (New York: New American Library, 1970) p. 111.

20. Kate Chopin, *The Awakening* (New York: Capricorn, 1964), p. 14; first published 1899.

21. Cora Sandel, *Alberta Alone,* trans. Elizabeth Rokkan (London: Peter Owen, 1965), p. 51; first published 1939.

22. C. Kerenyi, *Eleusis: Archetypal Image of Mother and Daughter* (New York: Pantheon, 1967), pp. 13–94.

23. *Ibid.,* pp. 127–28.

24. *Ibid.,* p. 130.

25. *Ibid.,* pp. 132–33.

26. Margaret Atwood, *Surfacing* (New York: Popular Library, 1972), pp. 213–14, 218–19, 222–23.

27. Jean Mundy, Ph. D., "Rape—For Women Only," unpublished paper presented to the American Psychological Association, September 1, 1974, New Orleans, La.

28. Clara Thompson, " 'Penis Envy' in Women," in Jean Baker Miller, ed., *Psychoanalysis and Women,* (Baltimore: Penguin, 1973), p. 54.

29. Robert Seidenberg, "Is Anatomy Destiny?" in Miller, *op. cit.,* pp. 310–11.

30. Tillie Olsen, *Tell Me A Riddle* (New York: Delta Books, 1961), pp. 1–12.

31. Evelyn Reed, *Woman's Evolution: From Matriarchal Clan to Patriarchal Family* (New York: Pathfinder, 1975), pp. 12–14.

32. Adrienne Rich, "Jane Eyre: The Temptations of A Motherless Woman," *MS.,* October 1973.

33. Lillian Smith, *Killers of the Dream* (New York: Norton, 1961), pp. 28–29.

X. VIOLENCE: THE HEART OF MATERNAL DARKNESS

1. The story recounted here is a true one; the statements quoted are from actual newspaper reports. For obvious reasons of privacy, I have not used actual names or locations.

2. George H. Williams, "The Sacred Condominium," in John T. Noonan, Jr., ed., *The Morality of Abortion* (Cambridge, Mass.: Harvard University Press, 1970), p. 150.

3. Oscar H. Werner, *The Unmarried Mother in German Literature* (New York: Columbia University Press, 1917), p. 21.

4. *Ibid.*, pp. 24–25.

5. *Ibid.*, p. 1.

6. *Ibid.*, pp. 26–27, 96.

7. *Ibid.*, pp. 1–4.

8. Ben Barker-Benfield, "Anne Hutchinson and the Puritan Attitude Towards Women," *Feminist Studies*, Vol. 1, No. 2 (Fall 1972).

9. Edward Moor, ed., *Hindu Infanticide. An Account of the Measures Adopted for Suppressing the Practise of the Systematic Murder by Their Parents of Female Infants* (London: 1811).

10. Lawrence Lader, *Abortion* (Boston: Beacon, 1967), pp. 76–79.

11. Elizabeth Cady Stanton, letter to *Woman's Journal*, quoted in Alma Lutz, *Created Equal* (New York: John Day, 1940), p. 234. I am indebted to Elizabeth Shanklin's unpublished paper, "Our Revolutionary Mother: Elizabeth Cady Stanton" (Women's Studies Program, Sarah Lawrence College) for this and the following reference.

12. Lutz, *op. cit.*, pp. 162–63; Elizabeth Cady Stanton, Susan B. Anthony, and Matilda J. Gage, eds., *History of Woman Suffrage* (New York: Source Book Press, 1970), I: 597–98.

13. "Infanticide in Japan: Sign of the Times?" *New York Times*, December 8, 1973.

14. May E. Fromm, M.D., "Psychoanalytic Considerations on Abortion," in Harold Rosen, ed., *Abortion in America* (Boston: Beacon, 1967), p. 210.

15. Henry J. Myers, M.D., "The Problem of Sterilization," in Rosen, *op. cit.*, p. 93.

16. Milton H. Erickson, M.D., "The Psychological Significance of Vasectomy," in Rosen, *op. cit.*, pp. 57–58.

17. Jane Brody, "Birth Control Devices: What Studies Show About Side Effects," *New York Times*, March 4, 1975; Harold

Schmeck, "F.D.A. Warns Birth Pill Raises Heart Attack Risk," *New York Times*, August 27, 1975.

18. Noonan, *op cit.*, p. 4.

19. *Ibid.*, p. 16.

20. *Ibid.*, pp. 29–30.

21. Lader, *op. cit.*, pp. 76–79.

22. *Ibid.*, p. 17.

23. For examples, see Garrett Hardin, *Mandatory Motherhood: The True Meaning of the Right to Life* (Boston: Beacon, 1974); Frances-Myrna, "Abortion: A Philosophical Analysis," *Feminist Studies*, Vol. 1, No. 2 (Fall 1972); Judith Jarvis Thomson, "A Defense of Abortion," in M. Cohen, T. Nagel, and T. Scanlon, eds., *The Rights and Wrongs of Abortion* (Princeton, N.J.: Princeton University Press, 1974), pp. 3–23.

24. Mary Daly, *Beyond God the Father: Toward a Philosophy of Women's Liberation* (Boston: Beacon, 1973), p. 112.

25. Susan Griffin, "Post-Abortion Interviews," *Scanlan's Monthly*, Vol. 1, No. 5 (July 1970).

26. Harold Rosen, M.D., "The Hysterectomized Patient and the Abortion Problem," in Rosen, *op. cit.*, p. 54; Joann Rogers, "Rush to Surgery," *New York Times Magazine*, September 21, 1975.

27. Flanders Dunbar, M.D., "A Psychosomatic Approach to Abortion and the Abortion Habit," in Rosen, *op. cit.*, p. 27; Lader, *op. cit.*, pp. 22–23.

28. Lader, *op. cit.*, pp. 121–22.

29. Carl Djerassi, "Some Observations on Current Fertility Control in China," *China Quarterly*, No. 57 (January–March 1974), pp. 40ff.

30. Rev. George W. Clarke, *Race Suicide—England's Peril*, pamphlet published by the Duty and Discipline Movement (London: 1917).

31. Deborah S. Rosenfelt, ed., "Learning to Speak: Student Work," *Female Studies* X (Old Westbury, N.Y.: Feminist Press, 1975), p. 54.

32. Tillie Olsen, *Yonnondio: From the Thirties* (Boston: Delacorte, 1974), p. 9.

33. Alta, *Momma: A Start on All the Untold Stories* (New York: Times Change Press, 1974), pp. 72–73.

INDEX